Red Pepper and Gorgeous George

FLORIDA GOVERNMENT AND POLITICS

UNIVERSITY PRESS OF FLORIDA

Florida A&M University, Tallahassee
Florida Atlantic University, Boca Raton
Florida Gulf Coast University, Ft. Myers
Florida International University, Miami
Florida State University, Tallahassee
New College of Florida, Sarasota
University of Central Florida, Orlando
University of Florida, Gainesville
University of North Florida, Jacksonville
University of South Florida, Tampa
University of West Florida, Pensacola

Red Pepper and Gorgeous George

Claude Pepper's Epic Defeat
in the 1950 Democratic Primary

James C. Clark

Foreword by David R. Colburn and Susan A. MacManus

University Press of Florida

Gainesville | Tallahassee | Tampa | Boca Raton

Pensacola | Orlando | Miami | Jacksonville | Ft. Myers | Sarasota

16 15 14 13 12 11   6 5 4 3 2 1

Library of Congress Cataloging-in-Publication Data
Clark, James C., 1947–
Red Pepper and Gorgeous George : Claude Pepper's epic defeat in the 1950
Democratic primary / James C. Clark ; foreword by David R. Colburn and
Susan A. MacManus.
p. cm.—(Florida government and politics)
Includes bibliographical references and index.
ISBN 978-0-8130-3739-4 (acid-free paper)
1. Pepper, Claude, 1900–1989. 2. Smathers, George A. (George Armistead),
1913–2007. 3. Florida—Politics and government—1865–1950. 4. Primaries—
Florida—History—20th century. 5. Political campaigns—Florida—History—
20th century. 6. Political culture—Florida—History—20th century.
7. Political culture—United States—History—20th century. 8. Anti-communist
movements—United States—History—20th century. 9. Democratic Party
(U.S.)—Biography. 10. Legislators—United States—Biography. I. Title.
E840.8.P38C55 2011
975.9'06092—dc23   [B]   2011018979

The University Press of Florida is the scholarly publishing agency for the State
University System of Florida, comprising Florida A&M University, Florida
Atlantic University, Florida Gulf Coast University, Florida International
University, Florida State University, New College of Florida, University of
Central Florida, University of Florida, University of North Florida, University
of South Florida, and University of West Florida.

University Press of Florida
15 Northwest 15th Street
Gainesville, FL 32611-2079
http://www.upf.com

Along the way, many people have blessed me with
their friendship, a helping hand, or a chance.
To them, this book is dedicated. Without them, my
life would have been so much poorer.

Mary Stokes, Beverly Kees, David Colburn, Evans
Johnson, Carl Leubsdorf, Pye Chamberlayne, John
Chambers, Jim Donna, John S. Marshall, Mike
Freeman, Cindy Treherne Borga, Susan Scanlan,
Juliet Van Scoyk, Eloise Nicholls Roberts, William
Edward Clark, Louise Covington Clark, David Burgin,
Randy Noles, William Morris III, Eddie Bradford,
Carolyn Huff, Jerrell Shofner, Dick Crepeau, Robert
Zieger, Vicki Tolar Burton, Samuel Proctor, Ed
Kalina, Rose Beiler, Jane Tolar, Rob Wood, Charles
Brumback, Susan Walker, Mary Mount, Jim Squires,
Pamela Noyes, Marty Steinberg, Kenneth S. Allen,
and James D. Clarke.

Contents

Illustrations

Foreword

Florida has held a unique place in the American mind for more than six decades. For many retirees, its environment has been like a healthy elixir that allowed them to live longer and more vigorous lives; for others, it served as a place of renewal where all things were possible; and for immigrants, it offered political freedom and access to the American dream. Historian Gary Mormino described Florida as a "powerful symbol of renewal and regeneration." Others have suggested that, if Florida had not been available to Americans after World War II, they would have been much poorer for it. Those who watched the 2000 presidential election unfold, however, wondered if that were in fact so.

During World War II, Americans from all walks of life discovered Florida through military service, and it opened their eyes to the postwar possibilities. With the end of the war in August 1945, Florida veterans returned home, where they were soon joined by hundreds and then thousands of Americans who were ready to pursue a new life in the Sunshine State. In the sixty years between 1945 and 2005, 17 million people moved to Florida, increasing the state's population to 18.5 million people in 2005.

Florida's population growth, the settlement patterns of new residents, and their diversity had a profound effect on the state's place in the nation as well as the image Floridians had of themselves. Prior to 1940, Florida was the least populous state in the South and one of the poorest in the nation. Its society and economy were rural and agricultural, biracial and segregated. Most residents resided within forty miles of the Georgia border, and their culture and politics were consequently southern in orientation. Like its neighbors, Florida was a one-party state with the Democratic Party dominating politics from the end of Reconstruction in 1876 to 1970.

All that changed in the fifty years following World War II. In less than an average life span today, Florida became by 2005 the most populous state in the region and fourth in the nation, a haven for seniors and foreign residents, and a dynamic multiracial and multiethnic state. Most Floridians now reside closer to the Caribbean than they do to Georgia, and, for most of them, their image of themselves and their state has changed dramatically to reflect this new geographic orientation.

As Florida changed, so too did its politics. Voters threw out the Constitution of 1885 in favor of a new document that would speak to the needs of a new state in 1968. They then gradually abandoned the Democratic Party in favor of a dynamic two-party system. By the 1990s, Republicans took their expanding constituency and their control of the districting process following the 1990 census to secure majorities in the state legislature and the congressional delegation. These were remarkable political developments and reflected the transformative changes in the state's population. However, in statewide races for governor, U.S. senator, and elected cabinet positions, as well as in presidential contests, Democrats remained competitive with their Republican counterparts, in large part because they held a 6 percent lead in registered voters (42 percent to 36 percent for Republicans).

Such a politically and demographically complex and diverse population has made Florida today something other than a unified whole. The political maxim that "All politics is local" is truer of Florida than most other states. Those who reside in North Florida have little in common with those living in Central or South Florida. While those residing in Southeast Florida see themselves as part of the "new America," those in North Florida view Miami as a foreign country. Ask a resident what it means to be a Floridian, and few can answer. Ask a Floridian about the state's history, and even fewer can tell you that it has operated under five different flags, or that its colonial period began much earlier than that of New England or Virginia. Perhaps one in ten or twenty can tell you who Democrat LeRoy Collins was, despite Republican Jeb Bush's acknowledgment of Collins as the model for all governors who followed him. It is literally a state unknown and indefinable to its people. Such historical ignorance and regional division become major obstacles when state leaders try to find consensus among voters and solutions that address the needs of all citizens.

An essential purpose of this series is to put Floridians in touch with their rich and diverse history and to enhance their understanding of the political developments that have reshaped the state, region, and nation. This series focuses on the Sunshine State's unique and fascinating political history since 1900 and on public policy issues that have influenced the state and nation. The University Press of Florida is dedicated to publishing high-quality works on these subjects. It welcomes book-length manuscripts and is also committed to including in this series shorter essays of twenty-five to fifty pages that address some of the immediately pressing public policy issues confronting Florida.

In this important book, James C. Clark, magazine publisher and faculty member in the University of Central Florida's History Department, depicts two of the most important political figures in the post–World War II political history of Florida—George Smathers and Claude Pepper—and the intersection of their political careers in the U.S. senatorial contest of 1950. As these two men went toe-to-toe in the Democratic primary for the U.S. Senate seat, they gave voice to many of the critically important issues facing the state and nation. At this point in Florida's history, even as migration began to change its politics, only Democrats were elected to statewide office. But these two men represented more than the thinking of Democrats; their platforms spoke to political issues that were beginning to divide the nation. The debates between Pepper and Smathers about the future of the New Deal and about the threat communism posed to the United States and to the free world highlighted issues that were pulsating through both political parties and would define both for a generation.

Clark offers readers a wide-ranging perspective on the personalities and ambitions of these two men, developments leading up to this election, and how they reflected the political dynamics of this age. Clark observes that the campaign not only spoke to foreign policy issues, it also reflected growing concerns about the breadth of the New Deal, civil rights reform, and the role of government regulation in the private sector and in the lives of citizens. In many ways, the campaign was as much about the New Deal and Pepper's dedication to it as it was about the threat of communism.

Pepper had been a leading New Dealer throughout his political career and, according to Clark, he feared the communist issue would derail the New Deal's economic and social programs. Unlike many Americans, Pepper did not view communism as a threat to world peace. Clark notes that Pepper traveled to Russia to meet with Stalin and came away believing that he was "a man Americans could trust."

Pepper and Smathers could not have been further apart on this and other issues. Smathers, a Marine Corps veteran of World War II, regarded communism as a grave threat to freedom and world peace and urged the nation to focus its energies on halting communist aggression in the world. Clark writes that Smathers also opposed civil rights reform, laws protecting the rights of labor, health care reform, and government regulation of business, all of which Pepper favored. In this single campaign, issues that would polarize the nation and define political campaigns for much of the late 1940s, the 1950s, and 1960s would play themselves out.

For all their mutual loyalty to the New Deal, Harry Truman and Claude Pepper did not like one another. Clark notes that in 1948 Pepper, who aspired to be president, had led the efforts to sabotage Truman's presidential candidacy. Truman never forgot Pepper's attempted insurgency and was determined to get revenge, even though the two shared many legislative interests. Ironically, Truman's support of Smathers would subsequently undermine much of the president's legislative agenda. As Clark recounts, Truman urged Smathers, then a congressman from Florida, to run against Pepper in 1950. Clark notes that Smathers had been thinking about challenging Pepper, and the president's urging to "beat that son-of-a-bitch" was all he needed to announce for Pepper's seat. Subsequently, Truman and his supporters worked quietly behind the scenes to aid Smathers's victory.

Despite the opposition of Truman, Pepper had a large following in Florida, particularly in South Florida among senior citizens who had

recently retired to the state from the Northeast. Many of them remained avid New Dealers, and Pepper's support for national health care
addressed an issue near and dear to them, as health care and the costs
associated with it threatened the financial stability of their retirement.
They eagerly embraced Pepper's candidacy and would remain loyal to
him throughout his political career.

Pepper lost this race by only 60,000 votes, even though he was opposed by the Democratic establishment as well as most of Florida's
prominent business community. Ed Ball, who headed the Du Pont Corporation's large Florida landholdings and industrial interests, including the Florida East Coast Railway, detested Pepper and his support
of the New Deal's labor reforms. Ball's financial support underwrote
Smathers's victory, but it was not easy.

In the aftermath of this election, there have been numerous articles
written about the two candidates and the allegations and actions each
undertook to defeat the other. Clark brings his formidable research
skills to bear on these issues, noting that Smathers's campaign was re-
markably sophisticated when compared to Pepper's and that Smathers
was the first of the postwar candidates to successfully brand his opponent as a communist sympathizer. But Smathers's campaign had many
facets to it, Clark notes, including a humorous side reflected in the cards
he distributed at rallies: "Bring prosperity to Florida. Join and support
Florida's fastest growing industry, Canning Pepper."

As Clark points out, this campaign between two formidable politicians was fascinating and influential enough without all the bogus lore
that was attributed to it. Allegations that Joe McCarthy was instrumen-
tal in Smathers's victory were simply wrong, as were tales of Smathers
denouncing Pepper's wife for being a "thespian" before their marriage
and even performing in front of paying customers.

For Clark, the political careers of these two men and their campaign
against one another established the framework for Florida politics in
the 1950s. The issues they raised in this campaign appeared over and
over again in state and local campaigns in Florida and also on the national stage. For the first time in its history, Florida became a focal point
for political developments nationally—and that would remain true
through the succeeding decades. The shifting landscape in Florida as a

result of massive in-migration led to a significant evolution in its politics and in its influence on the national political scene. The Smathers-Pepper senatorial contest in 1950 marked the beginning of the state's political reach beyond its border.

Clark's book offers a compelling portrait of this political era through the careers of two men who dominated state politics for much of the Cold War period and whose political views helped define the debate between the two parties and among voters nationally. It is a book rich in detail about Florida and about the changes that were unfolding in the immediate postwar era. It is also highly entertaining, with wonderful portraits of Smathers and Pepper and important insights into the politics of the Cold War. The book is a must read for Floridians and for scholars and students of state and national politics who seek to understand the changes that redefined Florida in those years and continue to shape it today.

David R. Colburn
University of Florida

Susan MacManus
University of South Florida, Editors

The Making of a Liberal

As the election returns began to come in on May 5 in 1950, Claude Pepper learned early that he would not be returning to the United States Senate. For the first time since becoming a state a century before, Florida voters turned out an incumbent senator, rejecting a man they had elected three times before, and who would later become a national figure. His political career was apparently coming to an end. His opponent, George Smathers, won a convincing victory and would go on to serve three terms in the Senate.

The voting that night had significance far beyond the borders of Florida. Throughout the country, politicians were watching the results and figuring how they could turn them to their advantage. In Washington, President Harry S. Truman gleefully watched his political nemesis go down to defeat and celebrated the election of a man he considered to be a friend. In North Carolina, Willis Smith, seeking to ignite his failing Senate campaign, followed developments in Florida closely and believed the results offered him a path to victory. In California, Congressman Richard Nixon, a friend of Smathers, duplicated his strategy and won a Senate seat six months later. Barry Goldwater, an Arizona businessman, used what he learned from the Smathers victory to successfully take on another incumbent two years later. Even though Smathers was a Democrat, the Republican National Committee interpreted the results as a repudiation of the Truman administration and a formula to win other elections.

Yet, while the election had lasting significance, it turned out that Pepper's political career was not finished. Over the next half century, Pepper returned to Congress, became known throughout the nation, appeared on the cover of *Time* magazine, coauthored a popular autobiography, and—on what would have been his hundredth birthday—was honored by the United States Postal Service with a commemorative stamp. No one could have foreseen this on the night the Florida voters soundly rejected him.

But then, no one could have foreseen that Claude Pepper would ever move beyond the crossroads community of Dudleyville, Alabama, where he was born in 1900. Over his lifetime he would work to solve many of the problems his family faced. Pushing for power projects to light rural homes, water for indoor plumbing, education funding, and provisions for the elderly would in every way benefit the Pepper family. But his political career was brought down in 1950 largely as a result of events half a world away from Dudleyville.

Claude was the son of Joseph Wheeler Pepper and his wife, Lena, née Talbot, who spent their lives trying, and usually failing, to stay ahead of creditors. Joseph Pepper's family came from Ireland or England, probably around the time of the American Revolution, although he was never sure. Lena Pepper's family came from England in the late 1700s. For generations their families farmed in the South. Both of their fathers left the family farm just once, to fight for the Confederacy.[1]

The couple tried to make a success of their small farm near Dudleyville during a hardscrabble time of unpredictable food prices and twelve-hour days. Claude was their fourth child, but the first one to live beyond infancy. In 1904 the family moved to Texas, looking for a new start and more fertile soil. But within a year the family returned to Alabama, struggling to produce a cotton crop and hoping that the buyers would pay them enough to cover their costs. When Claude was ten, the family gave up farming to move to nearby Camp Hill, Alabama, a town of 1,500. It meant a better school for Claude, but the family's economic situation remained precarious. Joseph Pepper tried his hand at business, first in a general merchandise store, then in a furniture store, but both went bankrupt. A series of jobs followed, and finally Joseph Pepper became a deputy sheriff.[2]

Claude Pepper lived to be nearly ninety, and over his lifetime hundreds of stories were told about his childhood. With the retellings, the details often changed. Sometimes the events were altered slightly, other times the characters and the locations, depending on who was telling the story and when. But what emerges is a bright boy whose talent for talking was discovered at an early age. Pepper said that when he was five, he went to the post office in Milan County, Texas, and started telling stories to the old men. Pepper recalled that the men clapped when he finished and give him pennies.[3] Most of his stories involve interaction with adults, not children his own age. There was the local attorney who let Pepper use his office and typewriter for his homework, the banker who came up with money a number of times to help Pepper with college and law school, and the teacher who devoted extra time to him.

Claude took odd jobs to help support the family, but he was also encouraged to finish high school. He graduated in 1917, receiving his diploma in a suit that was clearly too small, an indication of the family's limited financial means.[4] He worked briefly as a hat cleaner, traveling as far as West Point, Georgia, to clean hats. But the life of cheap rooming houses and customer conflicts was not for him, and he abandoned it after a few weeks.[5]

Although barely out of high school and only sixteen, Pepper took a job teaching in a Dothan, Alabama, grammar school. The second semester, he taught at the high school, where some students were older than he was. His year as a teacher has a simple explanation: World War I. The war created a teacher shortage, but as soldiers and those who had found work in military-related jobs began coming home, the demand for Pepper's services ended. He moved on to a Birmingham steel mill, working twelve hours a day, sometimes seven days a week, loading heavy pig-iron ingots onto a conveyor belt.[6] The grueling work convinced Pepper that he needed more education to get ahead.

In September 1918 he enrolled at Howard College, a small Baptist school in Birmingham, but stayed only one night before deciding that the school was not a good fit. He gave up a scholarship there and transferred to the University of Alabama. To pay his tuition, his family borrowed money from a banker, who saw Pepper's potential and overlooked the family's poor financial situation.[7]

When Pepper arrived at the University of Alabama in the fall of 1918, he enlisted in the Student Army Training Corps, and without leaving the campus he became a veteran of World War I. During his fifty-seven days of military service, he injured himself lifting ammunition boxes, qualifying him for veterans benefits.[8] The loans and the government allowance were not enough to pay his expenses, so Pepper took a job in the school power plant, rising before dawn each morning to shovel coal for three hours before class. (Shoveling alongside Pepper was another future senator, John Sparkman.)

Despite having to work, he was one of the most active students on campus, serving as editor of the college newspaper, working on the school yearbook, and briefly running on the cross-country team. His ability as a speaker brought him his greatest fame on campus: as a member of the debate team he represented the university at competitions in North Carolina and Missouri.

Soon his passion for politics began to show. He talked about politics in the school dining hall and served on the student government executive committee during his freshman year, though he failed in an attempt to win the student body presidency. He admired Woodrow Wilson and saw in Wilson's Fourteen Points the hope for a better world. In 1921 he received his degree after just three years, and was elected to Phi Beta Kappa, but he was unable to afford a new key and purchased a used one.[9] The University of Alabama yearbook held a prediction for Pepper: "Watch this boy. He's bound for a seat in a J.P. [Justice of the Peace] court or the gubernatorial chair."[10]

In the fall he enrolled at Harvard Law School with another loan from the Camp Hill banker and his $50-a-month veterans benefit. At Harvard his poverty showed, from his shabby clothes to his glasses. When a classmate asked about the glasses, which were provided free by the government, Pepper was evasive. "I didn't tell him I was a vocational student," he wrote in his diary, adding that "one has a sort of pride in family having means. And it takes courage to stand up & admit your poverty."[11] But the students eventually learned of his status, and Pepper heard that some of his classmates laughed about it. "Damn them, they would have got it [payment] if possible," he wrote. "Mine was legitimate. I'll be somebody when they are still laughing, but they won't laugh then."[12]

Pepper also used the veterans benefits to seek a cure for a lifelong skin condition. His face carried deep acne scars, made more noticeable by his large red nose. He consulted Dr. Townsend Thorndike, one of the nation's leading dermatologists, but Thorndike said nothing could be done about the scars. Pepper wrote to his parents, "How I would be if my face had been smooth & all, how different would I have been."[13]

As he had at Alabama, Pepper talked often about Woodrow Wilson, his first political hero. Even after Wilson left the presidency in 1921, Pepper continued to discuss Wilson's domestic and international programs with his classmates. It is easy to see why Wilson appealed to Pepper. Both were native southerners who went north but retained their love of their native region. Wilson supported the progressive reforms Pepper admired, including the eight-hour workday, the Rural Credits Act to help people like Pepper's parents, the Kern-McGillicuddy Act establishing workmen's compensation, the Keating-Owen Act regulating child labor, and tariff revision. Pepper also approved of Wilson's leading the United States into World War I, and of Wilson's doomed proposal that the United States play a role in international affairs for the first time through the League of Nations. Pepper wrote in his diary that he felt "bitterly towards Republicans for [their] treatment of Wilson."[14] In 1922 Pepper became involved in his first political campaign, not in his native Alabama but in Massachusetts. Colonel William Gaston challenged Republican senator Henry Cabot Lodge, who had opposed Wilson's domestic agenda and the call to join the League of Nations. Pepper campaigned for Gaston, making speeches in Concord, Boston, and Lexington in a losing cause.

His candidate had lost, but it was the start of a political career that would span seven decades. Wilson dreamed of a career in education and later turned to politics, but from the start Pepper thought of little but politics. When he was fourteen and was studying in the office of the local attorney J. H. Rogers, Pepper wrote, "Someday Claude Pepper will be United States Senator."[15] At the University of Alabama and at Harvard, his classmates nicknamed him "Senator."[16] In the Harvard dining hall, his friends called him "the future Senator from Alabama."[17] He said of his friends and professors, "They seemed to take it as an inevitable fact that I . . . was destined for Senate."[18] Pepper encouraged such speculation. His conversations in the dining halls centered on politics and his hope for a political career.

In 1924 Pepper graduated from Harvard in the top third of his class and returned to Alabama. While his classmates flocked to big cities with their prestigious degrees, Pepper headed home. Most of his classmates saw the South as backward, but Pepper wanted to help his family and the region. He wrote in his diary of his desire to "go back home and help the poor in the South. It makes me sad to see the plight of people, hair drawn, sallow, emaciated, unhappy, wearied they all seem. The dirt, the sorrow, the tragedy of it all." He wrote that he wanted to see it made better.[19]

He had done well at Harvard, and the citizens of Dudleyville held a homecoming ceremony for him. His skills as a speaker on that occasion earned him an invitation to speak at Camp Hill welcoming some visiting officials from the Alabama Power Company. That speech impressed a company official, who offered Pepper a job with a large Birmingham law firm. But Pepper already had accepted a one-year position teaching at the new University of Arkansas School of Law.[20] There were only two faculty members, Pepper and the dean, Julian Seesel Waterman.[21]

Pepper enjoyed his year in Arkansas—one of his students was future senator J. William Fulbright—but he turned down an offer to stay, opting to join the thousands flocking to the Florida land boom. From 1920 to 1930, Florida's population increased nearly 50 percent. Land that in 1915 had been given away was selling for hundreds of thousands of dollars a decade later. The ever escalating prices were based on speculation, and often property changed hands half a dozen times a day.[22]

In 1925 Arthur Trumbo, an Oklahoma banker and the father of one of Pepper's students at Arkansas, invited Pepper to go to Perry, Florida, as a consultant in a Florida land deal. The Perry attorney for the land syndicate, Judge William Barnett Davis, formed a temporary association with Pepper.[23] The plan called for Pepper to start working in Perry and then move to Homosassa, on Florida's west coast, to direct the syndicate's business dealings there. Pepper could make enough money to slowly pay off his college loans, help his still-struggling parents, and for the first time in his life be able to enjoy life's pleasures. He wrote to his parents that he could "send you all enough money every month to pay your bills and living expenses."[24]

Pepper arrived in Florida on June 30, 1925, just in time for the collapse of the state's land boom. Four months before Pepper arrived, the *New York Times* reported a slowdown in the boom, and just days after Pepper moved to Perry, *The Nation* pronounced that the boom had turned into a bust. Those stories were followed by a disastrous hurricane in South Florida in 1926 and a citrus crop infestation by the Mediterranean fruit fly. Florida banks began to fail, land sales collapsed, and hundreds of developments turned into overgrown fields.[25] There was no need for Pepper to move to Homosassa, and he remained in Perry to practice with Davis. The prospect of making big money evaporated, but Pepper found his law practice interesting, and he made enough money to gradually pay off his debts and help his parents. Soon he got his first major case, one involving the method used to claim title to land. The case reached the Florida Supreme Court, where Pepper won.

Florida was a state of newcomers. Yesterday's new arrival could become an instant millionaire, or be elected to office. In 1928 Pepper launched his political career as a candidate for the Florida House. The county where he had settled, Taylor County, on the Gulf of Mexico where the Panhandle turns into the peninsula, was one of the state's most lightly populated, with fewer than 15,000 people when he ran for election. Nearly half were African American and could not vote. Pepper won by pointing out that the incumbent, W. T. Hendry, failed to vote on a bill requiring farmers to dip their cattle to remove ticks. It is difficult to imagine an issue such as cattle dipping determining an election, but it was a major issue throughout the South. If cows became infested with ticks, the ticks could spread until entire herds were wiped out. Dipping solved the problem of ticks, but it created a raft of other problems. Dipping tanks had to be build, and that cost money. More than 3,000 tanks were erected in Florida, including 81 in Taylor County in 1928, the year of Pepper's election. In rare cases, dipping could kill the cows; many farmers complained that it damaged the cow's hide, and even in 1928 there were already complaints about the role of government in ordering individuals to do something. In Florida, there were also problems with the effectiveness of the program. Florida had no laws requiring cattle to be fenced in, and rounding them up for dipping was difficult. Pepper never took a stand on the bill but was able to appeal to both supporters and opponents of the legislation merely by saying that the voters needed someone to vote on important issues. He upset Hendry and, as a result of his election, was named to the State Democratic Executive Committee.

As a member of the committee, Pepper received a form letter from Franklin Roosevelt seeking advice on reforms in the Democratic Party. Roosevelt was the newly elected governor of New York and already thinking about running for president. The mass mailing was an effort to reach elected officials throughout the nation. Pepper wrote to Roosevelt, "I want the Democratic Party genuinely to become the Liberal Party of this Nation."[26] In 1928 Pepper campaigned for the Democratic presidential nominee, New York governor Al Smith. But Smith, a Catholic who favored the repeal of Prohibition, lost to Herbert Hoover, the first Republican presidential candidate since Reconstruction to carry Florida.

After just one term, Pepper lost his bid for reelection. He refused to rule out support for a retail sales tax, while his opponent stressed opposition to any such measure. But Pepper later blamed his defeat on his failure to support a resolution censuring the wife of President Herbert Hoover for inviting the wife of a black congressman to the White House.[27] When First Lady Lou Hoover invited all of the congressional wives to a reception at the White House, there was nothing unusual in the event itself, but in 1929 the congressional wives included Mrs. Oscar DePriest, whose husband was the first African American to be elected to Congress from the North. The invitation outraged many in the South and led to the introduction of resolutions in southern legislatures condemning it. In Florida the resolution passed easily, but Pepper became one of thirteen House members voting against it. Pepper said he did not think it a proper matter for the Florida Legislature to consider.

Pepper's opponent did not mention the race issue during the campaign, focusing only on the sales tax. Pepper carried just one precinct.[28] Not only did he lose his House seat in 1930, but the Great Depression began to affect him. The bank in Perry failed, and Pepper lost his small savings account. He also lost most of his law business. Like millions of

Americans, he faced the prospect of remaining where he was, without much hope for a better future, or moving. In 1930 Pepper moved to Tallahassee to start over, forming a partnership with Curtis Waller, a former aide to Senator Pat Harrison of Mississippi.[29]

In 1932 Pepper campaigned on behalf of the Democratic National Committee, traveling throughout Florida for Roosevelt, who easily won Florida and the presidency. Pepper had never met Roosevelt, but those speeches were the beginning of a relationship that extended for more than a dozen years and become the foundation for Pepper's political philosophy. Pepper became both the most enthusiastic and the last of the New Dealers. From 1932 to 1989, there were few Pepper speeches that did not mention Roosevelt and the New Deal.

Hoover was not the only political victim of the election. The Republicans lost control of the House of Representatives in 1930 and the Senate in 1932. Americans demanded action, and the old politics and the old answers were not sufficient. Florida's two United States senators had held elective office since the nineteenth century and were no longer popular with the voters. They had been installed in an era when the Florida Legislature selected U.S. senators, then held on to their seats when the voters were given the power to choose. The senior senator, Duncan Upshaw Fletcher, had been in the Senate for thirty-four years, rising to chair the Senate Committee on Banking and Currency. The junior senator, Park Trammell, became mayor of Lakeland in 1899, moved through the state legislature, served as Florida attorney general, and became governor in 1912. He was elected to the U.S. Senate in 1916 and reelected in 1922 and 1928. While Fletcher was generally respected, a Washington newspaper named Trammell as "the Senator least inclined to work."[30]

In 1934 Pepper decided to run against Trammel. A decade earlier, it would have been difficult to envision Pepper or anyone successfully challenging Trammell, but the Great Depression changed the rules of American politics; officeholders with decades of faithful service were voted out. Pepper had served only one term in the state legislature, lived in the state for less than ten years, and had no money, but candidates such as Pepper were winning office throughout the country. "The sentiment of our people demands that a candidate be free of reactionary tendencies and have a point of view boldly in sympathy with the New

Deal," Pepper said in making his announcement. There were three other candidates in the race, but Pepper quickly established himself as the strongest Roosevelt supporter. "I am with Franklin D. Roosevelt and shall give him aggressive and helpful cooperation. The cornerstone of the New Deal is the welfare of the common man. Upon that cornerstone I shall make my campaign."[31] The state had been in a depression since the collapse of the land boom in 1926, so Pepper's platform made his campaign more promising.

By embracing Roosevelt and the New Deal, Pepper set himself apart from the other challengers. The same strategy worked for other candidates, most notably Lyndon Johnson in a congressional campaign in Texas. In a multicandidate race during the Great Depression, the one who established the closest rapport with Roosevelt and the New Deal could usually do well. The largely rural population stood to benefit from the dozens of New Deal programs, and even businessmen thought the plan could save their struggling firms. Pepper also received endorsement from John H. Perry, the owner of the *Jacksonville Journal*, who complained of Trammell's "absolute inaction in Congress."[32] Pepper made Trammell the issue by pointing out that of the eighty-one bills Trammell introduced during his third term, just four minor bills became law.[33]

In the first primary, Trammell received 81,323 votes, but to the surprise of many, Pepper finished close behind with 79,396 votes. The other three candidates received a total of 53,000 votes, forcing a runoff election.[34] In the second primary, Trammell made race the main issue, pointing to Pepper's vote against the resolution condemning Mrs. Herbert Hoover for inviting a black woman to the White House: "HOOVER DINES NEGRO, PEPPER SAYS O.K.," read the headline on the handbill the Trammell supporters circulated.[35] Trammell also claimed that because Pepper attended a Northern school—Harvard University—he must be in favor of racial equality.[36] Pepper's campaign promoted a pension for anyone over seventy years of age and emphasized his support for labor unions. But primarily he talked about his support for Roosevelt and the New Deal.

Pepper lost the runoff election by 4,050 votes, 103,028 to 98,978.[37] "I extend to you my best wishes," Pepper telegraphed. "If I can in any way aid you to serve the people of Florida be ever free to command me."[38]

But others were not so willing to accept the results. It was clear after the first primary that there were irregularities in the voting in Tampa. In a state with little in the way of strong political organizations, the Tampa political machine could produce a significant number of votes. Although Pepper publically dismissed the reports of corruption, he spent part of the runoff day in Tampa visiting the suspect precincts. He said he saw Trammell supporters voting repeatedly while his supporters were prevented from entering the polls by heavily guarded election officials.

After the runoff, Edwin Dart Lambright of the *Tampa Morning Tribune* wrote that he believed that 6,000 of Trammell's votes were fraudulent. In one Tampa precinct, Trammell received 446 votes to one for Pepper. In another, Pepper received 75 votes while Trammell got 715. In all, Trammell received 6,511 votes to 360 for Pepper in the questionable Tampa precincts. Lambright wanted Pepper to call for an investigation, but Pepper accepted the results and returned to his law practice.[39] Any challenge was doomed: Trammell had friends in Washington and Tallahassee who could be counted on to come to his aid. Around the state, Pepper's popularity increased as the result of his gracious acceptance of defeat. The *Orlando Morning Sentinel* editorialized that "someday, in some election, the people of Florida are going to give Pepper another break, or rather a new deal. That is the general feeling. It is now Saint Pepper."[40]

On May 8, 1936, Trammell died in Washington, creating an opportunity for Pepper. Newspapers also speculated that Judge Charles O. Andrews of Orlando and former governor Doyle Carlton of Tampa might be candidates. The State Democratic Executive Committee was responsible for deciding whether to hold an open primary or have the committee select the nominee. Before they could decide, the state's other senator, Duncan Fletcher, died. Pepper announced his candidacy for Fletcher's seat, while Carlton and Andrews competed for Trammell's seat. Pepper went to the Senate without opposition. Andrews upset former governor Carlton 67,387 to 62,530. The *Leesburg Commercial* said, "As soon as Claude Pepper has time to learn the ropes, he will be recognized as one of the really great men of the Senate."[41]

The Junior Senator

By the time Pepper arrived in Washington in late 1936 as a champion of the New Deal, it was all but over. He had run on a platform supporting a New Deal that was running out of steam. There had never been a grand New Deal strategy, but rather a hodgepodge of legislation thrown at Congress starting in 1933 to see what might help end the nation's economic nightmare. In his first two years as president, Roosevelt worked to salvage American industry, then he moved to help unions organize (Wagner Act) and to create the Works Progress Administration, the Civilian Conservation Corps, and most famously Social Security.

Nevertheless, 1937 began with Roosevelt's second inauguration and high hopes. Roosevelt intended to use his overwhelming reelection as a mandate to continue his New Deal programs. "I see one-third of a nation ill-housed, ill-clad, ill-nourished," Roosevelt said in taking the oath for his second term. He could point to a series of dramatic accomplishments in his first term: industrial output had doubled since 1932 and farm income increased almost fourfold.[1]

But at the outset of his second term, Roosevelt made a major political miscalculation. He proposed a complicated program to allow him to name more justices—presumably sympathetic to his programs—to the Supreme Court. During his first term, Roosevelt did not get to name any justices, and the court was loaded with aging conservatives who struck down many of his New Deal proposals. His plan touched a raw nerve in the nation, gave the undermanned Republicans a rallying cry, and divided the Democratic Party. Although many Americans did not even know how many justices were on the court, the idea of disturbing an American institution alarmed voters.[2] Still, there are many who contend that while Roosevelt lost the battle, he won the war. Shortly after Roosevelt made his proposal, the court switched directions. In a 5-to-4 decision, the court upheld a minimum wage case almost identical to one it overturned earlier, then upheld the Wagner Act by the same 5-to-4 margin. Despite these favorable court rulings, Roosevelt lost considerable public and political support for his attack on the court.[3]

Also in 1937, Roosevelt ordered cuts in federal spending in an attempt to balance the budget. He cut the relief rolls and nearly eliminated public works spending. Roosevelt and his advisers, principally Secretary of the Treasury Henry Morgenthau, thought that the economy could stand some fiscal restraint, and they were nervous about the size of the federal debt. It was a bad decision; the economy collapsed as industrial activity dropped sharply and unemployment soared.

But Pepper went to Washington to fight for the New Deal, and he continued to be its champion even as others deserted the cause. His own life convinced him that many Americans needed help and that the government should provide that help. He was certain that he could not have attended Harvard without the federal aid he received, and he knew firsthand what life was like for poor farmers in the South. He believed Roosevelt's New Deal held the answers to the problems he personally experienced.

Pepper arrived in Washington in time for a debate on an issue that presented problems for him throughout his Senate career, a bill to make lynching a federal crime. Pepper fell in line with his fellow southerners, denouncing the debate as a waste of time and saying that there were more important issues to be considered. For the rest of his career, Pepper wrestled with the conflict between his desire to be a national political figure and the need to keep his constituents in Florida placated by opposing civil rights legislation.

During debate on a farm bill, Pepper found a way to link farming and civil rights. He argued that blacks were being lynched in the South for economic reasons and that improving the lot of all southerners would cut down on lynchings. "There is an actual correlation between the number of lynchings and the price of cotton," he told the Senate.[4] But in the next session Pepper took part in a filibuster against the antilynching bill, talking for six hours one day and five the next. In one speech, Pepper questioned the place of blacks in society, saying that giving the vote to blacks in the South would "endanger the supremacy of a race to which God has committed the destiny of a continent, perhaps of a world."[5] The filibuster worked, and the antilynching bill died.

It was routine for southern senators to take their place in the filibuster rotation when civil rights legislation was being considered, but during the course of the filibuster, Pepper drew surprising criticism from two liberals. Pennsylvania senator Joseph Guffey warned Pepper that criticizing blacks endangered his chance of playing a role in national politics, and Tommy Corcoran, a Roosevelt aide, urged him to take a temperate tone or risk losing his liberal credentials.[6] Fortunately for Pepper, Roosevelt did not make civil rights an integral part of the New Deal because he did not want to challenge the powerful Southern Democrats. In general, blacks benefited from New Deal programs only when they were not excluded from broad-based programs designed to aid the poor.[7] That meant that Pepper could support the entire New Deal program without offending Florida's white voters.

In addition to the farm program, a major part of Roosevelt's plan for his second term was the fair labor standards bill. The bill called for a minimum wage of forty cents an hour, and a maximum working week of forty hours. It was opposed by much of industry, including Florida's large timber interests. Pepper said he was opposed to the original bill and worked for change in the Senate Education and Labor Committee.[8] He reshaped the bill to exempt many of Florida's workers, including those in agriculture and in the turpentine industry.[9] But he failed to get an exemption for the lumber industry, and the timber owners worried that the weak law could become stronger over time. The fair labor standards legislation was one of those bills on which few wanted compromise. Business wanted no restrictions on its ability to set hours and wages, while workers wanted both. Pepper's work at crafting a compromise gained him few friends, and the weakened form of the fair labor standards bill angered many in Florida and played a dominant role in Pepper's 1938 campaign.

Pepper's life became a constant political campaign. In 1936 he ran in two losing primaries, in 1937 he won an election, and now in 1938, just months after being sworn in, he faced the voters again. In little more than two years, he ran in five elections.

On January 2, 1938, Pepper and Congressman James Mark Wilcox announced their candidacies for the Senate seat. Wilcox, a three-term representative from South Florida, had never lost an election. A third candidate, former governor David Sholtz, had burst onto the Florida political scene in 1932, but once he took office, his popularity fell rapidly amid reports of corruption. Having failed to secure what he considered a decent job in the Roosevelt administration, he was trying for a political comeback.[10] Like Pepper, Sholtz was running as a champion of the New Deal. Findley Moore, a Lake City businessman running on an antiblack and anti-immigrant platform, also announced his candidacy, as did Thomas Merchant, who wanted a national referendum held before the nation went to war.

The Florida primary election was important to Roosevelt, who was anxious to prove that the New Deal still had life and was popular with the voters. Florida held its primary in May, before other states, and both political parties saw it as a bellwether. On February 6, 1938, the president's son James Roosevelt announced that, while the administration did not want to tell the voters of Florida what to do, "it is our sincere hope that he [Pepper] will be returned to the Senate."[11]

For a variety of reasons, Pepper became the poster boy for the New Deal. He supported every single New Deal measure and he was a southerner. Roosevelt faced his most difficult time with Democratic senators from the South. Wilcox was an early New Deal supporter but parted with Roosevelt over adding Justices to the Supreme Court and the wage-hour measure and labeled Pepper a "rubber stamp" for the president.[12] A Pepper victory might convince other members of Congress that the public wanted the legislation passed.[13]

It was during this campaign that Pepper first met George A. Smathers, the man who would defeat him twelve years later. Smathers was a law student at the University of Florida who agreed to direct Pepper's reelection campaign on campus. Smathers found that the Pepper campaign in surrounding Alachua County was in disarray and ended up directing the campaign for the entire county. Pepper was impressed by Smathers and wrote, "You and I are young men and there is a lot to be done. Nobody would appreciate more than I the privilege of working with you."[14] Smathers responded by writing, "Anytime, anyplace . . . that I can aid your campaign please let me know."[15]

Just before the primary, *Time* magazine put Pepper on its cover with the caption "A Florida fighting-cock will be a White House weather vane."[16] Pepper won with 58.4 percent of the vote. He received 242,350 votes to 110,675 for Wilcox and just 52,785 for Sholtz.[17] Pepper did well in North Florida, winning the rural vote, and in Central Florida. His strongest opposition came in Florida's Gold Coast, the counties around Palm Beach where the state's wealthier voters lived. Pepper sent a telegram to Roosevelt saying, "The true principles of democracy as exemplified by your great leadership have just received a striking vote of confidence and approval in Florida."[18]

Pepper returned enthusiastically to the Senate in 1939 with a full six-year term, but he soon encountered more frustrations. The New Deal stalled during 1937 and by 1939 was in full retreat. Pepper condemned what he saw as "the unrighteous partnership of those who have been willing to scuttle the American Government and the American people and to jeopardize the peace of the world because they hate Roosevelt and what Roosevelt stands for." Pepper pointed to the United States Chamber of Commerce and the National Association of Manufacturers as the villains, and criticized those in Congress who "prostituted their power to serve" them.[19] Although Pepper was a loyal New Deal supporter, he was unable to sway votes in the Senate. He lacked seniority and was not popular with his colleagues, many of whom saw him as a publicity seeker who was quick to criticize others in order to gain attention. *Time* magazine reported in 1940 that "He was not well liked in the Senate, had no great influence there."[20] After reading the magazine, Pepper wrote in his diary that he "couldn't be [popular] and have done what I have to step on their toes."[21] He was bitter at the recognition others in the Senate received. He wrote to a friend, "Too often people like Senator [Harry] Byrd and his type, who prattle about economy, are thought of as being statesmen and my kind of fellow, who wants to see the people educated, healthy and with a chance to work as the irresponsible and radical one."[22]

Meanwhile, the focus on the nation's economic problems was gradually giving way to the war in Europe. The end of World War I seemed to hold great hope for world peace, but the Treaty of Versailles quickly turned from a bold vision to just another political dispute. At the time, the Senate rejected appeals from President Wilson and chose not to join the League of Nations. Isolationism dominated American foreign policy during the Depression years, and in 1937 Congress passed sweeping neutrality legislation to keep the United States from being pulled into another European war. A 1937 survey asked if America should take part if another war came to Europe. Of those surveyed, 95 percent said "No," and the same percentage wanted the United States to do "everything possible to keep us out of foreign wars."[23]

Pepper was one of the few in Congress who correctly identified the threat Adolf Hitler posed to the world. In 1939, while most of his colleagues quietly watched from the sidelines, Pepper sounded the alarm. Pepper feared the United States would become "hemmed in between a dominant Japan on the West and a dominant Germany on the East." He began lobbying to allow Great Britain to purchase arms on a cash-and-carry basis. But other senators felt that the United States was dragged into World War I because it was too willing to serve as arms merchant and banker for Britain and France. They rejected Pepper's argument and retained the neutrality laws.

Although few paid attention to Pepper's proposals, he was not discouraged, introducing a new resolution in 1939 to allow Roosevelt to send virtually every type of military equipment to the Allies. Pepper pledged to make a speech a day on the subject until something was done.[24] Despite the worsening situation in Europe, and the note of alarm in Pepper's speeches, he gained just one supporter in the Senate, Joseph Guffey of Pennsylvania.[25] Other senators, including Scott Lucas of Illinois, Josiah Bailey of North Carolina, and the venerable Burton K. Wheeler of Montana, responded with attacks on Pepper. Most of those who spoke out against Pepper were isolationists, but even those who thought the United States should play a role in the world did not come to his aid. It seemed that no one was listening to Pepper, although his constant calls for action were making him known throughout the country. An isolationist group calling itself Mothers of America hanged Pepper in effigy outside the Capitol. The coconut-headed dummy was given to Pepper as a souvenir. Still he pushed on, urging the construction of 50,000 airplanes, the creation of a three-million-soldier army and a two-ocean navy, and the transfer of American destroyers to Britain.[26] However, Roosevelt knew that isolationist sentiment in the country remained strong and that aiding England could damage his attempt for an unprecedented third term as president.

Pepper's problem was that he was so closely linked to FDR. Even those who agreed with his concerns about Germany saw him as little more than a Roosevelt mouthpiece. The *New York Herald Tribune* said that "when the White House has an important trial balloon to send up, it invites Senator Pepper to supply the necessary oratorical helium for the ascension."[27] *Time* magazine said, "Claude Pepper was the only one whom Franklin Roosevelt considered anywhere near fit to expound the Administration's foreign and defense policies."[28] But although he routinely informed Roosevelt before taking a stance, Pepper often acted without White House approval.

Speaking shortly before Germany invaded Poland, Pepper warned that the war would require the nation to turn all of its attention to "defense and security."[29] Pepper always maintained that if Congress had listened to his plea, Hitler might have been dissuaded from attacking.[30] After the German attack on Poland in September 1939, Roosevelt called Congress back into session to deal with the Neutrality Acts. From that moment, Pepper focused on world affairs.

The isolationism that was so strong in the Midwest was not a factor in Florida, and Pepper's position did not hurt him among the state's voters. But being right on military preparedness did not obscure the fact that he alienated many of his fellow senators with his critical remarks during debates. None of the senators who opposed him wanted to be reminded that they were wrong about Adolf Hitler. What did hurt Pepper in Florida was the growing opposition to the New Deal, primarily among the state's leading businessmen.

The South and the New Deal were always an odd couple. When the New Deal began in 1933, Southern Democrats were its most dedicated supporters. The South looked to Washington for help in building highways and providing flood control and electric power, just as it had looked to the North in the past for help.[31]

Roosevelt's election radically changed the status of Southern Democrats. Before 1933, Southern Democrats were the largest single bloc in the party, faithfully providing their electoral votes for Democrats as Republican presidential candidates rolled to victory. But with the Roosevelt election, and with newfound Democratic strength in the North, the importance of the Southern Democrats within the party began to decline. Southern Democrats went from a majority faction in a minority party to a minority faction in a majority party.[32] In 1918 the South controlled 26 of the 27 Democratic Senate seats and 107 of the 131 Democratic House seats in Congress, but by 1936 the South had 26 of the 75 Democratic Senate seats and 116 House seats out of 333 the Democrats held. The elimination of the two-thirds rule for nominating Democratic presidential candidates also eliminated the South's power to veto presidential nominees. Even in the general election, the South lost influence. If Roosevelt had failed to carry a single southern state, he still would have won all four of his presidential elections.[33]

But a bigger concern for the Southern Democrats was the makeup of the Roosevelt coalition—the Northern labor unions, big city machines, blacks, immigrants, and intellectuals. Gradually the southerners in Congress began to move away from Roosevelt's New Deal and toward the conservative Republicans. Because of their seniority, the southerners rose to committee chairmanships and used those positions to block legislation they did not like, including bills outlawing lynching and the poll tax. In 1935 Roosevelt told Felix Frankfurter, "I will have trouble with my own Democratic party from this time on in trying to carry out further programs of reform and recovery."[34] The movement away from the party was clear by 1936, when 43 of the 102 congressional Democrats from the South deserted the party on votes more than half the time.[35] Many southerners thought the worst of the Great Depression was over and saw no need for the New Deal's expanding welfare state and federal bureaucracy. The Roosevelt programs to help the South drew unwanted blacks to the Democratic Party.[36]

In 1943 the Southern Democrats and Republicans joined forces to try to savage New Deal programs. They were aided by the 1942 election results, in which the Democrats lost 42 seats in the House of Representatives and 12 seats in the Senate. The losses came from outside the South, which gave the southerners a greater voice in the Democratic Party. The new coalition of southerners and conservative Republicans attacked the Civilian Conservation Corps, the Works Progress Administration, and the National Youth Administration.[37]

Roosevelt still had loyal followers from the South in Congress, but often they were out of step with the political situation in their home states. At first glance, the list of New Deal supporters in the South seems impressive. Besides Pepper, there was Congressman Lyndon Johnson in Texas, Governor Olin Johnston in South Carolina, Governor E. D. Rivers in Georgia, Senator Lister Hill in Alabama, Governor Dave Sholtz in Florida, Congressman Maury Maverick in Texas, and Governor Burnet Maybank in South Carolina. But a closer look shows that there was little to support the notion that the South was becoming more liberal during the New Deal. Rivers was replaced after four years by the anti-Roosevelt racist Eugene Talmadge; Olin Johnston lost his first bid for the Senate to an anti–New Dealer; Hill moved to the political right to keep his seat; Sholtz was discredited; Maverick lost his seat after two terms; and Pepper eventually lost. Only Maybank and Hill managed to hold on without a defeat.[38] Although Pepper and the other southern New Deal supporters were often considered too liberal for their constituents, they were hardly true liberals, especially in civil rights.

Still, the voters in the South remained loyal to Roosevelt. In 1944, southern voters gave Roosevelt 69 percent of their votes, compared to about 50 percent in the Northeast and Midwest. It was a strange contradiction: among voters, Roosevelt found his greatest support in the South; among Democratic senators and congressmen, he found his greatest opposition in the South. At the same time, businessmen who had begged for help in 1933 began to see the New Deal as a threat to their economic well-being by 1937. As the businessmen turned against the New Deal, they also turned against its supporters, including Pepper.

New Deal critics have maintained that Roosevelt's failure to back liberals and challenge the conservative power structure of the South was caused by a lack of will. But when Roosevelt tried in 1938 to challenge thirteen incumbent Democrats in the South and West, it turned into a political embarrassment. The Florida primary was in May, followed by primaries in Georgia and South Carolina, where Senators Walter George and Ed Smith were seeking reelection. Both were obstacles to a number of Roosevelt measures, and Roosevelt was supporting opponents. If Pepper could win, it might send a message to voters in Georgia and South Carolina. But both used the Roosevelt intervention as a campaign issue and won reelection.

Making Enemies

All politicians make enemies, and the more controversial a politician becomes, the more likely the number of enemies will increase. Throughout his career, Claude Pepper managed to alienate people with long memories and large bank accounts. At the top of Pepper's enemy list was a onetime supporter, Ed Ball, the most powerful man in Florida. What is surprising is not that Ball and Pepper became bitter enemies but that the two ever thought they could work together. They were so very different, it is difficult to find anything these men had in common. Pepper believed that government was the instrument that could make things better, while Ball viewed private enterprise as what made America better and saw government as the enemy of the businessman.

Ball's biographers, like Pepper's, have relied a great deal on memories of the subject, and the stories have become embellished or changed over the years. For example, in their Ball biography *Confusion to the Enemy*, authors and friends Raymond K. Mason and Virginia Harrison wrote that Ball's father was once attorney general of Texas, which was untrue.[1] Ball was born in 1888 in a rural area of Virginia, the son of a Confederate veteran. He dropped out of school after the eighth grade and went to work in a series of jobs. Around 1900 he first met Alfred du Pont, a member of the Delaware du Ponts who was estranged from his family. Du Pont came to Virginia to hunt but soon developed a friendship with the Ball family.

Ball and most of his siblings moved to Los Angeles, and Ed Ball became a salesman. He sold cars, law books, and office furniture. He claimed that as a furniture salesman on the West Coast he earned $18,000 a year—about half a million dollars today. Again, a questionable claim.[2]

Alfred du Pont and his second wife had a difficult and distant relationship by 1920. At the same time, his exchange of letters with Ed Ball's sister Jessie became friendlier, although they had not seen one another for fourteen years. He decided to head to California to see Jessie, while his wife traveled to South Carolina. When he arrived in California, he received a telegram informing him that his wife had died unexpectedly in Charleston. One year later Alfred du Pont married Jessie Ball, and they soon moved to Florida.

Du Pont hired Ed Ball as an assistant, and over the next six years they came to dominate politics in Florida. After du Pont's death in 1935, Ball took over the operation of the du Pont fortune, which Alfred du Pont intended to go to help crippled children, but which instead was used primarily to build up the power and wealth of Ed Ball. In 1974 reporter Curtis Wilkie of the *Wilmington News* reported that the charity Ball controlled earned $15.2 million in income in 1972, but just $2.8 million went to help children; most of the rest ended up in the accounts of the bank Ball controlled and partially owned.[3]

Ball's empire came to include 1.5 million acres of land, more than two dozen banks, and railroads. From his Jacksonville hotel suite, he also controlled the Florida Legislature. Because of inequitable apportionment, control of the Florida Legislature passed to a small group of men who came from the lightly populated Florida Panhandle. Ball controlled those men and thereby could dictate which taxes were passed—or eliminated—and the fate of legislation. While Claude Pepper spent a lifetime advocating programs to help others, Ball spent his life enriching himself.

For half a century, Ball continued to run the du Pont empire for his own advantage, neglecting the crippled children that Alfred du Pont wanted to help. Ball simply did not like to be told "no." For Ball, court challenges were a sport. He tried to cheat others in the de Pont family, dragging parts of du Pont's will through the courts for three decades to deny them what amounted to a small fraction of the estate. In his suite in the Robert Meyer Hotel in Jacksonville, he ruled his empire from a living room full of hotel-issue furniture with few personal touches. Among business associates—he had few true friends—he always made his trademark toast over bourbon: "Confusion to the enemy."

While Alfred du Pont had moved to Florida in 1925 to take advantage of an amendment to the Florida Constitution—there could be no personal income tax in Florida without a constitutional change—Ball concentrated on taking advantage of the skewed apportionment favoring North Florida. Representatives of just 10 percent of the state's population controlled the fate of the other 90 percent. Ball dominated North Florida, and the legislature did what he said.

Like many businessmen during the 1930s, Ball was an initial supporter of Franklin Roosevelt's New Deal, but as the economy began to recover, Ball became increasingly critical of government bureaucracy, although he remained a Pepper supporter until 1944.

Ball supported Pepper in 1936 and 1938 and later said he "helped the buzzard get elected."[4] As 1944 began, the two were still relatively close, although Ball had abandoned his support of Roosevelt's New Deal policies. When Ball was seriously injured in a train accident in North Carolina, Pepper wrote him a friendly letter. Ball thanked Pepper, saying the letter "Did much to cheer me up." But Ball could not resist an opportunity to criticize the New Deal: "The only thing that I know that is tougher than a train wreck has been surviving in business through the depression and the regulations and regimentations of the New Deal; so, having survived both so far, I really feel that I have a right to be optimistic."[5] It was their last friendly exchange for the rest of their lives.

In 1944, three events dramatically changed Pepper's once-friendly relationship with Ball into one of hatred. In one year, Pepper attacked Ball's business interests twice and launched a personal attack based on incorrect information.

The first incident involved a tax bill to raise money to fight World War II. In 1943 Roosevelt asked Congress for $11 billion in new taxes. It seemed a simple matter; surely no one would deny money to help win the war. But Congress was in a rebellious mood. The Republicans had posted significant gains in the 1942 elections, and many Democrats refused to follow Roosevelt's lead.

In what should have been a routine piece of legislation, both Democrats and Republicans began hacking away at the Roosevelt tax plan, butchering his request to just $2 billion, of which only $1 billion represented new revenue. Then they began tacking on amendments to give tax advantages to selected businesses, including major benefits for Ed Ball and other Floridians.

The first benefit for Ball involved "renegotiation," a complex bureaucratic system allowing the government to reduce the amount paid to a company after the work was done. The idea was to prevent war contractors from profiteering. If a company's profit on a war-related contract was found by government auditors to be excessive, the government could renegotiate the contract. One of the amendments to the Roosevelt tax bill exempted many businesses from the process. Ball's St. Joe Paper Company made boxes and containers for companies shipping war supplies. Under the old rules, his company faced the renegotiation process, but under the legislation passed by Congress, the company was exempt. That meant that no matter how much money St. Joe Paper made, it was not subject to government review.[6] It could be a huge windfall for Ed Ball.

The second amendment that benefited Ball involved taxing provisions for bondholders. This obscure amendment, designed to benefit only a handful of people, saved Ball money because of his purchase of Florida East Coast Railway Company bonds. More important, it helped him in his battle with the Atlantic Coast Line Railroad in acquiring the FEC. The FEC was in bankruptcy, and its bonds were all but worthless. Ball began buying them for pennies on the dollar. No interest was being paid on the bonds, but the railroad claimed a deduction of the unpaid interest, and when the Internal Revenue Service questioned the deduction, leaving open the possibility that the railroad might owe substantial back taxes, it became an expensive proposition for Ball.[7]

Finally, the bill contained an amendment to aid Ball's vast timber interests. The provision allowed Ball to treat profits from lumber as capital gains instead of ordinary income, giving him a lower tax rate.

Ball stood to be one of the biggest winners in the country from the legislation. He would be spared the new taxes Roosevelt requested, be assured that no government bureaucrats would question his war-related profits, be guaranteed tax breaks on his bonds in the Florida East Coast Railway, and be taxed at a lower rate on his lumber profits.

Helping Ed Ball was certainly not Roosevelt's goal when he asked Congress for new taxes. When the results of this amendment process became known, Roosevelt told congressional leaders that he would veto the bill—and he did, declaring that the legislation "is not a tax bill but a tax relief bill providing relief not for the needy but for the greedy."[8] Roosevelt singled out two of the exemptions that benefited Ball, the reclassification of timber profits and the tax breaks for bondholders.

The president's decision provided opponents in Congress with an opportunity to assert themselves. There were just too many features benefiting too many factions for Roosevelt's veto to hold. The lobbying was intense as supporters of the legislation fought for the dozens of tax breaks. Ball hired Charles Murchison to lobby Pepper. Murchison was a Harvard classmate of Pepper's, a cocounsel in a major case, and, in December 1936, best man at Pepper's wedding to Mildred Webster.[9]

With the veto, Pepper was forced to choose between supporting Roosevelt and backing Ball and hundreds of other Florida businessmen. The House overrode the veto 299 to 95, far more than the number needed, and sent the bill to the Senate. Pepper was in Florida campaigning for reelection when the matter came up. He had three options: vote to uphold the president's veto, vote to override the veto, or stay in Florida and simply not return for the vote.[10]

Pepper's staff sensed that he wanted to support the president and knew that doing so would be politically damaging. They urged him to stay in Florida. Before returning to Washington, Pepper went to St. Augustine to have dinner with Herbert E. Wolfe, a friend of Ball's, a major player in Democratic politics, and a road builder who also stood to benefit from the bill. Wolfe pressed Pepper to vote to override Roosevelt's veto. Wolfe left the dinner believing that Pepper agreed with him, which made the subsequent vote even more difficult for Wolfe and Ball to accept.[11]

Despite Wolfe's impression, Pepper returned to Washington with his mind made up to support Roosevelt. Although Pepper knew that the tax was unpopular, he saw Roosevelt's stand as "making a magnificent liberal fight."[12] Not only did he decide to vote to uphold the president, but he tried to rally others. He was the only one in the Senate to speak in favor of Roosevelt's veto. Even the Democratic leader in the Senate, Alben Barkley, spoke against the legislation. Pepper wrote in his diary, "Bumbling Barkley has bumbled again." According to Pepper, FDR did not regard Barkley as a strong enough leader to be fully trusted. "He is not a natural leader, sometimes lacks industry."[13] Ironically, as Pepper's political career was in decline in 1948, the Democrats selected Barkley as their vice presidential nominee, a post Pepper coveted. While his fellow senators yelled out, "Vote, vote," Pepper urged his colleagues to support the president. It was a losing cause, as only twelve other Democrats and a single Republican voted to sustain the veto.[14]

The second conflict with Ball was more personal and involved an attack based upon incorrect information. In early 1944, as the tax bill moved through Congress, Pepper visited West Palm Beach, staying with a friend. Traditionally the Florida tourism season began on the first Sunday in December as visitors began arriving to spend the winter months. In 1941 the opening Sunday was the same day the Japanese attacked Pearl Harbor and thrust the United States into World War II. Florida hotels initially worried that the war might hamper tourism. But the mild weather was a major attraction to the military seeking training sites. Pilots and soldiers could train year around, and sailors found plenty of water. The army began throwing up barracks but could not meet the demand. Soon the government was leasing tens of thousands of hotel rooms. The list included every type of hotel from the most basic to the state's finest resorts such as the Don Cesar in St. Petersburg Beach and the Breakers in Palm Beach.

At the Breakers, the government leased some rooms for convalescing soldiers while regular guests occupied other rooms. The hotel's ownership situation was murky. It was owned by the Florida East Coast Hotel Corporation, a subsidiary of the bankrupt Florida East Coast Railway Company. The company also owned the railway, but the hotel and railway were operated as separate entities. At the time, Ed Ball was acquiring bonds in the railroad, and he eventually came to own it, but he did not own the railroad in 1944, and even if he had, this would not have given him ownership of the hotel.

During his visit, someone told Pepper that the wounded soldiers were not allowed to stray more than two feet off the sidewalks around the neatly manicured golf course. It was never certain whether what Pepper was told was true, and he did nothing to obtain more information. He saw a chance to link the poor treatment of wounded soldiers to his nemesis, Ed Ball. In April the army announced plans to close the military hospital at the Breakers because of the high operating cost. The patients were to be moved to other hospitals. With just a month to go before the 1944 primary election, Pepper turned the closing of the hospital into a campaign issue with a scathing attack on Ball. He claimed that Ball wanted to make more money by renting the rooms to the wealthy.

In a telegram to Roosevelt, Pepper said the closing "has been influenced either by the present management of the corporation which owns the hotel, or by a mistaken policy of economy by the War Department."[15] He wrote incorrectly that "the corporation is headed by Edward G. Ball of Jacksonville, brother of Mrs. Alfred I. DuPont, and in charge of the DuPont interests in Florida."[16] There is no indication that Pepper or his staff did any research into the case. It sounded compelling—the case of a businessman making wounded veterans suffer to please wealthy people. Certainly nothing could be worse than the charge of turning one's back on wounded soldiers in time of war, but Ball did not have anything to do with the operation of the hotel. It was the type of reckless charge that marked Pepper's political career. During the 1944 presidential campaign, he linked the law firm of prominent Republicans Thomas E. Dewey and John Foster Dulles to Adolf Hitler. Although Pepper later complained of unfair and reckless charges against himself, he engaged in them throughout his political career.[17]

Ball sent Jacksonville attorney A. Y. Milam, who once worked with Pepper, to Washington to explain the situation and demand an apology. Pepper refused to see Milam, who was left to explain the facts to a Pepper aide. Pepper was informed of his mistake and issued a retraction that fell short of the apology Ball wanted, further enraging him.[18]

Raymond Mason, who became a Ball business associate, said, "Nothing ever got Mr. Ball's blood boiling quicker than this erroneous statement, for in fact neither Ball nor the du Ponts had any connection with the hotel either prior to or at the time of the incident."[19]

Finally, Ball and Pepper clashed over the Florida East Coast Railway, which eventually cost Pepper not only Ball's support but also that of many union members. The state's other senator, Spessard Holland, later wrote, "I could never understand why [Pepper] would get into that fight. . . . I think it will haunt him for the rest of his life."[20]

For most people, the Florida East Coast Railway financing defied understanding. The original railroad was built between 1885 and 1896 by Henry Flagler, who also developed hotels along Florida's east coast. In the 1920s the railroad floated $150 million worth of second general mortgage refunding bonds to expand. Florida was in the midst of a boom, and the railroad was overwhelmed by the demands for freight hauling and needed to build a second track from Jacksonville to Miami. The railroad was hugely profitable, and the business decision appeared to be a sound one. But the boom collapsed in 1925 and the fortunes of the railroad declined.

The railroad might have survived the collapse, but the Great Depression eliminated any chance that it could repay the bonds. The railroad defaulted on the bonds in 1930 and, in 1931, collapsed amid a worsening depression. It was placed in receivership, and the value of its bonds declined dramatically.

Ed Ball began buying up the bonds for pennies on the dollar in 1940, and eventually he acquired effective control of the line. In an unbelievable statement, the Ball forces denied that they had any thought of making money, but said they rather wanted to guarantee "the preservation of an efficient and serviceable railroad devoted to the welfare of the east coast of Florida."[21] But clearly, if Ball could purchase the railroad at bargain-basement prices, reorganize it, and make it profitable, he could further increase his fortune.

In 1941 the Interstate Commerce Commission began looking at possible reorganization plans for the bankrupt railroad. The ICC came up with a solution, but the United States District Court rejected it.[22] Ball kept buying the bonds, and by 1944 he owned 51 percent. Ball wanted the railroad for himself, but other bondholders thought a merger with the Atlantic Coast Line Railroad would be better. It looked as though Ball was about to win when Pepper stepped in and took the side of the Atlantic Coast Line. Pepper said putting the railroad in Ball's hands was against the public interest.[23] After the 1944 election, Pepper launched a campaign to deny Ball ownership of the railroad. Perhaps Pepper thought that with a six-year term to look forward to, and a friendly president in the White House, he could afford to take on the man who had become a political foe.

During the campaign, the Atlantic Coast Line Railway helped Pepper and his friends obtain train reservations. It was no small task to find a seat during the war, and it took considerable influence to get a sleeping berth on short notice. After the election, Pepper thanked the president of the Atlantic Coast Line for his help. By this time, the two were on a first-name basis.[24]

Ball launched a campaign to convince Florida East Coast Railway employees that a merger with the Atlantic Coast Line would cost many of them their jobs. The St. Augustine Chamber of Commerce, where the railroad had its headquarters, published a booklet supporting Ball.[25]

Pepper managed to draw fire from both Ball and the railway workers, and he then made the situation worse. The ICC agreed to hold a hearing on the matter in November 1945 in West Palm Beach, while Pepper was making an ill-fated trip to Russia. The president of the Atlantic Coast Line, Champion Davis, sent a cable to Pepper in Romania urging him to return to appear before the hearing. Davis said Pepper faced ridicule if he did not appear.[26] Pepper replied that he did not "deem it necessary" to appear at the hearing.[27] It was Pepper who had requested the November hearing in the first place, getting it delayed from August.[28] A lawyer for Ball later commented that Pepper failed to show up because he "was in Moscow learning about the party line."[29] The failure to appear brought Pepper widespread criticism, alienating everyone involved in the case. Still, he wrote to a friend, "In the long run, it will not have hurt me politically to have opposed Ed Ball and the Dupont interests."[30] The case dragged through the Interstate Commerce Commission and the courts. It remained a major story and made front-page news again when the United States Supreme Court upheld a ruling that the Interstate Commerce Commission could not force a merger. In 1961 Ball finally obtained control of the 572-mile railroad.

In 1944 Pepper initially faced the opposition of three minor opponents in the Democratic primary. Findley Moore and Millard Conklin were running on a racist platform, and Alston Cockrell of Daytona Beach sought votes by giving the impression that he was a member of a well-known Florida family, even though he was not related to the high-profile Cockrells.

With two months to go before the election, Pepper had not drawn a significant opponent. Wilcox, the loser in 1938, and former governor Doyle Carlton, a loser in a 1936 Senate race, declined to run. Just fifty-seven days before the May primary, Judge J. Ollie Edmunds of Jacksonville, a most unlikely challenger, announced his candidacy.

Edmunds, a native of Georgia and the son of an itinerant lumber worker, had put himself through Stetson University by working as a janitor, waiter, and newspaper reporter while earning his undergraduate and law degrees. In 1931 he was appointed to the county court in Jacksonville. He also invested in timber land and became wealthy. He supported Pepper in 1934 and wrote to a friend that he had a "high regard for Claude's ability," adding, "I should like to see him in Washington."[31] Edmunds was reelected judge twice, but he was not a natural politician. Although chosen by his fellow county judges as their lobbyist in Tallahassee in 1941, he was otherwise unknown outside of Jacksonville.

Edmunds was clearly a last-minute candidate put forward by his friend Ed Ball. The two had become acquainted when Edmunds presided over the probate of the du Pont estate. The case was complicated, and Ball and his attorneys made frequent appearances before Edmunds. Later Edmunds became president of Stetson University and Ball donated money for its duPont-Ball Library. Edmunds had almost no organization or campaign staff. He named Ronald Slye his campaign manager— an unusual choice because Slye had no political experience. Slye was a furniture salesman who traveled extensively throughout the state. His title was misleading, for his role was largely handling the luggage and making sure the candidate showed up for events on time.[32] Slye was not the only political novice in the Edmunds entourage; most of those involved were friends and neighbors who had never taken part in a political campaign.

Edmunds was a game candidate, working his way through every county in the state, usually making three to five appearances a day.[33] Political scientist V. O. Key found that "Edmunds lacked Pepper's histrionic skills and his managers handled his campaign ineptly."[34] Edmunds called for less government but made no campaign promises, while Pepper traveled the state making what the *Miami Herald* said were too many promises.[35] Edmunds had trouble remembering people's names, a serious failing for a politician, and was chronically late for appearances. Ronald Slye's wife remembered that her husband "was just prodding him all the time: 'come on, it's time to go, it's time to go.'"[36]

Opposition to Pepper was led by Associated Industries, the Florida branch of the National Association of Manufacturers, which was controlled by Ball. Ball hired Dan Crisp, a Jacksonville public relations man, to spearhead the fight against Pepper. "We just wanted to defeat Pepper. Those were my orders," Crisp said. Ball gave some money, but his real contribution was in getting others to give, including the U.S. Chamber of Commerce, the National Association of Manufacturers, the American Medical Association, and dozens of others.[37] But the opposition was far from united. Many businesses were receiving lucrative government contracts, and scores of military installations were springing up around the state, creating thousands of jobs.

As in 1938, the Pepper campaign was seen as a referendum on the New Deal and Franklin Roosevelt. A strong showing by Pepper could boost the fourth-term aspirations of Roosevelt. A United Press story predicted, "The showing Pepper makes in this election will serve in many quarters as a gauge for estimating Pres. Roosevelt's fourth-term support in the 'solid South.' . . . If Pepper gets a majority vote and is returned to the Senate without being forced into a second primary, it will be considered an overwhelming victory for the New Deal."[38] To help him, Roosevelt asked Bernard Baruch—one of the wealthiest businessmen in the United States—to send money to Pepper, saying it was important.[39] Baruch had made his fortune as a Wall Street speculator, then turned his attention to public service and backing the Democratic Party. He had served both Woodrow Wilson and Franklin Roosevelt.

Florida was a difficult state for a politician who was not already well known to the voters. The size alone favored the incumbent. Its population centers were far apart, and the areas in between were sparsely settled. Air travel was not yet practical, and it took many hours to drive from one place to another. The Democratic Party in Florida was not tightly organized, and candidates generally depended upon their own resources, ingenuity, and personality to woo the voters. There were few if any political groups that could deliver sizable blocs of votes. Incumbents with high name recognition benefited from this situation, but it hurt a candidate such as Edmunds, who needed to attract more than 100,000 voters in less than two months.

Even a candidate with a clear and convincing message and plenty of money would have had a difficult time, and Edmunds's campaign lacked both. He ran as an opponent of the New Deal, but his message was usually muddled, charging Pepper with indiscretions but providing no specifics, and calling Pepper "the most notoriously absentee senator in Congress," although the charge was not true.[40]

It was Conklin and Moore, the two white supremacists, who raised race as an issue and allowed Edmunds to exploit it. Conklin was confident that "the issue that will defeat Pepper is the issue of white supremacy in the South."[41] At issue was a 1942 appearance by Pepper at a black church in Los Angeles. During the campaign, pictures of Pepper at the church began appearing in fliers and in newspapers throughout Florida. Pepper explained the appearance through newspaper advertisements and in public statements. Under a large headline that read "Senator Pepper's Reply to His Opposition's Cheap and Vicious Political Trick in Connection With His Appearance Before A Negro Church Congregation," Pepper maintained, "The only speech I have ever given to any Negro audience in California is a patriotic one I made . . . in the pulpit of a Baptist Negro Church on a Sunday afternoon at the expressed request of the members of the church. I said nothing indicating that I believe in social equality because, of course, I do not."[42]

In the midst of the 1944 campaign, the Supreme Court ruled in *Smith v. Allwright* that it was unconstitutional for the Texas Democratic Party to bar blacks from participating in the primary. In Florida, as in other states throughout the South, the white primary system effectively disfranchised blacks since the turn of the century. Some blacks did vote, mainly for Republican candidates in the general election and nearly always in larger cities such as Miami, Tampa, Daytona Beach, and Jacksonville. But they were few in numbers and had little effect on the election results. In some Florida counties in the 1940s, there were no blacks registered to vote. Pepper had to react to the *Smith v. Allwright* ruling to establish his credentials as an opponent of racial equality. "The South will allow nothing to impair white supremacy," he said. Pepper advocated an end-run around the Supreme Court ruling by trying to rewrite the requirements for voting in the Democratic primary so that it could pass a constitutional test while denying blacks the right to vote.[43]

Edmunds tried to exploit the race issue, running newspaper advertisements calling Pepper "a man who stirs up racial strife and discord in violation of Southern tradition." The advertisements said Edmunds believed that "the party principle of white supremacy must be maintained."[44] But Pepper's strong defense of the white primary system and statements on white supremacy kept Edmunds from successfully exploiting the issue.

Edmunds's other major primary issue was Pepper's support of the New Deal. By 1944 the New Deal was controversial with many who believed it was costing too much, robbing the individual of rights, and creating a huge bureaucracy involved in every facet of American life. Speaking in Miami, Edmunds said: "The daily life of every one of us has been so affected by petty tyrants and bureaucratic dictators who are wasting billions of precious dollars."[45]

The strangest disagreement in the campaign came over funding. Although both candidates were running inexpensive campaigns, each accused the other of having huge slush funds. Edmunds said, "A slush fund to stagger the imagination has been raised by those who have grown rich from profiteering on war contracts. This fund, reported to exceed $250,000, is being lavishly spent by the largest political organization in Florida history. The war profiteers are opposed to Ollie Edmunds. I am proud of it."[46]

Pepper saw it the other way. It was Edmunds who had unlimited money provided by wealthy businessmen determined to drive Pepper from the Senate: "They have offered every financial inducement, including financial security after the campaign."[47] Columnist Drew Pearson, a friend of Pepper's, wrote, "The GOP is pouring piles of money into the race" to defeat Pepper.[48] Another columnist, Marquis Childs, wrote that Pepper had "the formidable enmity of wealthy Northerners who have established residence in the resort state."[49]

Actually, neither candidate had abundant funds. The financial status of the Edmunds campaign is perhaps illustrated by Crosby Haddock Sr., a dairy company employee, who was loaned to the Edmunds campaign as a driver and advance man by his employer. Haddock said that on more than one occasion he shared a hotel room with Edmunds, hardly a sign of a healthy financial situation.[50]

Both candidates followed a traditional pattern that included an automobile tour of the state and speeches at county courthouses. Both used radio to carry their speeches, although Pepper was more effective both in arranging for broadcast time and in his presentation. The one-minute or thirty-second commercial had not come to Florida, and newspapers were the principal vehicle for advertising. The real value of newspapers was not in the advertisements but in the news columns and editorial pages. Newspapers routinely used their news columns to voice support of a candidate, and this coverage could be vital. There were front-page editorials and cartoons either supporting a candidate or lampooning the opposition. Pepper received the support of nearly all of the state's newspapers, failing only to get the endorsements of those owned by Perry. With financing from Ball, Perry had bought daily and weekly Florida newspapers and soon owned a statewide media empire. Like his financier, Perry turned from a supporter into a vigorous opponent.

Martin Andersen, the owner-editor of the *Orlando Morning Sentinel*, was typical of the newspaper executives backing Pepper. Andersen wrote, "Can a citizen of Florida figure out any percentage in putting an anti-Roosevelt freshman into the Senate against a pro-Roosevelt young veteran who by 1949 easily may become one of the outstanding figures of the world?"[51]

The power of Pepper's relationship with Roosevelt was shown five days before the election. The Gandy Bridge, connecting Tampa and St. Petersburg since 1924, charged a thirty-five-cent toll. For two decades residents had complained, asking the federal government to take over the bridge and eliminate the toll. With the election days away, Roosevelt lifted the toll as a wartime measure. The honor of making the announcement went to Pepper. In Tampa and St. Petersburg there were celebrations, and the schools of St. Petersburg were closed the day after the announcement.[52] Edmunds maintained that the announcement killed his campaign.[53]

In the May 2 election, Pepper received 194,445 votes, Edmunds 127,157, Conklin 33,317, and the two other candidates a total of some 26,000 votes. Pepper was held to 51 percent of the vote, barely enough to win the primary outright. A shift of just 4,000 votes from Pepper to the other candidates would have forced a second round. It was not just that Pepper was nearly thrown into a runoff, it was that he lost support in every area of the state. Even though the state's population increased, along with voter registration, Pepper received fewer votes in 53 of the state's 67 counties than in 1938. In some counties his total declined by half. Pepper did well in Dade County—which was already becoming a haven for retirees—but in the Gold Coast counties such as Palm Beach, where wealthy Northerners were flocking, he did poorly.[54]

Pepper seemed unfazed by his close call. In 1936 he won without opposition, in 1938 he was renominated with 58 percent of the vote, and in 1944 he barely managed a majority. This was in an era when most Democrats in the South were routinely returned to office with little or no opposition. Pepper had another six years to mend his political fences.

Ball was angry with Edmunds for not attacking Pepper more. He said that he told Edmunds "he couldn't follow the Marquess of Queensberry rules in a barroom brawl, but he wouldn't listen."[55] But while Pepper won another six-year term, Ball was not done with his campaign to unseat Pepper. At his behest, Dan Crisp created the Florida Democratic Club as an umbrella group for all those who wanted to see Pepper defeated in 1950.

During his first full term in the Senate, Pepper had emerged as a national figure, known for his early condemnation of Hitler, his support of American aid to Great Britain, and his position as a devoted New Dealer. In the process, he managed to alienate some powerful interests in his home state, who could undermine his senatorial career and his national ambitions. However, he seemed unmindful of the political problems he was creating for himself as he resumed his seat in 1945.

4

The Search for Peace

Once World War II started, Pepper turned his attention to the post-war world. He accurately predicted that world affairs would dominate politics once the war ended. Seven weeks after the Japanese attack on Pearl Harbor, Pepper wrote to his friend Raymond Robins, a Florida resident who was close to the Soviet leadership, "Of course, I am concerned about winning the war. Very much concerned. But I am primarily beginning to think about the Post War period, economically, politically, spiritually. . . . I am doing what I can to foster an appreciation of the necessity of some kind of a world governmental structure to be built upon the Post War wreckage."[1]

In April 1942—five months after Pearl Harbor—Pepper submitted a resolution calling for the United States to join a world organization after the war.[2] For the remainder of the war, Pepper continued his efforts to form such an organization. He thought the issue would increase his standing in the Senate. He told his friend Sherman Minton he had "a feeling that I have gained somewhat in influence in the Senate. . . . I have usually had to be so far ahead of the Senate that I was constantly in an exposed position. . . . There is no need concealing the fact that all of them have never thought that I was the greatest person in the world."[3] To Robins, he wrote that there were liberal groups in Michigan, Indiana, Ohio, and Wisconsin to "work in the next Democratic Convention for a liberal platform and a liberal candidate." A friend from Harvard Law School began to work on a "plan for forming an organization on my behalf throughout the country."[4]

As part of his effort to become a national political leader, Pepper took a major role in getting Henry Wallace confirmed as secretary of commerce in 1945. Wallace had originally joined the Roosevelt administration as secretary of agriculture. By 1940, Vice President John Nance Garner was disenchanted with his role in the administration, and Wallace replaced him on the Democratic ticket. But his left-wing positions alarmed party leaders, who led an effort to drop him from the 1944 ticket and replace him with Harry Truman. As something of a consolation prize, Wallace was named secretary of commerce, but still his enemies lined up to deny him that post.

Wallace and Pepper were devoted to the ideals of the New Deal, emerging as Washington's leading New Deal supporters while becoming estranged from the Democratic Party. At the 1944 Democratic National Convention, Pepper was the one who fought to keep Wallace as the vice presidential nominee until the bitter end. Pepper gave a seconding speech for Wallace in which he denounced the political bosses who opposed his renomination.[5] Although Wallace led on the first ballot, it was not enough to win, and on the second ballot Truman emerged with the victory. The subsequent naming of Wallace to even a minor cabinet post brought out determined opposition. The Commerce Department was responsible for loaning money to foreign nations, and opponents raised the specter of Wallace funneling money to Russia. The Senate Commerce Committee voted 15 to 5 against confirming Wallace, as a coalition of conservative Democrats and Republicans joined forces. Pepper wrote in his diary, "The opposition is the Republicans and the Bourbon Democrats. They hate Roosevelt but can't defeat him."[6] Pepper helped engineer a compromise in which Wallace was confirmed but lost the power to lend money. Although Pepper believed it enhanced his standing in the Senate and in the White House, the battle also served to tie him closer to Wallace in the mind of the public.[7]

Roosevelt's sudden death in April 1945 was a severe blow to Pepper. Roosevelt was his political hero, and Pepper was always the first to rally to a Roosevelt idea and willing to lend his considerable oratorical skills to defend the president on the Senate floor. Pepper called it "a fatal day." He was on a train to Chicago when he first heard the news and initially thought it might be false. Three days before Roosevelt died, he responded to a letter from Pepper dealing with foreign affairs. It was a letter that shaped Pepper's postwar view, and eventually doomed his career in the United States Senate. Roosevelt wrote, "I like what you say and it is perfectly clear that fundamentally you and I mean exactly the same thing. I like to feel that we have really accomplished marvels in the matters of both our domestic and foreign policies in changing the point of view of a lot of people toward more liberal trends, not only here but throughout the world."[8]

Roosevelt's death was a double blow because it placed Harry Truman in the White House. Pepper believed that he or Wallace, not Truman, was the logical heir to the Roosevelt political legacy. Years later he told an interviewer, "I liked Harry Truman, but he was not someone to take seriously."[9] Underestimating Truman was an error on Pepper's part and eventually contributed to his 1950 defeat. Two weeks after Roosevelt's death, Truman met with Pepper in the White House. Truman told him, "You know, Claude, I was for Roosevelt before he became president and supported him in the Senate, but now I am responsible for the unity and harmony of the country. Therefore, I suspect more of the time you will find me about in the middle of the road." Pepper was not impressed and wrote, "I am not too keen about him and can't support him beyond my patriotic duty."[10]

Pepper was not the only one to underestimate Truman. *Time* magazine concluded that "Harry Truman is a man of distinct limitations, especially in high level politics. He knows his limitations. . . . In his administration there are likely to be few innovations and little experimentation."[11]

Many liberals saw disturbing signs in Truman's actions. The Roosevelt cabinet, with its strong liberal element, began to change under Truman. Within four months of his taking office, only Wallace and Interior Secretary Harold Ickes were left from the Roosevelt cabinet, and they were eventually cast aside. One study found that 80 percent of Truman's most significant appointments in 1945 and 1946 went to businessmen, corporate lawyers, bankers, and military men.[12] Roosevelt intimate Tommy Corcoran told Alabama senator Lister Hill that such New Dealers as Wallace, Pepper, William O. Douglas, and Hugo Black "had the world in their hands last year, and now they're just a bunch of political refugees . . . a helpless bunch of sheep."[13] Pepper and the other

New Dealers were on the outside, their advice no longer sought, their participation in the highest political councils no longer wanted. Under Roosevelt, Pepper was a frequent visitor at the White House and could count on the President for assistance.

Truman had reaffirmed his support for Roosevelt's policies, but his actions were not encouraging for liberals.[14] He seemed to be pushing liberal issues, and attracting liberal voters, without securing passage of liberal programs.[15] Still, he faced a Republican Congress beginning in 1947 and had little leverage in getting legislation passed.

Although the New Deal stumbled badly after 1936, its champions still saw it as the best hope for the future of America. They were confident that Roosevelt could engineer a comeback for the New Deal once the war was over. Liberals questioned whether Truman would continue Roosevelt's policies. Five months after Roosevelt's death, Truman urged a continuation of Roosevelt's domestic programs, an ambitious reorganization of the executive branch, an increase in the minimum wage, greater rights for collective bargaining, more public works, and a permanent Fair Employment Practices Committee. He also talked about better housing and health care. Truman said, "Let us make the attainment of those rights the essence of postwar American life."[16] Former New York mayor Fiorello La Guardia said, "Franklin Roosevelt is not dead."[17]

Truman had disliked Pepper since their days in the Senate. After becoming president, Truman discussed Pepper with Henry Wallace and other members of his cabinet. Wallace recorded that Truman "has a very deep animus against Pepper. He says Pepper's only motive is to get publicity." Truman recalled that during the war he was giving a radio address at the Bath Shipyards in Maine when Pepper tried to take the microphone away from him. Truman told his cabinet that "all that was necessary to get ninety percent of the senators against anything was to have Claude Pepper come out on the floor for it."[18]

Pepper must have wondered how Truman, a virtual stranger to Roosevelt, could have ended up as president. During the 1944 campaign, Roosevelt and Truman did not campaign together, and as vice president Truman held just three brief meetings with Roosevelt. During those three meetings, Roosevelt failed to give him any assignments or tell him what the administration was doing—especially the development of the atomic bomb—and made no effort to keep him informed on domestic or foreign policy issues.[19]

Early in his administration Truman faced huge problems. Millions of soldiers were clamoring to get out of the service, civilians were tired of doing without a long list of rationed items, businesses wanted to get back to producing consumer merchandise, and the labor unions were displaying increasing militancy. Beginning in late 1945, unions staged a record numbers of strikes as workers sought to gain the pay raises they felt were lost during the war. There were strikes in nearly every industry: steel, coal, lumber, shipping, railroads. In all, four and a half million workers walked off the job in more than five thousand strikes in 1945 and 1946.[20] In some cases the strikes forced Truman to take anti-union positions, alienating the Democrats' most faithful supporters.

Pepper's strong support of organized labor brought him into conflict with Truman when a nationwide strike of railroad workers disrupted the nation's transportation system. Truman seized the railroads under his wartime powers, but workers walked off the job. Truman asked Congress for the authority to draft the workers. The House went along, but the Senate balked, largely because of the opposition of the Senate Republican leader, Robert A. Taft, and of Pepper. Pepper said he saw nothing that "justified the effort which was made to rush, in a unseemly and hasty manner, this measure into law."[21]

Truman expected Taft's opposition, but he was angry about Pepper's. At a cabinet luncheon in late May, the discussion centered on the railroad legislation. According to Wallace, Truman said, "Pepper is purely opportunistic."[22] The resistance of Taft and Pepper slowed the stampede to draft the workers. The measure was defeated in the Senate 70 to 13. Although Pepper thought he had done the right thing, his union support did little to help him in Florida, and his position served to separate him further from Truman.

By July, Pepper was expressing more misgivings about Truman. To Wallace, Pepper "spoke at some little length about his disillusion about the way things were going. He seemed to think there was danger of the present administration making many of the same mistakes that the Harding administration made."[23]

On July 30, 1945, Pepper received an unsigned memorandum entitled

"Your Personal Future." The plan called for Pepper to join the Truman ticket as a vice presidential candidate in 1948, then become the presidential nominee in 1952. Pepper was urged to be "an independent party regular with a personal following." The memo advised him to become "the prophet of the future" and "the most active and best publicized liberal." But the memorandum cautioned that "the path of Pepper's significance does not lie in international affairs. It only lies specifically in the applications of the world trend in internal politics."[24]

While Pepper accepted some of the advice, he rejected significant parts, and that cost him dearly. Instead of working to get on a ticket with Truman, he did as much as he could to antagonize the president. Instead of concentrating on domestic issues, he devoted his attention to foreign affairs, using his seat on the Senate Foreign Relations Committee to push his views. Pepper may have felt that a domestic agenda could not advance his political fortunes. Some other southerners held a national reputation, but there was one reality all southern politicians faced: race. Northern Democrats, including the big-city political bosses and African Americans, would never accept as the leader of the party a Southerner who had run as a racist. Pepper thought he could get around that issue by staking out new ground. Although it proved to be his undoing, Pepper saw his only route to higher office through international affairs. If he could become a world figure, he might overcome his region's racial views and secure his national ambitions.

During World War II there was a feeling—and certainly a hope—that the United States and the Soviet Union might be able to maintain their good relationship after the war. *Fortune* magazine conducted a public opinion survey in 1943 that revealed that 81 percent of Americans thought the United States and Russia should work as equal partners after the war. There were attempts to make the Russians look like Americans. *Look* magazine, seeking to cast Stalin as a regular guy, published a cover story entitled "A Guy Named Joe." *Collier's* magazine in a special issue concluded that the Russian form of communism was not so bad, but simply a "modified capitalist set-up," moving toward democracy.[25] *Life* magazine called the Russians "one hell of a people, who look like Americans, dress like Americans and think like Americans." Stalin's brutal secret police were described as "a national police similar to the FBI."[26]

Pepper was one of the millions of Americans who hoped that Russia and the United States would coexist peacefully. As early as 1941, Pepper met with Soviet ambassador Constantine Oumansky and readily accepted the Russian explanation of the Nazi-Soviet Pact, which bound Germany and Russia together and allowed Germany to launch an invasion of Poland in 1939. After the lunch, Pepper wrote in his diary, "The Russians naturally feel that they have been dealt with harshly by Britain and ourselves before the beginning of the war."[27]

In a nationwide radio address in June 1945, Pepper spoke in favor of loaning money to Russia to rebuild when the war ended. "The next thing that we have got to understand with our heads and our hearts is that we cannot have world well-being unless we help one another economically. We cannot have full employment, we cannot have prosperity, we cannot have stable political conditions or economic conditions unless the world generally is well off." He told the nationwide audience, "It is just as necessary for our economic security for us to help Russia financially as it was necessary to our physical security to help Russia through Lend Lease."[28] It was a theme to which he returned time after time. Earlier in the year, on the same program, he told listeners: "I don't have to be an apologist for Russia, but I think the cold pages of history will show that Russia's record for international and collective security is about as good as that of any of us."[29]

In August 1945, one week after the war ended in Japan, Pepper left for a tour of Europe and the Soviet Union. Although he said he was going as a member of the Small Business Committee to look for foreign trade opportunities, he went at his own expense.[30] Exactly what sort of foreign trade opportunities he envisioned in war-devastated Europe is a mystery. To finance the trip, Pepper agreed to write a series of articles for the North American Newspaper Alliance, a press syndicate. The syndicate, in turn, sold the articles to a number of newspapers including the *New York Times* and paid him $1,000.[31] It was a most unusual arrangement: Pepper met with world leaders as a member of the United States Senate, then wrote stories as a journalist. The leaders he interviewed assumed he was approaching them in his official capacity, not as a reporter seeking a story.

He first visited London, Paris, Frankfurt, and Berlin. In Berlin he inspected Adolf Hitler's office in the Reich Chancellery and the air raid shelter "in which he and Eva Braun are supposed to have committed suicide. I don't believe either of them is dead."[32]

On September 14 he flew to Moscow to meet with Soviet dictator Joseph Stalin. The interview lasted one hour, but it haunted Pepper for the remainder of his Senate career. United States ambassador Averill Harriman was out of the country when Pepper arrived, and it fell to the deputy chief of mission, George F. Kennan, to arrange the interview. Kennan was clearly outraged that Pepper was traveling as both a senator and a journalist. Kennan thought he was setting up a private and confidential meeting with Stalin for a member of the Senate Foreign Relations Committee. On the evening before the interview, Pepper told Kennan about the newspaper deal. "I recall only a sense of hopelessness I experienced in trying to explain to the Russians why a distinguished statesman, discussing serious problems of international affairs with a foreign governmental leader, would be interested in exploiting for a very minor private gain whatever value the interview might have," Kennan wrote.[33]

But Pepper was not the only one exploiting the meeting. The Russians were able to use it to obtain something sorely needed—positive publicity. Pepper went on Soviet radio to make a speech, which was printed and distributed by the Russians. In his radio address he called Stalin "one of the great men of history and of the world" and predicted that "Russia's greatest era lies not in her glorious past but in her future." He concluded by praising the Russians for working toward "the destruction of tyranny and the restoration of freedom and independence in the world." He said visiting Russia was a dream of his and added he had "long been a friend of the Soviet people."[34]

His statement about the restoration of freedom was in sharp contrast to the realities the world faced. The Russians were establishing puppet governments in the sovereign nations of Eastern Europe, and there were Russian troops as far West as Germany. The Soviets had abandoned their pledges to allow Eastern European nations self-determination and seemed poised to continue their advance, perhaps into Greece, or Turkey, or Iran.

In one of Pepper's syndicated columns he wrote that he was "privileged to talk with the single most powerful man in the world, the man who is going to determine in a large way what kind of world ours is to be."[35] In a story on the front page of the *Times*, he wrote that he told Stalin "that he was very much admired in the United States and often in the most cordial manner is referred to as 'Uncle Joe.'"[36] Most Americans believed that it was the president of the United States who was the most powerful man in the world, not Stalin. In his regular column to Florida newspapers, Pepper continued to praise Stalin and the Russians: "The Russians like the Americans. They are generally a friendly agreeable people." Pepper said he did not think the Russians had aggressive intentions and urged the United States to cooperate with them.[37]

In his private notes Pepper wrote, "As for foreign policy, the objective of the Soviet Union was to collaborate with other nations of the world in keeping peace."[38] He said that when he and Stalin first met, Stalin asked his age. Pepper said he was forty-five years old. Stalin said, "I envy you." Pepper replied, "There are a great many who envy you, too." As a present, Pepper gave Stalin a copy of a Henry Wallace book, *Sixty Million Jobs*.[39]

His statements drew increasing attention from the *Daily Worker*, the Communist Party newspaper, with his trip abroad receiving regular coverage. When Pepper visited Paris, the paper reported, "Senator Claude Pepper urged in Paris that the atom bomb be placed at the disposal of the Military Staffs Committee of the United Nations."[40] Along the way, Pepper criticized two leaders widely respected in the United States, Charles de Gaulle and Winston Churchill.

He concluded his tour with visits to Belgrade and Prague—two cities in the process of falling behind the Iron Curtain. In December 1945, Pepper returned to the United States after four months in Europe and encountered a strong wave of criticism in Florida. The *Fort Lauderdale News* said, "Claude Pepper believes in Communism. WE DO NOT. That's why we suggest that the sooner you realize he is NOT a part of OUR AMERICAN WAY OF LIFE the better off we all will be."[41] Even Pepper's friends were alarmed at the trip and its results. One wrote to a Pepper aide, "The Florida crackers are not interested in statesmanship, and they are not interested in Europe and world affairs. They are principally selfish and they think the Senator should be devoting his time and talent to the narrow interests of the state of Florida only, and it is going to take some good work . . . to overcome the ground that has been lost by his prolonged trip to Europe.[42] One constituent advised Pepper to "spend more time in Florida and devote more attention to local problems."[43]

However, even with the reaction at home, Pepper was convinced his trip could "make a greater contribution to future peace . . . and even if defeat should be the price still I would have no complaint." He said he thought constituents "are going to complain always when I don't devote my whole time to their petty, personal matters," and he felt he had five years to repair his base in Florida.[44] Indeed, if he had begun mending his relations with Florida voters then, perhaps he could have recovered by 1950 and won reelection. But for Pepper, things only got worse. He was never able to admit that the trip was a political mistake.

While he was away, there was a sea change in public opinion about the Soviets. Beginning in late 1945, the leaders of the West came to believe that the Soviets did not want peace, but rather wanted domination.[45] Secretary of State James F. Byrnes reached what he thought was an understanding with the Russians over the structure of the governments in Romania and Bulgaria to include more noncommunists. But many thought Byrnes was going too easy on the Russians. Within the State Department there were cries that Byrnes did not do enough for the Eastern European nations, and Republicans in Congress complained that Byrnes gave too much to the Soviets in agreeing to share some atomic controls. Truman himself was angry because Byrnes made the decisions without consulting with the White House. When Byrnes returned to Washington from Europe, Truman told him, "I do not think we should play compromise any longer. . . . I'm tired of babying the Soviets."[46] Truman resolved not to make further concessions to the Russians.[47] He saw a shift in American attitudes toward Russia and saw the Republicans making it a campaign issue in 1946.[48] Stalin stoked the fires with a rare speech in February 1946 in which he said communism and capitalism were incompatible.[49]

The change in attitude could be seen in the magazine headlines. No longer did they recommend cooperation with the Russians and praise Stalin. Now they cried to "Turn the Light on Communism," or warned that "Reds Are After Your Child." Hollywood turned out movies such as *I Married a Communist*, *The Red Menace*, and *Guilty of Treason*.

As 1946 began, the liberal movement in the United States split over the question of how to deal with the Soviet Union, and eventually two wings emerged. One supported Truman's hard-line policy toward the Soviet Union and was led by the Americans for Democratic Action. The ADA saw the Soviet Union as a military threat but supported continuation of the New Deal. The other, the National Citizens Political Action Committee (NC-PAC), believed the key to peace was through the maintenance of good relations between the United States and the Soviet Union. That group was willing to overlook Soviet aggression in Eastern Europe to maintain peace. They supported Soviet-American unity and were allied with much of organized labor through the Congress of Industrial Organizations. Both Pepper and Henry Wallace became frequent speakers at NC-PAC events. Wallace was committed to NC-PAC, and Pepper certainly agreed with its goals.[50] It wasn't long before NC-PAC and the Independent Citizens Committee of the Arts, Sciences, and Professions merged to form the Progressive Citizens of America. The PCA counted a number of communists and fellow travelers among its members, but that did not deter Pepper from speaking at its rallies. The group could turn out thousands to cheer for Pepper, crowding his schedule with appearances throughout the country. As United Auto Workers union president Walter Reuther once observed, "Communists perform the most complete valet service in the world . . . they provide you with applause, and they inflate your ego."[51]

On February 27, 1946, Pepper spoke at the Red Army Day dinner in Chicago to raise money for Russian relief. According to an account in the *Daily Worker*, Pepper "wished a long life to the Red Army as a warning to all tyrants who might attempt conquest." Pepper said that the Soviet people want friendship, but "our handling of the atom bomb does not ease their minds."[52] There were hopes that the United States would share the secret of the bomb, perhaps through the United Nations, but any chance of placing the atomic bomb under international control died with the growing anti-Soviet feeling.

The anti-Soviet sentiment received a boost early in 1946 when former British prime minister Winston Churchill arrived in the United States for an extended vacation. In March he spoke in Fulton, Missouri, and, as Truman looked on, warned that "an iron curtain has descended across the Continent." He seemed to be seeking an Anglo-American alliance to stand up to the Soviets. The following day Pepper and two fellow senators, Harley M. Kilgore and Glen Taylor, criticized Churchill's speech. They said such an Anglo-American alliance would "cut the throat" of the United Nations.[53]

On March 20, 1946, Pepper attempted to explain his views in a major Senate speech. He urged the United States to "destroy every atomic bomb which we have, and smash every facility we possess which is capable of producing only destructive forms of atomic energy." He also urged an immediate summit meeting among Britain, Russia, and the United States.[54] The speech received little coverage from mainstream newspapers in the United States, but was embraced by the *Daily Worker*. The front-page headline read "TREAT U.S.S.R. AS FRIEND PEPPER URGES," and the story said that Pepper "collided head on with the anti-Soviet hysteria now gripping the capital."[55] On April 4, Pepper made another Senate speech, this one entitled "Peace Through Equal Justice for All Nations." He criticized the foreign policy of Great Britain, calling the United States the "guarantor of British imperialism." Pepper's speech implied that it was Britain, not the Soviet Union, that was responsible for the problems in the world.[56]

The speech brought him the greatest backlash of his career, unleashing a stream of negative publicity that continued until his 1950 defeat. He was out of step with the American people, who increasingly believed that the United States was too soft in dealing with Russia.[57] In March 1945 a public opinion survey showed that 55 percent of Americans said the United States could trust Russia. One year later, the figure was down to 35 percent.[58]

The day after Pepper gave the speech, Florida's senior senator, Charles O. Andrews, demanded an apology. Andrews said Pepper's speech "does not represent the feeling and sentiment of the great mass of people of Florida." Andrews singled out Pepper's charge that the United States and Britain were "ganging up" against Russia, but said he did not agree with "any part of his statement."[59] Pepper did not respond to Andrews, and did nothing to slow down his criticism of American foreign policy and general praise of the Soviet Union.

In the United States, the only praise Pepper received came from the *Daily Worker*. In an editorial, the paper said Pepper's speech "can well be studied by every patriotic American. . . . It should raise to new heights the fight for an affirmative foreign policy for our nation."[60] Russian newspapers gave Pepper's remarks more attention than a major speech by Truman in Chicago.[61] The *Washington Post* carried an editorial entitled "Red Herring." It was the first time the word "red" was used in print in connection with Pepper. The editorial said, "If he keeps it up, he will be making a strong bid for the distinction of being America's number one white-washer of aggression. . . . We don't see how the Senator's constituents can avoid asking him where his loyalties lie."[62]

Before the controversy quieted over his April 4 speech, Pepper set off another firestorm with an April 8 article in the *New Republic*. In it he wrote, "The United States is nursing exclusive possession of the atomic bomb, seeking globe-girdling military bases and considering military conscription." Pepper again proposed the destruction of all atomic weapons, called on the United Nations Security Council to establish the joint occupation of all strategic bases outside their own homelands, and equal access to raw materials for all nations.[63]

In Moscow, Pepper's article received extensive coverage in the Russian newspaper *Pravda*. A telegram to Secretary of State James F. Byrnes from the American embassy in Moscow noted that the Russian newspaper "prominently publishes abbreviated translation of Pepper's *New Republic* article." The telegram also noted the Russian newspapers reported on a Pepper speech "in which he accuses the British of 'desiring to force US to shed American blood so that British may rule Palestine as a colony,' and asserts that US too often supports British in British-Soviet conflicts on interest in Europe and Middle East."[64]

Pepper's remarks and writings also brought scrutiny from the Federal Bureau of Investigation. The Bureau prepared a memorandum about Pepper's association with groups suspected of being communist fronts. The May 1 memo from FBI official D. M. Ladd to Director J. Edgar Hoover included a note, "I thought you would be interested in the following information further pointing out Senator Pepper's pro-Russian attitude." At the bottom of the note Hoover wrote a personal order that the report be sent to Truman aide Harry Vaughan at the White House.[65] "I thought the President and you would be interested in the following information . . . concerning the continued pro-Russian attitude of Senator

Claude Pepper about whom previous information has been furnished to you by me."[66]

A second memo from Ladd to Hoover contended that "Senator Pepper has been associated with, given approval to, or spoken before at least twenty-three Communist Front organizations. . . . Pepper has consistently followed the general Communist Party line in his political views since as early as 1940."[67] The memo also noted that "a number of his speeches since early 1946 have been written by individuals who are prominent Communists or who travel in high Communist circles."[68]

The speechwriter this memo referred to was Charles Kramer, also known as Charles Krivitsky and Charles Krevisky, who worked for Pepper's House Subcommittee on Wartime Health and Education. Kramer began working for the Communist Party in 1931 and joined the party two years later. Kramer was editor of the communist publication *New Masses* until 1931 and was identified as a communist and a member of the "Soviet espionage apparatus." He worked at a number of middle-level government posts before going to work for Senator Kilgore in 1942. His role was to pass sensitive Senate documents to Soviet agents, although most of his information was little more than warmed-over Washington gossip. In 1945 Kramer moved to Pepper's staff. Beginning in 1946, the FBI placed Kramer under surveillance. In March the surveillance showed that Pepper held a meeting in his office with Kramer and three other men suspected of being involved in Soviet espionage. In 1947 the surveillance took them to Pepper's Washington apartment, where Pepper met with Kramer and three others with communist links for more than six hours.[69]

It is not known whether Pepper knew of Kramer's ties to the Communist Party, or those of his associates. But for a man already linked to left-wing causes, hiring someone such as Kramer only served to rouse the interest of the FBI. After leaving the Senate, Robert M. La Follette published an article in which he said that four Senate committees, including Pepper's, had been infiltrated by communists. La Follette wrote that the staff of the Pepper subcommittee "probably did great harm to the cause of improved health in this country by its reckless activities."[70] When Kramer's past became public, Pepper fired him.

Pepper managed to further tie himself to communists with an ill-advised decision to write the introduction for a book entitled *The Great Conspiracy Against Russia*, a blatantly procommunist book published by the International Workers Order. Pepper wrote: "A continuation of the disastrous policies of anti-Soviet intrigue so vividly described in this book would inevitably result in a Third World War."[71]

Pepper believed Truman was pursuing a disastrous course. He wrote to Raymond Robins complaining, "This that we are doing now is essentially American imperialism as the imperialists of McKinley's day. . . . They want the United States to dominate the world's economy and with our own force give shape and direction to the whole trend of things on earth."[72]

The early postwar period was a heady time for Pepper. He met with world leaders, including Stalin, fought and won a battle with President Truman, had a calendar full of speaking engagements throughout the nation, and had his opinion routinely sought by journalists. His political successes fueled his ambition for higher office. Amid all of this, Pepper failed to see that his actions were hurting him in Florida and imperiling his reelection in 1950.

The Controversial Politician

From 1944 to 1950, Claude Pepper received a stream of negative publicity for his support of the Soviet Union. Except for the Soviet newspaper *Pravda* and the newspaper of the American Communist Party, the *Daily Worker*, it is difficult to find a pro-Pepper article from that time in any newspaper or magazine. *Time*, *Newsweek*, *United States News*, and nearly all of the Florida newspapers criticized Pepper harshly and often. As for his hope of being a national candidate, only the *Daily Worker* saw him as viable. In early June 1944 a *Worker* story said, "Senator Claude Pepper, rather than Henry Wallace, is the figure most often mentioned as a possible standard bearer. . . . The Floridian has caught the public imagination."[1]

In the wake of his speech about Britain and his stand in the railroad case, it was rare to pick up a magazine or newspaper and not read about Pepper. The day after the *Daily Worker* article appeared, the conservative newsweekly *United States News* carried a story on Pepper that was unflattering in both its tone and its selection of facts. "Senator Claude Pepper has bobbed up suddenly as an outstanding hero of the labor unions and leader of the country's liberal to leftward groups. . . . In such circles and among labor leaders, Senator Pepper's name now is being bracketed with that of Henry A. Wallace when 1948 presidential campaigning is discussed."[2]

The stories about Pepper were increasingly hostile. A *Washington Times-Herald* columnist sought to link Pepper to the communists for speaking to the American Slav Congress, a group with strong communist ties. "I heard from the lips of that great soldier, that dynamic leader, the man that drove the Nazis out of Yugoslavia, Marshal Tito, the story of the partisan struggle in Yugoslavia. . . . I saw a republic being born in Yugoslavia," Pepper told the group.[3]

At the end of August 1946 the *Saturday Evening Post*, one of the largest-circulation magazines in America, published an article entitled "Pink Pepper" that said, "The Communist press whoops it up for Pepper because he has been taking Russia's side in international disputes. . . . When he first came to the Senate he followed the straight Roosevelt line. People said he was a stooge, a mere loud mouth from the South. But that still leaves Pepper himself unexplained. What is he up to?"[4] It was a good question. With the election still two years away, Pepper tried to cast himself as a running mate for either Truman or Wallace, and as a presidential candidate himself.

Newspaper editorial pages throughout the country criticized Pepper's positions. In Connecticut the *Hartford Courant* concluded that Pepper must have converted "to Communist since he visited Russia."[5] Pepper noted the criticism in his diary. "Fla. Tampa Trib & other papers keep after me and Russia. Terrific anti-R[oosevelt] sentiment in the country. Lots of sniping at me at home."[6]

Three months after carrying a critical profile of Pepper, *United States News* again reported on Pepper's activities: "Senator Claude Pepper, a foremost advocate of a go-easy with Russia policy, is emerging as the forthright leader of America's more extreme or radical liberals. . . . Mr. Pepper more recently has been building a record that led some to accuse him of following the Communist line. . . . The Senator, of course, has his eye on the Presidency."[7]

The same week, *Newsweek* also contained an unflattering article: "Months ago talk on the left fringe of American politics had begun to revolve about Pepper as the best for Democratic Vice President or third-party leader in 1948. At 46, Pepper appears to regard himself as a man of considerable destiny." *Newsweek* repeated Pepper's praise of Tito in Chicago.[8]

In October 1946 there were two more critical articles in national publications. The *American Mercury* ripped him as "Claude Denson Pepper of Florida—the current darling of the ultra-left wing press . . . the fellow who made a pilgrimage to the Kremlin for a cozy, confidential chat with Comrade Stalin barely a year after he campaigned for the Senate re-election on a platform that included white supremacy for the South." The magazine became the first to write Pepper's political obituary: "Pepper's career has probably reached its zenith. Though the United States electorate makes mistakes, it is usually quick to tell the synthetic or imported from the genuine."[9]

The second unflattering article appeared in a magazine with a small circulation but a major impact. *Medical Economics* was read primarily by doctors, who were already suspicious of Pepper's views on government-funded medical care. "He represents not Florida, but that vague area known as the left-of-the-CIO-PAC, the American Labor Party, and the 'friends of the Soviet Union.' . . . The big red faced gentleman from Florida has an uncanny talent for making the opposition look bad. And he has no compunction about selecting facts to gain an end."[10]

Despite the criticism, Pepper continued to attack American foreign policy and urge support for Russia. In a May 1946 speech to the American-Soviet Institute, an organization with strong communist ties, he said, "When the history of this tragic era is written . . . the onus of failure to achieve disarmament and collective security will not fall upon the Soviet Union." He went on to praise Stalin as a great leader.[11]

A few months later, speaking at a Labor Day rally in Los Angeles, Pepper said, "These foolish people who tell us we can never get along with Russia and encourage us to widen instead of bridge the gap between the two nations, who want us to go back to the Hoover and Coolidge and Harding enmity for Russia instead of the Roosevelt friendship, will divide the race of Man into two mutually destructive forces."[12] Pepper saw himself as pursuing Roosevelt's plan for the postwar world. As *Newsweek* observed, "His colleagues believe he has become convinced that he is heir to FDR's big mantle, especially in matters concerned with foreign policy, and that he speaks today as FDR would have spoken."[13]

Time after time, Pepper took to the Senate floor to explain his position on U.S.-Soviet relations in lengthy speeches. He became a leading voice in urging the United States to loan money to help Russia rebuild from the devastation of World War II. In 1943 there were discussions about a loan to the Russians, who wanted a billion dollars. The loan had widespread backing, including support from Treasury Secretary

Henry Morgenthau Jr. and the president of the United States Chamber of Commerce, but the loan clashed with Truman's increasingly hostile view of the Soviets. The Russians filed a loan request in August 1945, but seven months later the State Department, in a preposterous statement, announced that the application had disappeared.[14] Pepper called for Truman to meet face to face with Stalin—no American president met with a Soviet leader between 1945 and 1955—but no one was willing to listen. Just as when he called for greater military preparedness before World War II, Pepper was ridiculed and isolated.

Despite the negative publicity, Pepper began to discuss openly his national ambitions. A small publication, *Reader's Scope*, carried a series of articles about possible presidential candidates and included Pepper. He received encouragement from Francis Townsend, the father of the pension plan that bore his name. Townsend wrote, "I think you are the logical choice for the Democrats as candidate for the presidency."[15] Pepper also began to get questions from reporters about his political ambitions. In August 1946 he talked with reporters about the 1948 presidential election. The United Press story showed Pepper to be aligning himself with anyone willing to support him. He said he would "not run away" from the Democratic presidential nomination, although he predicted a Truman reelection. Pepper also offered himself as a vice presidential candidate for either Truman or Wallace, but said he preferred Wallace. "I would be happy to be on a ticket with anyone." The wire service story caught the eye of Truman's staff and was placed in the files of Truman's secretary.[16]

Pepper saw the 1946 congressional elections as a referendum on his views. Victories by liberal Democrats would show that there was support for his position, he believed. He traveled throughout the country in the summer and fall of 1946, campaigning for Democratic candidates. But Pepper's tour was a disaster. Although he bragged about his many speaking invitations, most were from far left-wing groups. In Boston on October 9 his speech was boycotted by the Democratic candidates he was supposed to be speaking for.[17] In Michigan he was heckled when he spoke on behalf of a candidate opposing Republican senator Arthur H. Vandenberg.[18]

The most memorable appearance came in September 1946. The left-wing National Citizens Political Action Committee and the Independent

Citizens Committee of the Arts, Sciences, and Professions planned a huge political rally at Madison Square Garden as part of the campaign against New York governor Thomas Dewey's reelection. NC-PAC, a creation of those who wanted close relations with Russia, later evolved into Wallace's Progressive Party.[19] Pepper was a favorite at NC-PAC events. The main attraction was Wallace, with Pepper also a featured speaker.

Wallace planned to speak on Republican obstructionism in Congress, but the rally organizers learned that he had privately urged Truman to change his thinking on American-Soviet relations, and Wallace was asked to talk about that.[20] Wallace cleared the speech with Truman, but while it generally agreed with the administration's foreign policy, it was different in significant ways. Before 18,000 people, Wallace criticized what he said was British imperialistic policy in the Near East. "The tougher we get, the tougher the Russians will get," Wallace warned.[21]

The Wallace speech was far milder than the speech Pepper gave. Pepper held nothing back in his criticism of the Truman administration. "With conservative Democrats and reactionary Republicans making our foreign policy as they are today, it is all we can do to keep foolish people from having us pull a Hitler blitzkrieg and drop our atomic bombs on the Russian people." He added, "I think we ought to remember, however, that the last two fellows who tried to get rough with the Russians—you may remember them from their first names, Napoleon and Adolf—did not fare so well."[22]

The crowd at Madison Square Garden cheered wildly for Pepper, who asked, "What do you expect in a foreign policy which really meets the approval of Senator Vandenberg and John Foster Dulles?" Wallace's more temperate remarks often brought boos and catcalls. In the Soviet Union, it was the Pepper speech that drew the most attention and praise for his opposition to those who "undermine the foundations of peace, poison the international atmosphere and provoke conflicts among great powers."[23]

Even though Truman initially approved Wallace's remarks, the president began to backpedal. Secretary of State James F. Byrnes was in Paris for a Council of Foreign Ministers meeting. With Byrnes in Paris was Republican senator Arthur Vandenberg, the subject of the Pepper attack. Truman and Byrnes worried that Vandenberg, and other Republicans, would drop their support of the president's foreign policy and turn the entire incident into a campaign issue. The meeting represented the first use of the get-tough policy Truman adopted for dealing with the Russians. On September 20, Wallace received a letter from Truman asking for his resignation. Despite his bungling of the situation, Truman had little choice but to fire Wallace. If he kept Wallace, Vandenberg might have ended the bipartisan unity on foreign policy.[24]

The Wallace firing drew criticism from liberals, who saw Wallace as the last true New Deal member of the Truman administration. A *Chicago Sun Times* editorial spoke for the left: "The New Deal as a driving force, is dead within the Truman administration."[25] Although Wallace was disliked in the South, the firing did little to help Truman. He was getting rid of Roosevelt's advisers but not his policies.[26]

In Florida, Pepper's remarks drew a great deal of attention. An editorial in the *Lakeland Ledger* said, "The Russians liked Senator Pepper's Madison Square Garden speech a great deal more than they liked the one by Secretary Wallace, although the Florida Senator and the former vice president have been running neck and neck for leftist honors."[27] But for Pepper, the biggest mistake was not what he said but who he was seen with. A picture taken at the rally showed Pepper with Wallace and Paul Robeson, one of the best-known blacks in the country and a known communist sympathizer. The picture was circulated throughout the state.

Just how far Pepper had moved from his party's position on Russia became clear on September 21 when Congressman John J. Sparkman, the head of the Democratic National Committee's Speakers Bureau, dropped Pepper as a speaker for the national party during the 1946 campaign. Sparkman, who was also running for the United States Senate in Alabama, said, "Certainly we don't want to send out anyone who is advocating the election of Republicans to Congress, as it appears from the press dispatches that Mr. Pepper has done. Certainly we don't want to send out anyone who is going to stab the President; we don't want those stabs, whether from the right or the left. And certainly Mr. Pepper has been attacking the President."[28] Sparkman also dropped Wallace as an official representative of the party.

Pepper was in Tallahassee when the announcement was made, and he quickly responded. He said his removal from the speakers' list showed "a determination to have a purge of all those who believe in progressive leadership." He said Sparkman's announcement "is not very likely to have any practical effect on what I do," adding that he had more speaking invitations than he could fill.[29] The Wallace firing brought Truman even more criticism and imperiled the Democratic campaigns for the House and Senate just seven weeks before the November election. Party leaders could not tell whether removing Pepper as a speaker could help or hurt. They decided it might hurt, especially in the North. The day after Sparkman read Pepper out of the party, Robert E. Hannegan, the chairman of the Democratic National Committee welcomed him back in. Hannegan denied that Pepper was removed from the speakers' list. In fact, Hannegan and Pepper held a series of what were described as "peace talks" to work out Pepper's role in the fall campaign. Under the plan, Pepper concentrated on liberal groups.[30]

In a sense, Pepper was lucky. Wallace's remarks at Madison Square Garden and his subsequent firing by Truman received nearly all of the attention. Instead of realizing that he had avoided more negative publicity, Pepper was disappointed that his speech "was lost generally under the Wallace speech."[31] Even before the furor over the Madison Square Garden events died, Pepper gave another controversial speech. He told a union convention in Jacksonville that Truman was being advised in foreign policy by the same type of reactionaries that were advising him on domestic issues. At the same time he kept up his praise for Wallace, calling him a "great American statesman."[32] While nearly everyone saw Wallace as representing the Democratic Party's left wing, Pepper disagreed. "I don't know exactly what a left-winger is, but I regard Wallace as just a good Democrat who believes in democracy and wants to see it become effective."[33] Pepper held Truman in growing contempt. He wrote to his friend Raymond Robins, "The presidency is just over his head and he not only is not big enough for the job, but not good enough for the job."[34]

Pepper ended his 1946 campaign swing in New York, where he encountered some of the most serious criticism of his tour. He was there to address a street rally sponsored by the communist-influenced Fur and Leather Workers Union. The *New York News* said his appearance meant "the radical part of the Democratic mixture is grooming Wallace and

Pepper for President and Vice President in 48."[35] But the most stinging criticism came from the right-wing *New York Mirror*, which used the term "Red Pepper" for the first time and said he was from "Florida, where he stands for Bilboism—for inequality in America—for 'white supremacy.'"[36] The *New York Times Magazine* said that "it is a good bet that if Mr. Pepper had to run now he would face an extremely difficult campaign for re-election. However, 1950 is a long time off." The lengthy article appeared two days before the election and repeated the "rumor circulated in the Capitol Hill cloakrooms by the anti-Pepperites that the Senator from Florida is after something bigger. They say he would like to be a 'labor president'—at least a Vice President—of the United States."[37]

Despite the critical comments, Pepper was encouraged by his reception as he stumped for Democratic candidates. He wrote to a fellow senator, "I am convinced by everything I have seen that we can and will win again a Democratic Congress by a good margin. . . . I have found an overwhelming sentiment among the people to retain and extend the gains of the Democratic administration both at home and abroad."[38]

Pepper could not have been more wrong. The 1946 election was a disaster for the Democrats in general and for the candidates Pepper backed in particular. In New York, James M. Mead and Herbert Lehman both lost, and Vandenberg was easily reelected in Michigan. The Republicans won control of the House of Representatives for the first time since 1931, with a margin of 246 to 188, and of the Senate for the first time since 1933 by 51 to 45. The Democrats lost 55 House seats and 12 Senate seats. But the losses and the string of critical articles had no apparent effect on Pepper. He blamed the losses on the firing of Wallace. "The last link with Roosevelt," he noted in his diary, was "now willfully cast out by Truman."[39] He could not see that he might have played a role in the losses, even though the candidates he campaigned for either lost or avoided the rallies where Pepper spoke.

But Pepper did realize he had lost some support. In early 1946 he noted in his diary that "about 10% of those who have previously supported me have left me."[40] In the wake of the 1946 election losses, he began to feel that he could not win in the South and might do better to move to a more liberal state. He wrote in his diary, "Can I survive in the South and give liberal national leadership? . . . If not, and I have such an ambition would not the earliest defeat and removal to NY or Calif. be preferable?"[41] This diary entry shows how out of touch he was with political reality. To believe that any state in the North would elect a candidate who had run as a white supremacist and had filibustered against antilynching legislation was unrealistic, if not absurd.

Pepper also continued to believe that he had a future in national politics, and that relations between the United States and Russia would improve. In December, Pepper met with William D. Pawley, a leading Democrat and ambassador to Brazil. Pawley asked Pepper about his pro-Russian views. Pepper said that he would not change his stand and did not want to talk about the matter anymore, adding that Franklin Roosevelt was a man who could look ahead five years and that Pepper believed that "in the not too distant future the entire world, including the United States, would be supporting Russia wholeheartedly." Pepper said that "when that day arrived, he wanted it to be known that it was Senator Pepper who championed close, friendly, and cooperative relations with Russia." Pepper declared he "naturally wanted to take advantage of the prestige he would reap, stating he would have hopes of being considered as a Presidential candidate."[42]

Pepper also received encouragement for his views from Charles E. Marsh, a newspaper publisher and backer of Lyndon Johnson, who wrote a memo entitled "Thoughts on Pepper." In it he presented a five-year plan aimed at putting Pepper in the White House. Marsh said he considered Pepper a "noble man, the best we've got in this country" but added that Pepper was "really a dawdler when he is not kicked in the butt. He loves the good things of this life, but above all loves to bask in his achievements and compliments of little people."[43]

Among the other people Pepper turned to for advice were William Carleton, a left-wing University of Florida professor who urged greater cooperation with the Russians, and Raymond Robins. Robins, who had moved to Florida after a lifetime of fascinating experiences, had made a fortune as a mining engineer, worked for Theodore Roosevelt's Progressive Party in 1912, then joined the Republicans. He had been a Congregational minister, an evangelist, and the Progressive candidate for the Senate from Illinois in 1914. As a member of the Red Cross Commission sent to distribute supplies to Russia after the fall of the czar in 1917, he became vitally interested in the fate of that country. During the nearly fifteen years that the United States did not have diplomatic relations with the Soviet Union, Robins served as an unofficial ambassador. In that role he met frequently with Bolshevik leaders; when he returned to the United States, he urged recognition of the Soviet Union. Robins never became a member of the Communist Party, but he was certainly a fellow traveler who admired Lenin and Stalin. He wrote to Carleton that "all of Lenin's prophecies have now been fulfilled," and said that for peace to be assured the United States needed to recognize the Soviet Union as "the first power of Europe."[44]

Robins moved to Chinsegut, an estate near Brooksville, Florida, and in 1937 he began writing to Pepper. Soon the two were communicating regularly. Robins saw Pepper as "a dark horse . . . to take his place in time among the great presidents."[45] As late as 1949, Robins was predicting that Pepper would be president.[46] Unfortunately for Pepper, nearly every piece of advice Robins gave him turned out badly. It was Robins who suggested that Pepper write the introduction to *The Great Conspiracy Against Russia*.[47] Robins and Carleton became Pepper's closest confidants in foreign affairs and constantly pushed him to support Russia as a means of securing the presidency. The three men reinforced one another. Carleton wrote to Robins, "Your position will become sounder and sounder as historical perspective plays upon the great events of 1917."[48]

As the 1947 session opened, Pepper lost his seat on the Senate Foreign Relations Committee to Senator Carl A. Hatch of New Mexico, who was placed on the committee as part of an effort to force Pepper off. One newspaper said he had been "squeezed off the Committee by a neat little bit of technical legerdemain."[49] Pepper wrote to Robins that "by a skillful intrigue I was removed from the Foreign Relations Committee by a Senator who had some seniority in the service of the Senate over me."[50] It was never clear whether Truman was involved in the decision to push Pepper from the Foreign Relations Committee, or whether Pepper's fellow Democrats in the Senate had made the decision. It was yet another instance in which his own party was isolating him. Pepper took a seat on the Agriculture Committee but clearly missed the Foreign Relations Committee. The *Tampa Morning Tribune* editorialized that "while Russia loses a friend in Foreign Relations, Florida gains a friend in Agriculture."[51]

Although Pepper was off the Foreign Relations Committee, he continued to devote most of his time to the subject. Nearly all of his speeches dealt with foreign affairs and his continuing campaign for better relations with Russia. The result was that the publicity he received throughout the country dealt almost exclusively with his stand on Russia.

In March, Pepper's connection with the extreme left wing was again spotlighted when the *Chicago Star*, a Communist Party newspaper, announced that Pepper had agreed to write a column for the newspaper: "Sen. Claude Pepper, Florida's fighting liberal, is a hard hitter. His courageous and often brilliant speeches confound his reactionary enemies in Congress. . . . Look for 'Pepper Pot,' a new Star column!"[52] The National Catholic Welfare Conference criticized Pepper for furnishing the *Star* with the column, calling Pepper "next to Wallace the Communists' main front man."[53] Pepper claimed that the column was one he sent to a regular mailing list of newspapers and radio stations, but he ordered the *Star* taken off the mailing list.[54] *Newsweek* commented that Pepper's "colleagues now call him 'Red' Pepper. But the pro-Communist left returns his affection. Only Henry A. Wallace outranks Pepper on their popularity scorecard."[55]

Early in 1947 the British informed the United States that they could no longer provide military and financial support to the Greek government. Truman wanted the Republican-controlled Congress to appropriate money for the United States to take over the British role, but the Republican leadership was leery of spending tax dollars to help the Greeks. Even administration officials knew that the Greek government was corrupt and inept, and that there was little evidence that the Russians were directly involved in trying to overthrow the Greek government. It was a difficult sell, and forced Undersecretary of State Dean Acheson to sound the alarm of communism. He warned the Republicans that communism was on the march; Greece was just one step on the road leading through Turkey and Iran, then Africa and all of Europe. The strategy worked, and the Republican leaders promised Truman their support.[56] Historian Melvyn P. Leffler argues that the Soviet actions "hardly justified the inflammatory rhetoric Acheson and Truman used."[57]

In March, Truman proposed an aid package to Greece and Turkey that became known as the Truman Doctrine. When the Senate held hearings on the Greek-Turkish aid bill, Pepper arranged to rejoin the Foreign Relations Committee as a guest, a practice that allowed senators with a special interest in a subject the opportunity to ask questions. When

Acheson testified before the committee, most of the questions were friendly except for Pepper's. Pepper said he thought the Truman Doctrine would "destroy any hope of reconciliation with Russia."[58] To make it clear he was opposed to the spread of communism, Pepper said he wanted to "stop Russian aggression wherever it exists . . . but that does not mean that we are going to intervene in every country where there is communism."[59] In a column to Florida newspapers he wrote, "Should we commit ourselves to fight Communism in every country of the world with unlimited money and, if necessary, with military force?"[60]

Pepper came up with his own version of the Truman Doctrine, calling for aid to Greece but not Turkey, as well as the exclusion of military supplies and the administration of the program through the United Nations. For the first time in several years, he was not alone. John Knight, publisher of the *Miami Herald*, wrote, "For once, I agree with Senator Claude Pepper in his suggestion that the Greek question be referred to the United Nations."[61]

After speaking against the bill, Pepper pledged to vote for it. He realized that to vote against the measure eliminated any standing he enjoyed in foreign affairs within his own party. He wrote to his friend Robins that he was voting for the measure as "a personal sacrifice of my convictions on the measure as a part of the price of attaining greater future usefulness in international affairs."[62]

As the vote drew closer, however, Pepper continued to speak against the bill, and gradually he became a leading opponent of a measure he promised to support. Pepper pushed for his alternative—aid to Greece, but through the United Nations. He was joined by Senator Glen Taylor of Idaho, who became equally controversial for his support of Russia. During the debate over the Truman Doctrine, Taylor spoke to the National Press Club, and to the tune of "I'm Going Crazy" he sang:

Now we're scuttling the UN for Greece and Turkey
There's no one again' it but Pepper and me.

Pepper's speeches against the Truman Doctrine brought him more criticism. He responded by saying that, given the political climate, even Thomas Jefferson "would be afraid to speak his own mind" if he were alive.[63] In the left-wing journal *In Fact*, Pepper wrote: "We must constantly be reminded that Hitler and the Nazis built up their vicious system on the pretense of fighting Communism. Lots of people in this country are actually fighting democracy under that guise."[64]

Pepper's criticism of the Truman Doctrine, and his defense of Russia, became more pronounced as the vote drew closer. On April 17 Pepper spoke to the Senate about the aid package for four hours. He urged that the Senate adopt his substitute—a $100 million aid package with no military aid, just for Greece, and administered through the United Nations. One of the reasons the administration wanted to prop up Turkey was to keep the Russians out of the Dardanelles. But Pepper, in the midst of an increasingly angry debate, said, "The Russians have as much right in there as we have to be in Panama, to be perfectly frank." Pepper complained that "the Russian viewpoint" had been ignored.[65]

In late April, just before the final vote, Pepper attended a World Federation luncheon where the speaker talked about the importance of the United Nations. Pepper decided then "beyond any question that I would not and could not vote for the Truman Doctrine because I hated it and I knew it betrayed America and America's stand in the United Nations which was the hope of the world's peace."[66] On the day of the vote, Pepper announced his intention to vote against the measure.

The decision heartened Pepper, and he wrote, "I never felt better in my conscience than when I finally resolved against the most intense persuasion of some of my dearest and best friends." But he also realized the damage it would do to his political career in Florida. He found that the change made him "subject to constant harassment at home, and generally in the nation. . . . Whatever the consequences may have been or may be to me in Florida I would not change that vote."[67]

Pepper's stand on the Truman Doctrine brought praise from just two quarters, the *Daily Worker* and the Russian newspaper *Pravda*. Whenever one of the communist publications praised Pepper, an American newspaper or magazine reported the information, usually adding critical comments. When *Pravda* gave Pepper high marks, *Newsweek* reported that "*Pravda* last week counted Soviet Russia's many blessings one by one, and the results were gratifying. There was so much the Russians could be thankful for, the Moscow daily exulted, particularly their American friends," including Claude Pepper.[68]

1. Following the 1948 election, George Smathers became a regular visitor at the Little White House in Key West. He was one of the few elected officials in Florida to campaign for President Harry Truman's reelection. On this trip he met with Truman and Chief Justice Fred M. Vinson. Reproduced courtesy of Associated Press.

2. Pepper was an early advocate for military preparedness and warned of the
danger Adolf Hitler posed to the United States. His position brought him
opposition from antiwar groups who campaigned against passage of the peacetime
draft. Marie Randy, the president of Uncle Sam's Peace and Prosperity League, got
past Capitol Police and thumbed her nose at the door of Pepper's Senate office.
Reproduced courtesy of Bettmann/Corbis.

The Red Record of
Senator Claude Pepper

HERE
IS THE
TRUTH

HERE
ARE THE
FACTS

HERE
IS THE
EVIDENCE

A DOCUMENTED CASE HISTORY
FROM OFFICAL GOVERNMENT RECORDS
AND ORIGINAL COMMUNIST DOCUMENTS

3. A former FBI agent, undoubtedly backed by financier Ed Ball, compiled *The Red Record of Senator Claude Pepper*. Thousands of copies of the booklet linking Pepper to left-wing organizations were distributed throughout the state during the 1950 primary campaign. Reproduced courtesy of P. K. Yonge Library of Florida History.

4. Both Pepper and Smathers made several appearances each day, beginning in the morning and ending late at night. Pepper spoke to this nighttime rally in Gainesville shortly before the 1950 primary. Reproduced courtesy of Thomas D. McAvoy/Getty Images.

5. Ed Ball thought he had ended Pepper's political career in 1950. But when Pepper returned to Congress in 1963, he trumped Ball by pushing through legislation that forced Ball to give up his banks and restricted his business activities. In 1964 Ball testified before a Congressional committee considering the legislation aimed at him. Reproduced courtesy of Associated Press.

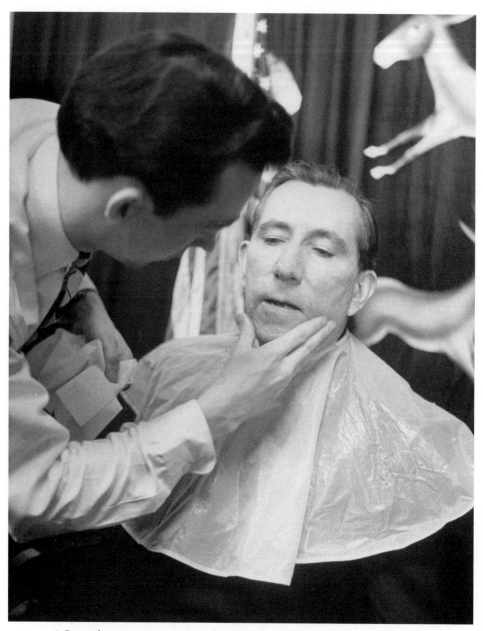

6. Pepper's attempt to oust President Truman at the 1948 convention brought him national attention. An NBC technician applied makeup before Pepper was interviewed on the new medium of television. The interview could not be seen in Florida, which got its first television station in 1949. Reproduced courtesy of Francis Miller/Getty Images.

7. Pepper climbed up to shake hands with an engineer for the Atlantic Coast Line Railroad, which backed Pepper. But opposition from Ed Ball's Florida East Coast Railway contributed to his defeat. Reproduced courtesy of Thomas D. McAvoy/Getty Images.

8. Truman did little to hide his dislike for Pepper. Pepper had attempted to deny Truman the vice presidency in 1944 and the presidential nomination in 1948. Reproduced courtesy of George Skadding/Getty Images.

9. Pepper and his wife, Mildred, slept on an election-eve flight from South Florida to their home in Tallahassee. Both Pepper and Smathers used private airplanes in 1950, their first widespread use in a Florida election. Reproduced courtesy of Thomas D. McAvoy/Getty Images.

10. Pepper appeared in 1946 with singer Paul Robeson and Secretary of Commerce Henry Wallace at a left-wing rally at Madison Square Garden. Wallace's speech resulted in his firing by Truman, and Pepper drew condemnation for his own speech. The photo was widely circulated in the 1950 campaign to support allegations that Pepper was overly friendly with an African American and with Wallace, whose support of Russia made him as controversial as Pepper. Reproduced courtesy of Bettmann/Corbis.

11. On a charter flight to Miami, Smathers read a newspaper with a political advertisement for Pepper on the back page. Like all Pepper ads, this one linked him with Franklin Roosevelt and prosperity. Reproduced courtesy of Hank Walker/Getty Images.

FIFTEEN CENTS   May 2, 1938

TIME

The Weekly Newsmagazine

Color photograph for TIME *by Paul Dorsey*

Volume XXXI

CLAUDE PEPPER
A Florida fighting-cock will be a White House weather-vane.
(See NATIONAL AFFAIRS)

Number 18

12. Pepper appeared on two *Time* magazine covers nearly half a century apart—
a unique distinction. Reproduced courtesy of Paul Dorsey/Time Magazine.

APRIL 25, 1983

$1.50

TIME

VIET NAM'S WOES An Exclusive Report

Spokesman For the Elderly

"They deserve much — and need much."

Congressman Claude Pepper

Reproduced courtesy of William Coupon/Time Magazine.

13. As the early returns showed Smathers taking a commanding lead, he embraced his wife at his Miami headquarters. Reproduced courtesy of Hank Walker/Getty Images.

14. In 1950 there were just two television stations in Florida, and the new medium played no role in the campaign. Instead, candidates primarily saw voters in small groups or, like Smathers here, individually. Reproduced courtesy of Thomas D. McAvoy/Getty Images.

6

Pepper and the 1948 Election

In August 1947, Pepper met with Truman as part of a congressional delegation and emerged to say, "The President should be and will be nominated and should be and will be elected." Pepper said he had given up the idea of supporting a third-party movement being considered by Henry Wallace: "I think Mr. Wallace can render his best service by continuing to be a private citizen who speaks his mind freely." When reporters asked who Truman should pick as his vice presidential running mate, Pepper did not name any names but clearly described himself: "Somebody who subscribes as completely as possible to the views of Franklin D. Roosevelt. He ought to be someone who can command not only the strong but the enthusiastic support of organized labor and the working people in general." *Time* magazine wrote, "No one doubted that Claude Pepper, friend of Russia and darling of the left wing, was looking in the mirror as he was speaking."[1] A few hours later, Pepper appeared on *Meet the Press* and again voiced his support for Truman. After the broadcast, Truman called Pepper to thank him.[2] Pepper wrote to former senator Sherman Minton, "You know there never was any question but that I was going to support the President."[3]

While Pepper was talking publicly about backing Truman for reelection in 1948, privately he was considering other options, including challenging Truman for the Democratic nomination or a third-party bid. He asked his friend William Carleton if the time was right for a third party, or "if the Democratic Party's liberal wing should be built up."[4]

Carleton wrote him, "If the situation shapes up in such a way in 1948 for you to make a contest for the Democratic presidential nomination, I hope to God you will seize the opportunity."[5] Pepper wrote to his friend Raymond Robins that he wanted to be able to rely on the support of the Florida delegation to the convention in case an opportunity for him should develop.[6]

In order to have any chance at a spot on the national ticket, Pepper needed to have his own delegation to the Democratic National Convention behind him. In 1940 and 1944, Pepper was chairman of the Florida delegation, but by 1948 the opposition to him had developed to the point that the question now was whether he even had enough support to go as a delegate.

The delegates to the convention were chosen during the May Democratic primary, with the voters selecting 28 delegates, of whom 12 had a full vote and 16 a half-vote.[7] In January 1948 the Democratic Executive Committee met in Jacksonville. The meeting seemed routine until the final fifteen minutes, when Pepper opponents complained about the procedures for electing executive committee officers. They moved to elect a new state Democratic chairman to replace Pepper's friend and supporter, Volusia County sheriff Alex Littlefield. The executive committee was dominated by Pepper supporters, including Littlefield, state railroad commissioner Jerry Carter, and Key West attorney William Albury. They might have been able to maintain control, but putting it to a vote was risky. The Pepper supporters suggested delaying the election of officers until June, one month after the primary, and their proposal was carried, by a vote of 58 to 55.[8] The *Orlando Morning Sentinel* called the victory a "typical Pepper coup. He learned of the danger, worked quietly to avert it until the day of the showdown, then appeared personally to ensure its safety."[9] Pepper had, nevertheless, come perilously close to being repudiated by members of his own party in Florida.

The Pepper opponents worked under a number of banners, primarily the Florida Democratic Club, which was organized in 1944 by Jacksonville public relations executive Dan Crisp with financing from Pepper's powerful enemy Ed Ball. The organization failed to oust Pepper in 1944 but continued to work for an eventual Pepper defeat. Its immediate goal was to control the 1948 delegation to the Democratic convention, but its true purpose was to unseat Pepper when he faced reelection in 1950. Two longtime opponents of Pepper, Charles E. Sheppard and Frank Upchurch, were selected as officers. Both men were close associates of Ball.

The group said it was opposing Pepper because his "official acts, and unofficial speeches and statements, since the 1944 election is conclusive proof that he had deserted the Democratic Party to promote the interests of the radical elements in their propaganda for the communistic ideology and communistic infiltration into our American governmental institutions and organizations." The group said that his call for destroying American atomic bombs and giving Russia financial aid showed that Pepper "is not a good American."[10] Referring to the activities of the Florida Democratic Club, Pepper's close friend Chester Dishong, the sheriff of DeSoto County, told him bluntly, "You better use your head a little, son, as you are in a hell of a spot."[11]

Whether he was listening to Dishong, weighing the impact of the contentious January meeting of the Florida Democratic Executive Committee, or seeing for himself the problems he faced as he met with voters, Pepper began to modify his positions and increase his presence in Florida. In February he wrote to a friend, "I suppose you may imagine I have been having my own troubles in Florida where reaction is very much entrenched and very vigorous. Hence I went to Florida three times in January, have just returned from a trip there, and am scheduled for every weekend this month to go there."[12] He also modified his stand on the Soviet Union. In March he criticized the Soviets for the first time: "The Soviet Union has been guilty of aggression which offends and affronts our sense of independence and dignity and freedom for the peoples of the world."[13]

In putting together delegate support, Pepper faced two problems: the opposition from the Florida Democratic Club, and his inability to come up with a candidate to support. He told Robins that he was putting together "a delegation to the convention which will be friendly to me, and of course, getting a group of friends to run as unpledged delegates. I am not so much concerned as to what their attitude will be toward the President as I am that they are friends of mine in case any opportunity on my behalf would develop, and they could be counted on. We are going to have a scrap."[14]

Pepper was realistic to see that a slate pledged to him was doomed to fail, and a slate pledged to Truman could not do much better. He needed to pledge his support to a candidate who might attract votes. On January 24, 1948, Pepper praised General Dwight Eisenhower's decision not to become a candidate: "It was laudable of Eisenhower to stay out of the political arena, as it was best that military officers do not enter the political fields."[15] But a few months later Pepper saw an opportunity to use Eisenhower to help elect a pro-Pepper delegation.

Despite the general's protests that he had no interest in politics, Pepper wrote to a friend that Eisenhower was "the only one between us and defeat."[16] Pepper envisioned Eisenhower as being more reasonable in dealing with the Soviets. "It is certainly a tragedy to see this great nation [Soviet Union] so full of hopeful potentialities being degraded as it is by those now dominant and seeking more arrogant power in the nation," he wrote in a letter to Robins.[17]

If Pepper was to have any chance of capturing control of the delegation to the Democratic National Committee, he needed Eisenhower. Eisenhower not only had tremendous popularity in the South but also had the advantage of having never taken a political stand. There was nothing he had said or done to alienate voters in the South. Pepper ignored Eisenhower's decision to stay out of the race. "He may be pulling the door a little closer to him, but I didn't hear the lock click."[18] In an April speech in Los Angeles he again mentioned Eisenhower as a possible candidate.[19]

Without consulting Eisenhower, Pepper decided to use his name. Pepper called his slate Loyal Democrats for Eisenhower and States Rights. Pepper hoped to use Eisenhower to attract votes for himself and threw in states' rights as an appeal to southerners alarmed by Truman's civil rights program.

Pepper's position on civil rights was complicated. He opposed civil rights legislation but did not join with his fellow southerners, who made race-baiting a major part of their agenda. His solution was to downplay civil rights as an issue in selecting the Democratic presidential nominee. "We are faced with a grave international crisis. War itself could come almost any day. As important as are these civil rights matters, they are not the only things that should be considered in choosing the Democratic nominee for President."[20]

While the Florida Democratic Club moved quickly to put together its slate, Pepper procrastinated, waiting until late April to assemble his delegates.[21] Despite knowing he faced a difficult fight, Pepper failed to campaign for his slate. It was a problem Pepper wrestled with throughout the 1940s: the choice between staying home to deal with political problems in Florida and answering the calls of those who saw him as a national figure and wanted him to speak throughout the country. Ten days before the May primary, Pepper went on a nationwide speaking tour that included stops in Montana, Nebraska, South Carolina, and California. Meanwhile he picked up another opponent when Governor Millard Caldwell offered his own slate. Caldwell said he was not trying to decrease Pepper's influence at the convention, but of course that was the result.[22]

Of the three Florida slates, none was pledged to Truman. The Caldwell slate was unpledged, and the Florida Democratic Club supported Mississippi governor Fielding L. Wright, an old-line states' rights champion. The Wright slate promised to "work as a team with other Southern States against Truman and against the so-called 'Civil Rights Program.'" In a slap at both Pepper and Truman, the club claimed, "The present leaders of the Democratic party in an appeal to radical minority groups in the large cities of the North, East, and Mid-West are determined to sacrifice our traditions and way of life in the South."[23]

Despite Eisenhower's name and the use of the term "states' rights," Pepper's slate fared poorly. The Florida Democratic Club slate won with 11 delegate votes, Pepper's slate captured 6½ votes, and Caldwell's slate took just 2 votes, with a half-vote uncommitted.[24] Pepper had decisively lost the support of his own delegation. Worse, two-thirds of the delegates not only were opposed to any presidential or vice presidential candidacy for Pepper but wanted him out of the Senate. The only good news was that the gubernatorial candidate Pepper favored, Fuller Warren, won the Democratic nomination. Still, Pepper did not see the delegate vote as a repudiation of his views. He wrote to Robins, "On the whole, the elections turned out very favorably for me, for a number of sheriffs in the big counties, some of whom I actively aided, were elected, and others who can be of value to us in 1950."[25]

It is difficult to see how Pepper could be encouraged by the results. Although a number of his supporters won local elections, and indeed might help him in 1950, the voters of Florida had rejected him and his slate. Although his friend Alex Littlefield was reelected state chairman, Frank Upchurch, a leading Pepper opponent, was chosen as chairman of the Florida delegation to the Democratic National Convention.[26] For the first time since being elected to the Senate, Pepper was not to be the chairman of the Florida delegation.

After the disastrous 1946 election, Pepper's public statements became more and more erratic. In early May he called Henry Wallace a good American and backed off his earlier prediction of a Truman victory.[27] Two weeks later he said he was "neither for nor against Mr. Truman," but pledged to support the Democratic nominee.[28] In late May he wrote to Robins that he did not believe Truman could win: "The national situation alternates as far as Democratic chances are concerned between confusion and hopelessness."[29]

The best hope, Pepper decided, was Eisenhower, who repeatedly made it clear that he did not want to be a candidate. Pepper's earlier interest in Eisenhower brought him into contact with Leonard V. Finder, the publisher of the *Manchester (N.H.) Union-Leader* and the man who first floated the idea of an Eisenhower candidacy. Finder told Pepper a strange story: Eisenhower did not want the Republican nomination because the Republican leaders were selfish and shortsighted, Finder said, but Eisenhower had told him privately that he was willing to run as a Democrat because he "felt differently about the Democratic Party."[30]

On June 26, as the Republican National Convention came to an end, Finder claimed he met with Eisenhower and that the general had not made up his mind about running for president but "would be greatly affected by the action of the Republican convention." The Republicans had already nominated Thomas Dewey when Finder wrote his letter, and Eisenhower gave no indication he was unhappy with the choice.[31] Pepper admitted to Robins that there was not much chance for an Eisenhower nomination but said he would continue to work for it.

While he was supporting Eisenhower, Pepper also saw himself as a potential candidate. He wrote to a friend that if he "were to follow the inclinations of my heart, I should be out fighting in the way that Henry Wallace is fighting."[32] Amid the dozens of conflicting stands Pepper took on his political future, it is unclear if he ever had a single, clear goal in mind. Did he really think that he would be Truman's choice for vice president after opposing Truman, and many of his programs, for four years? Did he believe an Eisenhower candidacy was possible, or was he using him as a stalking horse to mask his own ambitions? Did he believe that Eisenhower might select him as his running mate, or name him to a major job, perhaps secretary of state?

Pepper became a leader in the drive to dump Truman and recruit Eisenhower. The movement included people with little in common except a desire to nominate anyone but Truman. The unofficial leader was James Roosevelt, the California state chairman and son of Franklin Roosevelt. The list also included New York mayor William O'Dwyer, Minneapolis mayor Hubert Humphrey, Governor Strom Thurmond of South Carolina, Senator Richard Russell of Georgia, and Nebraska state chairman William Ritchie. On July 4 James Roosevelt sent a telegram to each of the 1,592 delegates to the Democratic National Convention inviting them to attend a special caucus on July 10 in Philadelphia, site of the convention.[33]

The Eisenhower effort had the quiet backing of the left-wing CIO Political Action Committee, one of the most active political organizations in the country. The union distributed literature and encouraged union locals to pass resolutions supporting Eisenhower. "It was quite clear," CIO officials believed, "that the movement had sufficient strength to assure a nomination of Eisenhower by the Convention in the absence of any statement in the contrary from him."[34]

The coalition had little hope of success, however, even if Eisenhower wanted to be president. It assumed that he would sweep the convention, although Truman controlled a majority of the delegates. While his backers agreed that Eisenhower was the best candidate, they knew little about his views. For example, where did he stand on civil rights? What would have happened to the support of southern senators such as Lister Hill and John Sparkman and Governor Strom Thurmond if it turned out that Eisenhower embraced a strong civil rights platform? And how would O'Dwyer, Humphrey, and organized labor have reacted if Eisenhower sided with the southern position on civil rights? The chances of the coalition holding together were very slim.

But the specter of an Eisenhower candidacy did worry Truman. He told Secretary of the Army Kenneth C. Royall to contact Eisenhower to work out the wording of a withdrawal statement.[35] On Monday night, July 5, Eisenhower issued a statement saying, "I will not, at this time, identify myself with any political party, and could not accept nomination for any public office or participate in a partisan political contest."[36] The statement seemed final, but a few die-hard Eisenhower supporters sought to keep the possibility alive. Roosevelt sent a telegram to Pepper interpreting Eisenhower's words to mean that he would not "seek partisan political office" but would accept the nomination as a "unity candidate."[37] Roosevelt said Eisenhower should still be a candidate "unless he refuses to accept after the convention nominates him."[38]

Pepper agreed with Roosevelt that there was still a glimmer of hope that Eisenhower might become a candidate. On July 6 he sent a telegram to Roosevelt saying, "This man cannot refuse a truly national draft to a truly national leadership in the salvation of his country." Pepper's idea was to "make the Democratic National Convention the expression of a national draft of General Eisenhower." He sent a copy of the telegram to Eisenhower with the note "You will understand that I neither expect nor desire either an acknowledgment or reply.[39]

Pepper released a public statement saying, "The Democrats must be prepared to let General Eisenhower be a truly national President." Not only would the Democrats have to give him their nomination, but so would the Republicans. "He could not be expected to accept the nomination if it narrowed him to the limits of a party candidate. The Democratic party's rewards would lie in the tributes it would gain for its magnanimity in a time of crisis." Pepper said Eisenhower should also be allowed to write his own platform and select his own running mate.[40]

But Eisenhower genuinely did not want to run for president. To the professional politicians, it seemed as if Eisenhower was merely being coy, a typical posture of denying interest while waiting for the right moment to become a candidate. Truman wrote in his diary that the Democrats opposing him were "double dealers all. But they'll get nowhere—a double dealer never does."[41]

For the third time in six months, Eisenhower was forced to deny he was a candidate. On Friday, July 9, he sent a telegram to Pepper: "I respectfully and earnestly request and urge that you drop such intention because I assure you that to carry it out would result in acute embarrassment to all concerned as well as confusion in the minds of many of our citizens. . . . I would refuse to accept the nomination."[42] Although Eisenhower said the telegram was "personal for you," Pepper quickly released it to the press, which, as Pepper knew would happen, "dominated the headlines."[43]

Nearly all of the Eisenhower support fell away, and most of those who opposed Truman now realized that his nomination was inevitable. But the hard-core Truman opposition remained, led by Roosevelt, Pepper, Americans for Democratic Action chairman Leon Henderson, Nebraska Democratic chairman William Ritchie, and the CIO-PAC leadership. Pepper did not realize that much of the opposition to Truman was personal, not political. Ritchie and Truman had a falling out, and even after Truman was nominated, Ritchie said, "I'm convinced that he cannot be elected. He has muffed the ball badly."[44]

Truman and James Roosevelt had been feuding for some time, and in June the two argued in a Los Angeles hotel suite. Roosevelt, who had been an assistant to his father in the White House, was best known for his love of fast cars and good times. Truman jabbed his finger into Roosevelt's chest and said, "But get this straight: whether you like it or not, I am going to be the next president of the United States. That will be all. Good day." With that, Truman turned and walked out.[45] Henderson did have influence, but with only about 120 delegates.

Some Truman opponents turned to Supreme Court Justice William O. Douglas as a possible candidate. Douglas was a strong supporter of the New Deal and was very popular. Henderson said that "the Democratic Party must choose Douglas or invite a disaster that will imperil the future of progressivism in America."[46] Douglas had expressed no interest in the nomination, and his views on many subjects were unknown. Those views that were known were very close to Truman's.[47]

Jack Kroll, the leader of the CIO-PAC, arrived in Philadelphia on Saturday, July 10, and met with James Roosevelt to discuss options and confirm a rumor that Pepper might become a candidate. According to detailed notes kept by Tilford E. Dudley, a CIO official, Kroll and Roosevelt then met with Pepper and several other union officials. Pepper told them the anti-Truman forces were falling apart. They needed a candidate, he said, and he was willing to serve as that candidate. Those at the meeting, however, did not embrace the Pepper candidacy, suggesting instead that Pepper conduct an informal survey of delegates to see if he had any support, and that he play "hard to get."[48] No doubt Kroll realized that Pepper was no improvement over Truman—and almost certainly a greater detriment to the party—but he would not want to offend one of the leading supporters of the labor movement. And there was an additional problem for Kroll and the CIO. Pepper was fine as a prolabor southern senator, but the CIO could not support a national candidate who had campaigned in his last election on a platform of racial superiority.

While waiting for Pepper to conduct his informal survey, the CIO decided to support Douglas. Two hours later a caucus of the remaining anti-Truman forces was held in the Bellevue-Stratford Hotel. Each time the anti-Truman forces met, the turnout was smaller, the options were more limited, and those in attendance were largely those who personally disliked Truman and who held little influence at the convention. The caucus, which became known as the Pepper Caucus, failed to agree on anything, but they kept open the possibility of a Douglas or Pepper candidacy.[49]

When the caucus adjourned, a smaller meeting was held with Roosevelt, Kroll, and Pepper. Roosevelt said that if Pepper could attract commitments from southern delegates, Roosevelt could deliver support from California and some northern states. Kroll again recommended surveying the delegates to measure Pepper's support. Pepper should have realized then just how weak his position was. Kroll had embraced Douglas, a candidate he had not spoken to and who expressed no interest in the nomination, while stalling Pepper. Roosevelt had sent him to seek votes among southern delegates, where Pepper's views made him highly unpopular. In exchange, Roosevelt held out the lure of a large bloc of votes from the California delegation, even though he could not deliver its votes to Pepper.[50]

That night at 10 p.m. another anti-Truman caucus was held, this time at the Drake Hotel. A small number of delegates from Nebraska, Kansas, California, and a few other states attended, along with Kroll and some other CIO officials. There was little enthusiasm after Eisenhower's firm withdrawal, but a committee was named to see how much support there was for Pepper. William Ritchie, the Nebraska chairman, was elected to lead the committee.[51] Even before he conducted the survey, Ritchie let it be known that Pepper would declare his candidacy the following day. The last of the anti-Truman advocates were so desperate that they were reduced to finding a candidate who met just two criteria: a "liberal," and willing to give "definite assurance that he will take the nomination."[52]

Pepper offered a different version of the events in his autobiography. He said that on Saturday a number of Democratic congressmen and columnists came to his room for breakfast to discuss a possible Pepper candidacy. At that breakfast, Pepper said, Ritchie agreed to lead a movement on his behalf. Pepper said that eventually "a large number of labor delegates and liberals filled a large room to overflowing and agreed that I should be the candidate to oppose President Truman."[53]

On Sunday, July 11, a CIO caucus was held. Nearly a hundred delegates who were either union members or close supporters attended. There was still a great deal of anti-Truman sentiment, but little support for another candidate such as Pepper or Douglas. That afternoon, Douglas said he had no intention of becoming a candidate and asked that effort on his behalf stop. Kroll held a news conference to announce support for an open convention. He said Pepper's entry as a candidate was welcome but said the CIO-PAC would not endorse any candidate.[54] Hours earlier, the CIO was ready to endorse a laundry list of candidates, most of whom they had never spoken with. Now they refused to endorse the candidacy of Pepper, who wanted the nomination and who was a strong supporter of the CIO.

On Sunday evening Pepper announced his candidacy at what had been the Eisenhower headquarters. In a large room, surrounded by the leftovers of the Eisenhower campaign, he said, "This is no gesture. This is a fight and I believe we can make it a winning fight, even if we are starting tardily."[55] He said, "This is not the time for politics as usual, for this nation is trembling on the brink of war and our national economy is threatened by an economic depression."[56] He said he was urged to run by members of the Ritchie Committee, even though it is unclear whether the Ritchie Committee ever found any support for Pepper. Ritchie was named as chairman of the Pepper campaign committee. Ritchie, like Pepper and Roosevelt, held little influence within his own delegation. That night, CIO officials met to discuss the Pepper candidacy. Pepper told a Kroll aide that he "hoped to pick up the support of individual delegates from the different states," but that he had no large commitments.[57] Pepper said he did not expect a CIO endorsement but did ask that they canvas delegates and rally people on his behalf. Kroll said the CIO-PAC would assist Pepper with the canvas.[58]

While proclaiming himself a liberal, Pepper made it clear he was a "practical" southern liberal and criticized Truman's civil rights program as "a snare and a delusion."[59] Pepper and his supporters also came out for restoration of the two-thirds rule. This rule, which had been in effect until Franklin Roosevelt became president, required that, to be nominated, a candidate win two-thirds of the vote, not just a majority. The anti-Truman forces believed that they could deny Truman the nomination if he had to get the votes of two-thirds of the delegates. The *New York Times* was sharply critical of Pepper's move, saying he "was so desperate yesterday that he talked about a move to amend the majority rule and require a two-thirds vote on the first three nominating ballots. This, of course, is anathema to the Northern liberals on whom he counted for some support and would increase the power of the Southern conservatives, whose votes Senator Pepper can't get anyway."[60] For decades, southern delegates used the two-thirds rule as a veto, guaranteeing that no candidate who was overly friendly on topics such as civil rights could win the nomination.

Pepper claimed to have enough support to deny Truman the nomination on the first ballot with votes from twenty-two states. Ritchie said there were between 300 and 400 first-ballot votes for Pepper. But when he was pressed for details, Pepper said he could count only on the 6½ votes from his home state. When Pepper sought support from the other Florida delegates, they sat silently and did nothing.[61] The *New York*

Times said the Pepper announcement was the "hottest and funniest" part of the convention. The newspaper observed that while the anti-Truman forces sought a name to unify the opposition, Pepper's name "had the directly opposite effect."[62]

Pepper always had his eye on the presidency. In 1940, while in Orlando to address a club meeting, he told one of the members, "In some strange way I should be president."[63] But this was certainly the strangest way, challenging an incumbent president who already had enough committed delegates to win on the first ballot.

The Florida newspapers had a field day. The *Fort Lauderdale News* referred to the "sad spectacle of Senator Claude Pepper nominating himself as a Democratic presidential candidate."[64] The *Miami Daily News* said, "Senator Pepper is not a proper candidate for the Democratic party."[65] The *Tampa Morning Tribune*, in a front-page editorial, called his candidacy preposterous.[66] John Knight, the publisher of the *Miami Herald*, wrote, "Some men in public life simply cannot resist the temptation to thrust themselves into the spotlight."[67]

Democratic leader James A. Farley called Pepper's candidacy "stupid and fantastic," and said Pepper was being laughed at by the delegates.[68] An attempt to stage a demonstration for Pepper was a failure.[69] Even those who seemed determined to nominate anyone but Truman rejected Pepper. Leon Henderson, the ADA chairman, said, "We have already had two dark horses shot from under us. Why the hell should we get up and ride on a red roan?"

Truman made no public statement about Pepper's candidacy, but in a letter to A. J. Angle, the collector of customs in Tampa, he wrote that "the antics of one of the Florida Senators is right in line with what he usually does at every convention. He is merely a publicity hound."[70]

Pepper had been swept up in the convention fever. He watched as people sought desperately to find a candidate to challenge Truman. When candidate after candidate refused, Pepper thought he could fill the breach, but no one wanted him. One day after declaring his candidacy, he withdrew. He tried to put the best face on his withdrawal. He said he met with four advisers who thought "the best thing for me to do was to issue a clear, courageous statement and withdraw my candidacy for President."[71] Even though he had found only a handful of delegates, he made his cause sound more impressive by telling reporters, "I release all promises of support and request that I not be nominated for any office within the powers of this convention."[72] On the floor of the convention hall, a twenty-two-year-old woman tried to ride a horse onto the floor but was stopped at the door. She said she was campaigning for Pepper. "Everybody likes horses, everybody likes Pepper," she told a policeman. The officer turned her away, saying she should have tried a donkey.[73]

While everyone else saw Pepper's candidacy as either lunacy or grandstanding, Pepper himself could not understand what happened. He wrote to his friend Carleton, "When reflective eyes are turned back to the convention, they will conclude that I offered the only way by which the Democratic Party could have saved the disunity which now appears to be fatal in the coming election."[74] He also viewed the rejection by his fellow southerners as a terrible mistake. "The South, had it rallied to me, who had never been extreme upon these matters, could have achieved the aim it was supposed to be pursuing of defeating the nomination of the president."[75]

In the end, Claude Pepper, who sought to be the liberal heir to Franklin Roosevelt, ended up casting his vote for Senator Richard Russell, arguably the most conservative member of the Democratic Party. Pepper voted for Russell to protect himself from criticism by segregationists, and all of the southern delegates except for a baker's dozen in North Carolina cast their ballots for Russell. But as soon as the votes were tallied, Pepper immediately endorsed Truman and called Truman's acceptance speech the "most magnificent address of his career. I had the strange feeling that some of the spirit and magnetism of Mr. Roosevelt had come back to the party."[76] In the fall Pepper campaigned for Truman, although a Truman friend urged that Pepper be kept out of Florida because "he will do more harm than good."[77] Angle told Truman that Pepper was drawing tiny crowds to his speeches in Florida and urged Truman to send Pepper "out west." Angle thought that Pepper was backing Truman only for selfish motives. He wrote to Truman that Pepper "figured this campaign would give him a splendid opportunity to appear before the people in your behalf and that it would strengthen his political fences. . . . You were exactly right when you sized him up as a 'publicity hound.'"[78] Pepper did campaign in a number of states including Illinois, Minnesota, and West Virginia, but as events showed, Truman did not forgive his actions at the convention.

Pepper was trying to have it both ways. If Truman somehow pulled an upset and was reelected, Pepper wanted to be on his good side. But if Truman lost, then a search would begin for new leadership, and that could mean a heightened role for Pepper and perhaps a presidential nomination in 1952.

Pepper realized that the fiasco might have hurt him in Florida, telling Carleton, "my course may prove fatal in the next election. Yet, as I said to President Roosevelt . . . 'We cannot stand for election always.'" Still, he saw a silver lining. "It may be, that by diligence and great exertions and the help of loyal friends and the upsurging of many liberal forces which are latent in our state, I can survive."[79] The *Fort Lauderdale News* thought Pepper's actions at the convention destroyed any chance he had for reelection in 1950. "When the Senator went crawling back to Truman after the acceptance speech, he lost what little following he had among Florida's political leaders."[80]

For the progressives, the 1948 election signaled an end to their political dreams. The idea of a liberal party, which seemed so promising two years earlier, was a failure. Truman won the election with 49.5 percent of the vote to Dewey's 45.1 percent. Thurmond took just 2.4 percent, but he was able to carry four southern states. Wallace finished fourth, with 2.3 percent of the popular vote and no electoral votes. In Florida, Truman won with 48.8 percent of the vote.

With his reelection in hand, Truman began to cultivate a friendship with George Smathers, a young Florida congressman. Truman wrote to Smathers's mother: "Had a good visit with George at Key West. He's the only public official I invited to see me! The others invited themselves."[81]

Pepper did not realize it, but he was a man without a party. When Wallace left the Democratic Party, he took with him the extreme left wing. That was also the core of Pepper's national support, the people who filled his calendar with speaking invitations throughout the country. He had alienated himself from the Democrats, and now he stood alone.

Pepper's isolation came as he began to reconsider his view of the

Soviet Union. In 1948 a number of events including the communist takeover of Czechoslovakia and the collapse of Chiang Kai-shek in China led him to attack what he called the "Russian onslaught." He said, "Hell is not hot enough for those Red criminals who have thrust upon a world still groaning from one war, another war." He now supported the North Atlantic Treaty Organization and called for increased arms appropriations.[82] But it was too little, too late. His own reelection was fast approaching, and Pepper's views on the Soviet Union posed a serious problem for him as relations between the United States and the Soviets deteriorated.

The Opponent

If Claude Pepper had someone who was his exact opposite, it was George Smathers. Life came easily to Smathers, who excelled at everything he tried. The most noticeable difference was their appearance. Pepper was short and unattractive. Even he thought often about his terrible acne scars. Smathers was so handsome that his political opponents tried unsuccessfully to dismiss him as a pretty boy. Where Smathers was agile and athletic, Pepper was awkward. Smathers stood ramrod straight, while Pepper seemed perpetually slumped over. Smathers was born to a wealthy family, while Pepper's family always flirted with financial disaster. Smathers got attention naturally, while Pepper seemed to have to seize center stage. While Pepper was unpopular in Congress, Smathers was well liked. It was a tribute to his ability to get along that two of his best friends in Congress were John Kennedy—he was in Kennedy's wedding—and Richard Nixon, who first visited Florida at Smathers's urging.

Smathers was born in New Jersey, where his father, Frank, was a successful attorney and a powerful force in Atlantic City's Democratic Party. In 1910 Frank made a decision that had an impact on the nation and the world. Smathers delivered Atlantic City's delegates for Woodrow Wilson in his quest for the 1910 Democratic gubernatorial nomination. A grateful Wilson named Smathers to the state circuit court, but Frank Smathers was troubled by chronic arthritis, and his doctor recommended that he go south for the warmer climate. In 1920 the Smathers family took the train from New Jersey to Miami. George was six years old, only a few years younger than Miami itself.

George grew to be six feet two inches tall by the time he reached Miami High School, where he was elected student body president, the first of more than a dozen elections without a loss. He excelled in basketball, football, boxing, and track. His performance on the football field drew the attention of the University of Illinois, which offered him a football scholarship. But Frank Smathers advised his son to skip the scholarship. Frank reasoned that if George hoped to go into politics in Florida, attending college in Illinois would be a mistake. (Indeed, before the decade was out, opponents of Claude Pepper used his attendance at Harvard University to attack him.) George Smathers decided to attend the University of Florida.[1]

Smathers breezed through college, as he did through life. Unlike many students, he was not affected by the financial hardships of the Great Depression. As an undergraduate he was captain of both the basketball and track teams, was readily accepted into the prestigious Blue Key society, and excelled in debate. After receiving his diploma in 1936, he went directly to law school, where he won the Best All-Around Man award in his first year. During his second year of law school, Smathers met the state's new United States senator, Claude Pepper, who was running for reelection. Smathers was impressed and volunteered to help run the Pepper campaign on the university campus. He found that there was little organization in the Gainesville area and soon was running the entire Pepper effort in all of Alachua County. While this brought Smathers to Pepper's attention, it might also have shown him how poorly organized the campaign was—a trademark of Pepper's political career.

After finishing law school, Smathers worked in his father's law firm for two years. In 1940 he applied for a job as an assistant U.S. attorney for Florida's Southern District. In later years there was a dispute over exactly how large a role Pepper played in helping Smathers obtain the job. Pepper did recommend Smathers, but the larger role was played by Pepper's colleague, Senator Charles O. Andrews. Smathers went to college with Andrews's son, Charlie, and the two were close friends.[2]

The job was a wonderful opportunity for Smathers. The Southern

District covered much of Florida, stretching from Tampa to Miami. The United States attorney was based in Tampa, giving the Miami staff a great deal of autonomy. Smathers took on high-profile cases and quickly began to make a name for himself. He recalled later, "When you are twenty-five and twenty-six, as I was, there is not much gray area. It is either all white or black. You are either right or you are all wrong and we put everybody in jail. Nobody was safe."[3] While serving as an assistant U.S. attorney, Smathers was blessed with a series of cases that propelled his name onto the front page. His cases fascinated the public, usually featuring sex, greed, and attractive women.

One of his first cases involved a white slavery operation run by Alice Reid Griffin, who was charged with bringing two women from Georgia to Key West for immoral purposes. In May 1941 Smathers faced Bart Riley, one of the state's most successful attorneys. Riley seemed to have every advantage: he enjoyed a lofty reputation, and he was appearing before a hometown jury. He was so confident of victory that he mounted no defense, failed to call Griffin as a witness, and relied on his closing argument to carry the day.[4] He underestimated Smathers. The two-day trial ended with a guilty verdict. The *Miami Herald* reported that "if Riley was depending upon the strength of his indubitably fine oratory, he reckoned without George, who is himself one of the finest orators Florida has produced in this generation." The newspaper noted that Smathers "prepared his testimony and exhibits with such care that Bart simply couldn't break him down."[5] Griffin received a three-year sentence and Smathers had his first courtroom victory.

The case was hardly earthshaking, but it did afford Smathers significant public attention because it involved corruption, sex, and often lurid details. He followed the Key West victory with an even more impressive win over Evelyn and Al Youst, the owners of the infamous La Paloma nightclub, a South Florida center for gambling and prostitution. La Paloma itself was a small, ramshackle building, but what went on inside quickly caught the public's attention in a big way, and the curious packed the courtroom. Like the Griffin case, this one was sure to draw newspaper reporters. Al Youst was charged with bringing five young women from Tennessee to Miami for immoral purposes. Spectators were sometimes barred from the courtroom, and the press used such phrases as "testimony went beyond all printable bounds."[6] First, there was Evelyn Youst herself. She was one of the five women Al Youst brought from Tennessee. She was just seventeen, and the job led to romance, pregnancy, and marriage to her boss. Al Youst was suffering from tuberculosis, and in deference to his health, the court sessions lasted just two hours a day. But any sympathy his condition might have gained disappeared when he was able to stand to plead not guilty. The short court hours served to drag the trial out and keep the story on the front page until Smathers obtained a conviction.[7] The four other women Youst brought from Tennessee were all attractive and provided detailed testimony of the exotic dances inside the club and the after-hours activities they engaged in. At first Evelyn Youst bought her infant to court, but that ended when the judge banned the chronically crying child. Evelyn Youst took the stand to describe herself as just a country girl from Chattanooga and called her performance at La Paloma "art." The jury saw it differently, and convicted Al Youst on ten counts of conspiracy. Youst had already been arrested thirty-six times in thirteen states. After he was convicted of a crime in New Jersey, the judge suggested he leave the state. "Go a long ways away. Go to some place like Florida," the judge told him. Youst took the advice and headed south, where he ran into George Smathers. The New Jersey judge who gave him the advice was William Smathers, the uncle of George Smathers. "I guess the Smathers family is bad luck for me," Youst said.[8]

The Miami Junior Chamber of Commerce named Smathers its Outstanding Young Man for 1940, and there was speculation about a political career. The *Miami Herald* predicted, "The bigwigs of the national Democratic Party are going to discover what a great logician, rhetorician and orator the party has in George Smathers."[9]

The *Herald* editors saw Smathers emerging as a candidate for office in 1944, but Smathers was thinking about something sooner. He considered running for Dade County solicitor, but before he could make a final decision, the Japanese attacked Pearl Harbor on December 7, 1941.

Smathers wanted to join the Marines, but as a twenty-seven-year-old federal prosecutor with a wife and son, he was low on the priority list, and the government wanted Smathers to concentrate on eliminating the threat of German espionage in South Florida. The Marine

Corps enlistment office was next to the federal building where Smathers worked, and he became a regular visitor. Soon a routine developed: Each day he stuck his head into the enlistment office and said, "Hey, fellas, when ya gonna take me?" In 1942 the Marines at last took Smathers and sent him to Parris Island, South Carolina, for basic training, then to Quantico, Virginia, for Officer Training School, and finally to the Pacific theater.[10] In November 1943 he finally saw action at Bougainville as a member of Marine Bombing Squadron 413. He served in Munda and the Admiralty Islands, but parts of his job caused him to develop ulcers. It fell to Smathers to notify families when their loved ones were killed in action and to debrief officers returning from missions. Smathers talked of "the torn and mangled bodies of young men lying in death agony—and strewn upon the beaches and battlefields of war."[11] Both were painful tasks. While many men continued to wear their uniforms after the war, using them to promote themselves in business or politics, Smathers refused to wear his. He stored it away and brought it out years later to give to another young man who was entering the Marines.

He returned to the United States with the rank of captain in early 1945 to a desk job he hated. The fighting was over for Smathers and, like millions of others, he wanted to get on with his life. He launched a campaign to get out of the military.

Smathers first contacted William Paisley, an aide to Attorney General Tom C. Clark, about getting back to his job as an assistant U.S. attorney. Before going to Washington, Paisley was an assistant U.S. attorney in Jacksonville and knew Smathers. Paisley passed along the request to Clark with a note saying Smathers "is an exceptionally able trial lawyer, well connected, and will be heard from."[12] Smathers also wrote to Pepper to see if strings could be pulled on that end. Finally Smathers wrote directly to Clark, declaring that his military job was inconsequential and seeking to return to the Justice Department.[13] Smathers got his discharge just days after the atomic bomb was dropped on Japan and the war ended. There is no indication that Pepper played any role in obtaining the discharge.

As soon as Smathers was out of the service, politics became a driving force in his life. He knew he could count on support from his friends from the University of Florida, where thirty of his classmates had gone on to serve in the Florida Legislature. He looked at the options, including a run for the United States Senate, but the next Florida senator up for reelection was Spessard Holland, who was extremely popular and impossible to defeat. Claude Pepper's seat was not available until 1950, and Smathers rejected a run for the Florida Legislature as not worth his time: "I wouldn't give two hoots in hell for all the seats in the legislature in Florida." But he noted that "a start has to be made," and settled on a seat in Congress as his first goal.[14]

The seat was held by Pat Cannon, who had served three terms without distinction, seemed to be popular, and certainly had the common touch. Cannon was raised on a South Carolina farm, won a football scholarship to Stetson University, joined the Miami Police Department in 1925 in the midst of the Florida land boom, and earned a law degree at the University of Miami while he worked on the force. He failed in two attempts to win a seat on the Miami city commission and lost a run for Congress before being elected in 1938. He was the largest man in Congress—weighing more than three hundred pounds—and probably the most self-effacing man in politics. He told his constituents he was "your fat friend,"[15] and said he was an "errand boy for the public."[16] Although Cannon did absolutely nothing of importance during his six years in Congress, he was well liked and there seemed to be no reason to remove him from office.

Smathers had been in the military for nearly three years, and he needed something to put his name back on the front pages of the South Florida newspapers. He found it in the case of John Henry Colt, the chairman of a local World War II Office of Price Administration panel. Colt was accused of taking bribes in exchange for favorable rationing decisions. Nearly all Americans suffered under wartime rationing, and the case was explosive. If a public official taking bribes was not enough to encourage newspaper coverage and public attention, Colt was also a man with a shady past. He had been convicted of insurance fraud in New York, receiving a suspended sentence, and was linked to showgirl Mary Barton, who committed suicide.[17]

It was perfect, save for one thing: it was not Smathers's case. An assistant U.S. attorney named Fred Botts was assigned to prosecute the case. But Smathers was not to be put off. He wrote directly to Attorney

General Tom Clark, telling him the Colt case was perfect for putting him "back in the public eye—and quick." Smathers wanted Clark to intervene and get the U.S. attorney for the district, Herbert S. Phillips, to put Smathers on the case. Smathers admitted that winning the Colt case would help his political career in 1946.[18] Smathers claimed that Phillips "would let me handle the case but quite naturally doesn't want to offend his assistant, and so I think he would welcome higher authority assigning the case." He also claimed that the FBI agents who were assigned to the case wanted him to handle the prosecution. Finally, he said that prosecuting the case would help him do what "my close friends in Washington want me to do [i.e., win] next spring." Whether there was any truth to the claims is unknown.[19]

Eventually a compromise was reached, and Smathers and Botts shared the case. They won, and Smathers garnered the headlines that went with the victory. He was back in the public eye just in time. The case took longer than expected, dragging on into January, just days before the February 1 filing deadline.

Cannon was not anticipating opposition in 1946. A *Miami Herald* columnist reported that only "tiny rumblings of opposition" were expected.[20] Smathers kept his pending candidacy a secret from nearly everyone, and Cannon announced his bid for reelection on January 25, unaware of what awaited him the following day.

On January 26, Smathers entered the race for Congress with this statement: "Since my return from the Pacific, I have strongly felt the need for aggressive representation of all the people of this district regardless of position or special interests. . . . I know I can represent this district in a progressive, honest and able manner."[21] Perhaps Cannon did not see what was happening throughout the country. A new generation of political leaders was springing up. Those who came of age in the Great Depression, and were tested during World War II, were now seeking power. A survey by the *Army Times* showed that the two major political parties nominated a total of 183 World War II veterans for Congress in 1946. Of those, 69 were elected.[22]

When Smathers resigned as an assistant U.S. attorney in January, Richard Danner, the head of the FBI office in Miami for much of the war, also resigned and signed on as Smathers's campaign manager.

Politically there was not much difference between Smathers and Cannon. Both were moderate Democrats whose South Florida district allowed them to largely avoid the race issue, but they did split over international affairs. In the months after World War II, the Soviet Union went from an ally to an enemy. The hope that the end of the war meant a world at peace quickly vanished. Smathers saw the threat that Russia posed, and said the United States had a major role to play to counterbalance Soviet aggression.

Cannon maintained that the problems of the world could not be solved by the United States, and certainly not by him. Cannon pointed to the ongoing plight of the Armenians, who, he said, "have been starving all my life. We cannot subsidize the world."[23] Cannon was equally unmoved by the rising Soviet threat, calling Russia a third-rate power.[24] At no point during the campaign did he seem to take Smathers seriously.

Smathers did his homework, poring over copies of the *Congressional Quarterly* to analyze Cannon's record. He hammered at Cannon for missing 37 out of 75 votes in 1945, including votes on veterans' housing, school lunch programs, and the controversial Office of Price Administration.[25] Smathers promised to be "a congressman willing to stick to the job. . . . And give Pat Cannon a chance to devote his full time to the thing which he seems best at—being absent."[26] Cannon tried to ignore the charge, saying he "answered every roll call that the American people would want me to."[27] But Smathers kept up his attacks, comparing Cannon's missed votes to "a man in the army saying, 'I know we are going to win the battle,' and not going out to fight."[28] Smathers was tireless, knocking on doors from early in the morning until late at night, and speaking to every group willing to listen. Of particular help in this campaign—and future campaigns—were his friends from high school, college, law school, the military, and the U.S. attorney's office. They pitched in and did the work of a hundred campaign staffers. Cannon branded them the Goon Squad as an insult, but Smathers liked the name, and for the next two decades the Goon Squad was there whenever Smathers called. One night he attended a series of meetings that went until 3 a.m. When he came out, he noticed milkmen on their rounds and began shaking hands. He was still at it three hours later when garbage men began making their rounds, and he greeted them in turn.[29]

Cannon tried without much success to attack Smathers's privileged background and his good looks. He referred to his challenger as pretty, and Cannon's followers began calling Smathers "Gorgeous George," the name of a popular wrestler.[30] Cannon also attempted to link Smathers to Pepper, who was increasingly unpopular in the state.

Cannon stepped up his personal attacks in the final days of the campaign. To the Dade County Young Democrats rally he said, "This young gentleman is beaten this very minute" and "has no more chance to go to Congress than a mountain goat. . . . Never, as long as time lasts, will that boy go to the American Congress."[31] As part of a smear campaign, his workers distributed handbills reading "Vote for George Smathers" but signed "Communist Party of Miami."[32]

To the Retail and Wine Dealer's Association, Cannon gave a rambling and ill-advised speech. "I can't understand why Smathers got the FBI to manage his election unless he wants to scare the hell out of the voters. . . . if I am so unworthy, why the hell don't you start indicting me?" Cannon was clearly talking about Danner, who was representing Smathers at the event.[33]

Smathers gained the endorsements of both the *Miami Herald* and the *Miami Daily News*. The *Daily News* picked up on the Smathers charge about Cannon's missed votes and an indifferent foreign policy.[34] On election day, Smathers won by a surprisingly large two-to-one margin. He won all but three of the ninety-two precincts in Dade County, carried Monroe County, and lost only in lightly populated Collier County. He ran a nearly flawless campaign, learning to keep attacking, work hard, and exploit the friendships he had made in Miami and at the University of Florida.

When Smathers took his seat in January 1947, the world was in the midst of turmoil and the Russian threat seemed to grow greater each day. It was the year Bernard Baruch coined the term "cold war," and newspaper columnist Walter Lippmann turned it into a household word with his book of the same name. It was also the year President Truman issued the Truman Doctrine, designed to help nations fight the spread of communism. Smathers thought the threat was real and the United States should be wary of Russia. While Pepper was the leading opponent of Truman's get-tough-with-Russia plan, Smathers wholeheartedly endorsed it.

Smathers began to gather influence in Washington, far beyond what was expected of a freshman congressman. In October 1946, even before taking the oath of office, he met with President Truman to discuss keeping the Opa-locka Naval Station open.[35] By any standard, his first term was a success. In the House he made friends with the large number of World War II veterans who were also new to Congress. But it was his endorsement of Truman for reelection—a rarity in the South—that brought him closer to the administration and earned him the support and friendship of the president.

In the 1948 presidential election, Smathers faced the same difficult choice as other politicians in the South. Truman was running for reelection but was clearly the underdog and had been written off by most politicians. He was beset with challengers. His Republican opponent, Thomas E. Dewey, the New York governor and racket buster, was a heavy favorite. But Truman also faced two challengers who threatened to splinter his own party. On the left, former vice president Henry Wallace hoped to steal the party's ultraliberal wing, while South Carolina governor Strom Thurmond sought votes in the South as a Dixiecrat by promising to uphold the region's traditions of segregation. Thurmond's strategy called for him to capture the electoral votes of the former Confederate states—140 votes in all—and deny Truman or Dewey an electoral majority.

Many Southern Democrats rushed to support Thurmond, while others, such as Pepper, sought alternatives to Truman, offered half-hearted support, or sat out the campaign. Smathers, however, endorsed Truman and campaigned for him. Smathers predicted a Truman victory in Florida, although most people thought it a lost cause. As historian David Colburn has observed, "The full consequence of the postwar migration into Florida revealed itself in the November election of 1948."[36] Truman easily carried Florida by a three-to-one margin over Thurmond, thanks to thousands of northerners who settled in South Florida and voted as traditional Democrats. Thurmond was held to a few dozen electoral votes as Truman upset Dewey. Smathers won the gratitude of the president. After the election, the *Miami Daily News* commented, "Representative Smathers can have virtually anything he wants in the House. As long as Mr. Truman is in the White House, the door will always be open to him."[37] What Smathers wanted was to advance to the Senate—where his uncle William had served in 1937–43 from New Jersey.

In early 1949 Pepper suspected that Smathers was preparing to challenge him. He wrote that Smathers "seems to be toying with the idea of running against me next year but he is not determined to do so and many of his friends are counseling him against it. I suppose, however, that some one or more will give me the usual race."[38] That spring, Pepper thought that either Governor Millard Caldwell or Smathers might enter the primary against him, but he thought both would back out "when the showdown comes."[39] Pepper did not understand how much trouble he was in. He wrote, "I feel, however, that the situation will work itself out."[40] By August Pepper believed that he had escaped a challenge by both Caldwell and Smathers. He thought they were "nearing a decision not to run against us next year." Pepper said it was because "they don't think they can win."[41]

Rather than trying to rebuild his bridges, Pepper seemed to go out of his way to alienate people. During hearings by the Public Welfare Committee, Ira Mosher, an official of the National Association of Manufacturers, the umbrella organization for Florida's Associated Industries and other state business groups, was testifying against the repeal of the Taft-Hartley Act. Suddenly Pepper blasted Mosher, saying that "it was the poor people whose sons went to the battlefields and a lot of the manufacturers' sons who stayed at home and got rich." Mosher became angry and replied, "I lost three members of my family in the war."[42] The *Washington Sunday Star* called Pepper's remarks "the all-time low," adding, "To put it bluntly, Mr. Pepper's performance was an affront to common decency, and it will be resented as such by every decent Senator and every decent citizen."[43] The *Tampa Morning Tribune* observed that Pepper was "driving away from his support those Floridians who would otherwise be inclined to favor his reelection."[44]

Caldwell decided not to run, telling reporters he preferred the "liberty of a private citizen" to a seat in the Senate.[45] But Smathers said there was another, more personal reason. Caldwell was a congressman before becoming governor, and during his time in Washington his son was killed in an automobile accident there. Caldwell told Smathers, "I don't want to go back to Washington because it brings back bad memories."[46]

In August, just as Pepper was deciding that Smathers would not be a candidate, President Truman intervened. Truman invited Smathers to the White House and told him to "go down to Florida . . . make a survey and report."[47] Smathers remembered Truman telling him to go out and defeat "that son-of-a-bitch Claude Pepper."[48] The president's secretary did not record any such words, but it is not difficult to imagine Truman using them. Smathers went to Florida and began talking to people about a possible Senate bid.

One of those he met with was Ed Ball, the longtime Pepper enemy. The relationship between Ball and Smathers was the subject of speculation for nearly half a century. Associates of Ball painted a picture of Ball pulling the strings behind the scenes for the Smathers campaign. For his part, Smathers seemed only vaguely aware of Ball and his role in the 1950 campaign. In scores of interviews over forty-six years, Smathers was consistent in maintaining that he barely knew Ball, and that the millionaire's role in the campaign was minor. He spoke of Ball operating separately from the campaign. Then, in 1996, Tracy E. Danese interviewed Smathers. Danese was working on his doctorate at Florida State University, but he was an unusual graduate student: he held a law degree and was a respected business leader in Ball's adopted hometown, Jacksonville. For Danese, Smathers told a different story, one in which Ball was intricately involved in the campaign from the start.[49]

The two first met in 1946 when Smathers and another attorney tried to get Ball to invest in Florida's first television station. Smathers recalled that Ball rejected the idea, saying, "We don't spend money on these damned foolish ideas."[50]

In 1950 Leonard Usina, the president of Ball's Florida National Bank in Miami, brought Ball and Smathers together at a boardroom lunch, but no firm endorsement ensued. In fact, Smathers remembered that Ball said very little. Herbert E. Wolfe, who was a leading road builder and one of the state's most well-connected people, arranged a second meeting. Wolfe was close to Ball, disliked Pepper, and persuaded Ball to support Smathers. At the same time, Wolfe volunteered to serve as Smathers's finance chairman. Smathers told Danese that during the campaign, he and Ball met again several times in Ball's Jacksonville hotel suite to share drinks and the names of people who might help defeat Pepper.[51]

Smathers looked closely at Pepper's 1938 and 1944 voting totals and found weaknesses. In 1938, Pepper defeated five candidates by a total of nearly 70,000 votes. In 1944 he overcame four candidates by a total of 9,600 votes. Smathers saw that while Pepper was thought to be strong in his home area of North Florida, he did not do well elsewhere, getting a minority of the votes in more than half the counties statewide in 1944.[52]

A September column in the *Orlando Morning Sentinel* said that three candidates were being mentioned as opponents for Pepper—Caldwell, Smathers, and former representative Emory Price of Jacksonville. "The dopesters now believe that 1944 will be repeated in 1950 unless some strong candidate emerges, who will define the issues right down the line somewhere close to the Dixiecrat platform, but without its label."[53]

Smathers said that he went to see Pepper before entering the race and warned him that he was in trouble. "Claude, you got to do something, somebody is going to beat you. And a lot of people have approached me about it." Smathers said that Pepper replied, "George, don't worry, if I go over the state and make speeches I'll turn the whole thing over." Smathers also said he went to see Pepper aide Bob Folks and said, "Somebody has got to rescue your guy or he is going to be defeated. . . . I'd like to be a senator some day and this is my chance."[54]

Smathers contacted the White House on October 26 and told Truman aide Matt Connelly that it was important that he see the president. He visited Truman on November 8, and although there is no written record of the meeting, it is clear that Smathers told Truman he would oppose Pepper. Within a week the *Miami Herald* reported that Smathers was all but declared, "now that [he] has seen the president."[55]

In later years Pepper accused Smathers of demanding a deal. According to Pepper, Smathers promised not to run in 1950 if he received an appointment as United States solicitor general, veto power over any appointments by the governor to fill empty United States Senate seats, and support for Smathers in the 1952 gubernatorial election. In his memoirs, Pepper says he rejected the deal immediately.[56] Pepper's memory seems questionable, however. There is no way Truman would have allowed Pepper to choose someone for a high government post. If Smathers wanted to be solicitor general, he would have a better chance by calling on Truman personally, or his close friend Tom Clark, now a Supreme Court justice. And there is no way Pepper could have controlled Senate appointments.

By October, Pepper realized that the Smathers threat was real: "He may win, although I don't think so, but I have regretted to see what has happened to him, already, spiritually."[57] Seven months before the primary, Pepper offered his friend Raymond Robins an analysis of the coming campaign: "It will be a spirited campaign, with his youth and handsome charm, energy and money, not to speak of all those selfish and shortsighted forces who will array themselves with him. But those people haven't been winning lately, and the people have a way of understanding the issues. I suspect they will pretty clearly understand this battle and its significance."[58]

Pepper was unable to find fault with himself and to view events realistically. He never blamed himself for his dramatic loss of popularity in Florida. Pepper knew the chances he took with his controversial stands. In 1948 he said, "Time and again I have gone contrary to public opinion. If they catch me at a moment when public opinion is against me they may throw me out, but I am going to continue to fight for what I believe to be right."[59] By 1950 Pepper had positioned himself contrary to Florida public opinion on a series of issues ranging from Russia to civil rights. The situation boded ill for his political future.

8

The Campaign Begins

Few states have benefited from war and military mobilizations as much as Florida. In the sixteenth century the Spanish showed scant interest in their seemingly worthless possession until the French staked a claim. Then Florida became a military center with a succession of ever-larger forts built at St. Augustine. In the American Revolution, British Florida remained loyal to King George and saw its population swell with refugees from the other colonies. After a series of wars, most of the Seminole Indians were displaced to Oklahoma and Arkansas, while a handful fled to the Everglades. But the wars led the United States to develop a series of roads and a communications system which lured new settlers and turned the frontier outpost called Fort Brooke into Tampa. In the Civil War the state was of little military value, but its salt and cattle were coveted by both sides, and once again it was a haven for those seeking to avoid the war, primarily Confederate and Union deserters, who knew that south of St. Augustine the state was largely uninhabited and they could vanish. The state's residents initially opposed the Spanish-American War, fearing that the state's proximity to Cuba might bring the fight to the port cities along the coast, especially the new city of Miami. Worse, if the war was successful, Cuba might be brought into the United States. Its prime industries of sugar, cigars, citrus, and tourism would pose an economic challenge to Florida. The government satisfied Florida by beefing up the military along the coast and agreeing not to make Cuba a territory of the United States. Tampa became the headquarters for the war and saw men and money pour into the state as military camps were set up along the coast.

In World War I, Florida's weather was the lure to train pilots for a new instrument of war, the airplane. But it was World War II that had the most dramatic impact on Florida. Even before the United States entered the war, the state was a training ground for British pilots. The German Luftwaffe made it nearly impossible to train pilots in England, and the year-round clear skies of Florida offered a perfect alternative.

Once the United States entered the war, more than two million men and women came for training in Florida. Nearly every crossroads could boast of some military facility. Camp Blanding, an army base, became the state's fourth largest city, and the coastal waters were used to train everyone from Navy Seals to PT boat commanders. Two future presidents, John Kennedy and George H. W. Bush, trained in Florida. Many liked what they saw and returned after the war. Others went home but remembered the lure of Florida and came back after their retirement.

The war poured billions of federal dollars into the state, reviving shipbuilding in Pensacola, Panama City, Jacksonville, and Tampa.[1] When the troops pulled out, they left behind developed land ready to be put to use for other purposes. Military airfields throughout the state became commercial airports. The airfield in Sebring became a racetrack for the Sebring Grand Prix. In Tallahassee, the barracks at the Dale Mabry Army Air Field became home to the first men to attend the Florida State College for Women, and later became Tallahassee Community College. A camp for German prisoners of war in Lake County became a community college, and bases were used for colleges in Tampa, Palm Beach, Miami, and Boca Raton. Members of the state's congressional delegation used their power to keep other bases open and poured money into the state economy. The war had also produced a host of German weapons including rockets, which seemed to represent the future of warfare. As the United States Army advanced across Germany, an elaborate program was established to capture the German scientists behind the rocket program. This led to America's efforts in space, and in 1947 the government selected a 15,000-acre site at Cape Canaveral for rocket experiments.

Two of the biggest boons for Florida, however, were not related to the war. Air-conditioning, a luxury once reserved for movie theaters and department stores, became practical for household use after World War II. In 1945 just over 1,000 room air-conditioners were manufactured; in 1946 the number jumped to nearly 30,000, and by 1950 it rose to 193,000.[2] Scientists also came up with a way to control the mosquitoes plaguing residents and tourists. Working at a government research laboratory in Orlando, scientists developed DDT in 1945 and were soon spraying the entire state. "Don't Get Excited—It's DDT Spray Plan," the *Cocoa Tribune* headline read in an effort to reassure new residents that there was no danger. There was, of course, danger, but it took years for scientists to prove the damage the spraying caused birds, fish, and water.

By 1950 in-migration had raised Florida's population to 2,771,305, an increase of 46 percent since 1940. Delta Airlines began flying to Jacksonville in 1945, and soon there were regular flights to Orlando, Leesburg, Ocala, Gainesville, and Lake City. Books with titles such as *How to Retire in Florida* and *Florida Today: New Land of Opportunity* attracted newcomers. In twenty years the state's population nearly doubled, while the population in the rest of the nation increased by just 20 percent. The influx also changed the population distribution of the state. In 1930, four out of ten people lived in North Florida, another four out of ten in Central Florida, and two out of ten in South Florida. By 1950, only a third of the residents lived in North Florida, with 37 percent in Central Florida and 29 percent in South Florida. During the 1940s, Dade, Duval, Hillsborough, Pinellas, and Orange counties added a total of half a million people, while the population in a dozen North Florida counties declined. The new arrivals were older; the percentage of those older than sixty-five years of age living in the state increased from 4.8 percent in 1930 to 8.5 percent in 1950.[3]

Something new was happening in the United States—retirement. Social Security, a product of the New Deal, made it possible for people to consider retiring. As late as 1950, two-thirds of American men older than sixty-five were still working, but that was changing, and Florida was the prime beneficiary. People could now afford to quit their jobs and, with Social Security checks arriving each month, start a new life in Florida.

An examination of the population shift shows that there was an in-migration of middle-class whites from the North, including elderly voters, who tended to be conservative and were more likely to favor Republican candidates. Finally, although the number of registered African American voters increased, the percentage of African American voters dropped dramatically from 44 percent in 1900 to about half that percentage in 1950.[4] It was a very different state from the one Claude Pepper found in the 1920s, different even from the one that reelected him to the Senate six years earlier. And unlike in his previous campaign, he no longer had a president vitally interested in his success.

Smathers and Richard Danner mapped out a well-organized campaign. Florida had never seen anything like it. Smathers decided to make his announcement in Orlando, a city in the center of the state. The city's coliseum was decked out as if it were a national convention, and an overflow crowd of three thousand packed the hall. Smathers urged his supporters from throughout the state to gather in Orlando, and motorcades arrived with hundreds of cars. Under the slogan "Make Yours a Double-Duty Vote, for Florida, for America," he spelled out the dominant theme for the campaign—anticommunism: "You will not find in me an apologist for Stalin, nor an associate of fellow travelers, nor a sponsor of communist-front organizations. . . . The people of our state will no longer tolerate advocates of treason." The announcement was followed by a parade through downtown Orlando.[5]

His announcement was carried on a network of twenty-two Florida radio stations. Although his opposition to communism was the dominant theme, Smathers pledged to attack Pepper's positions on national health insurance, race relations, unions, and government spending issues. Smathers promised opposition to the Truman administration's efforts to enact a civil rights program, pass a national health insurance plan, and repeal the Taft-Hartley Act, a Republican-sponsored measure aimed at limiting the power of labor unions.[6]

Pepper said he was hurt by Smathers's opening remarks and promised never to speak to Smathers again. Smathers fired back that "probably now neither Joe Stalin, Henry Wallace, nor Paul Robeson will speak to me again either. . . . All their minds must run along the same channel."[7]

Smathers knew that to win he needed to take some positions opposing Truman, especially on civil rights, but he wanted to make sure the president knew that he still supported the administration. In a letter to Truman aide Matthew J. Connelly, Smathers said, "I have supported the Administration more than has any other Florida congressman in the history of the state. . . . In every election Pepper has run, about a year before the primary comes off, he grabs onto the coattails of the President and clings there steadfastly until he is reelected, after which it is his custom to take off in all directions." Smathers asked that Connelly offer some protection from some of Pepper's "columnist friends."[8]

In the 80th Congress, his first term, Smathers supported the president's proposals 93 percent of the time, but in the first session of the 81st Congress, in 1949, his support fell to 84 percent. Pepper, who supported Truman 87 percent of the time in the 79th Congress, became Truman's most loyal supporter in the Senate in the 81st Congress, voting with the president 99 percent of the time.[9]

Despite the Smathers challenge, Pepper waited six weeks before announcing his candidacy. Perhaps he believed what the *St. Petersburg Times* said about his "uncanny knack for landing on his feet by always showing up at the eleventh hour to do and say exactly the right thing."[10] He appeared to be confident, predicting that Smathers was in for "the thrashing of his life."[11] Smathers replied, "He's a very nice man personally, but I disagree with his basic policies and that's why I'm against him."[12] There was reason for Pepper to believe that he could make amends with Florida voters. The *St. Petersburg Times* was not alone in its conviction that Pepper would always land on his feet. Six months before the primary, the landmark study *Southern Politics in State and Nation* was published. Author V. O. Key praised Pepper's "superb performance on the stump" and said the "professional politicians look with great admiration on his ability to come back to the state for a few weeks and wipe out the opposition in a whirlwind campaign."

Still, Key cautioned, "There are those who remark somewhat sadly that, 'Claude is not the same Claude that we knew when he started out back here in Florida,'" and "even Claude's most ardent admirers, as 1950 approached, were wondering whether he was going to be able to talk himself into another term in the Senate."[13]

Speaking to a large crowd in Miami and a statewide radio network, Pepper launched his campaign by hammering on the themes that had served him so well in the past. "For nearly fourteen years I have worked tirelessly in the service of every part of Florida. During that time the federal government has spent for the welfare of the citizens of Florida over a billion and a half dollars and has loaned almost a billion dollars more to our businessmen, to our farmers, and to our veterans."[14] He outlined his platform, which included a New Deal–like government benefit for nearly everyone. He promised price supports for farmers, aid for education, loans to businessmen and veterans, a pension for everyone over sixty, national health insurance, more hospitals for veterans, federal aid to fight beach erosion, and completion of South Florida flood control projects. And, for the first of hundreds of times during the campaign, he evoked the memory of the Great Depression: "You know what that crowd promised us back in 1928. . . . They promised us two cars in every garage and a chicken in every pot. What did we get? When we got them out, we didn't have any cars, we didn't have a garage, we didn't have a chicken. We didn't even have a pot."[15]

Pepper based his campaign on his seniority in the Senate, on the contention that Smathers was really a Republican running as a Democrat, and on telling voters that his opponents were trying to defeat not him but the New Deal. Seniority was to be treasured, especially in the South, where northern superiority in numbers meant that if the South was to have power, it needed to rely on southern politicians holding office for long periods and gaining committee chairmanships. Pepper pointed out: "At 49 years of age, I am the youngest Senator with nearly 14 years of experience and seniority in the Senate. I have just reached my greatest capacity for service to Florida."[16] Pepper was one seat away from being the chairman of the Senate Foreign Relations Committee, even though he was taken off the committee in 1947.

Smathers, however, turned the seniority issue against Pepper. "My opponent says he will continue fighting communism. Let us hope he will not fight it as he has in the past. . . . If he is re-elected, and one senator dies, he will become chairman of the Senate Foreign Relations Committee and will be the man to deal with Russia in seeking a lasting peace."[17]

No Pepper campaign speech was complete without a description of what he brought the state during his fourteen years in office. In Clewiston he pointed to the giant sugar mill; in Tampa he cited the lifting of the toll on the Gandy Bridge in 1944; in Plant City he told voters about securing funds for the hospital. Pepper promised to support Truman's domestic program, with the exception of the Fair Employment Practices Commission and civil rights. There was much Pepper could claim credit for. He had helped thousands of Florida voters with everything from routine requests for information to huge government contracts. One voter in St. Petersburg said, "I don't agree with Claude Pepper on a single national question but I'm going to support him because he did me a mighty big favor when nobody else seemed able to."[18] Pepper also had the support of the state Democratic committee chairman and the governor, Fuller Warren. Pepper had supported Warren's campaign in 1948, and he expected Warren to put the state bureaucracy behind his campaign. It was standard practice for both state and federal workers in Florida to campaign and contribute to the candidate of the political party in power. Pepper asked various federal agencies for the names of Floridians they employed, but the FBI rebuffed him. J. Edgar Hoover wrote to a subordinate, "No such list is to be furnished anyone least of all Pepper. H."[19]

Smathers poked fun at Pepper's constant promises, which he called the "promise derby." In Jacksonville he said, "If I should promise you a new twenty-seven-story federal building, he would come here tomorrow night and raise it to thirty stories."[20] Speaking in the rain in Lake Wales, Smathers said, "I know you need rain but unlike my opponent, who takes credit for everything. . . . I won't claim full credit for this. I will only say I hope I helped."[21]

On the same day that Pepper declared his candidacy, a third candidate, James G. Horrell of Orlando, withdrew and endorsed Smathers. The Horrell withdrawal was significant because it meant that there could not be a runoff election. One of the two candidates would win the May primary and the Senate seat. Horrell had done his homework in preparing to be a candidate, including research on Pepper's problems and the state voting patterns. Horrell recommended to Smathers that Pepper's opponent should "carry on a clean but strong campaign," but "it was also thought that a little mud and a little name calling by local supporters in the right places and at the right time would do some good." Horrell wrote that "in rural areas, particularly in West Florida, use of States' Rights, Civil Rights, [and] Communism [will] create a winning psychology and dispel the aura of invulnerability which Pepper has built up about himself." He also prepared a list of all the organizations identified as communist-front groups to whom Pepper spoke. Upon withdrawing from the race, Horrell gave the report to Smathers, who adopted much of the Horrell strategy and put to good use the list of communist-front groups.[22] Smathers also asked the House Un-American Activities Committee for information to use against Pepper, and the committee provided reports linking Pepper to a list of procommunist groups and individuals.[23]

In an era when television was still largely unavailable, political campaign appearances were a major draw, especially in small towns. Crowds turned out to listen to candidates, and few could top Pepper's oratory. Instead, Smathers turned his speaking tour into a show. Before he arrived, two sound trucks pulled into town. The large speakers were painted orange and blue, the colors of the University of Florida, with "Elect Smathers" written inside the speaker cones. "Vote American" was lettered on the side panels. The trucks played music and broadcast political messages as a crowd gathered. The campaign attempted to have a motorcade arrive with Smathers and always had a local resident make the introduction.

Smathers and Pepper both supported the European Economic Recovery Program, European military aid, the peacetime draft, the minimum wage, pensions for veterans, slum clearance, and agricultural price supports, but on some significant domestic matters they took different stands. Pepper favored a limited form of a national health insurance bill; Smathers was against it. Pepper was opposed to Taft-Hartley, and Smathers voted for it. Pepper was a leading supporter of federal aid to education, while Smathers opposed the idea. Pepper was opposed to a bill to limit the extension of Social Security benefits, and Smathers supported the limits.[24] While Smathers pointed with pride to his support of much of Truman's Fair Deal, Pepper remained committed to the more expansive New Deal philosophy.

Smathers made Pepper's stand on the Soviet Union—including Pepper's relationships with left-wing groups—the leading issue, emphasizing the theme day after day. He raised other issues, but communism was the club he used against Pepper in every speech. Smathers criticized

Pepper's very limited support for the Fair Employment Practices Committee, his relationship with the Congress of Industrial Organizations, and his stands on race relations, national health insurance, and the federal bureaucracy. In addition, Smathers knew that Pepper's involvement with the Florida East Coast Railway badly divided his usually reliable union support. And Smathers had the backing of the du Pont interests.

The basic approach to daily campaigning by the two candidates was very similar. They crisscrossed the state, giving as many as eight speeches a day. Before a candidate arrived, a car with a loudspeaker entered the town and urged people to turn out. Most speeches were given in front of the courthouse, although appearances at night were usually held in a hall. Sometimes the speeches were broadcast on local radio stations, and both candidates had national broadcasters on their side. Robert Montgomery and Fulton Lewis Jr. used their radio programs to boost Smathers, while Elmer Davis made frequent positive comments about Pepper on his network program. The American Federation of Labor sent two of its radio commentators to Florida in the final weeks of the campaign to broadcast appeals for Pepper.[25] Bands warmed up the audience and, for both candidates, the song "Dixie" was usually played. Pepper frequently spoke in front of huge portraits of Roosevelt, Truman, and himself, and talked about how he had fought beside Roosevelt and Truman for the past decade.[26] The candidates generally took Sundays off, although both usually attended church services and shook hands with parishioners. Television was still in its infancy and played no role in the campaign.

By April the campaign's hectic pace was beginning to wear on the candidates. Smathers told one audience, "They talk about the New Deal and the Fair Deal. Ladies and gentlemen, this is an ordeal." Smathers went through three pairs of shoes and lost eleven pounds by April 2.[27]

Humor occasionally appeared in what was otherwise a serious campaign marked by vicious charges. Pepper's opponents distributed horn-rimmed glasses and a large plastic nose to mock him. He joked about it: "They can call me a Red and a Black, but when they attack my beauty, that's too much, I think I'm getting mad."[28] The Smathers camp passed out cards reading "Bring prosperity to Florida. Join and support Florida's fastest growing industry, Canning Pepper."[29]

Smathers established his headquarters in Jacksonville as part of an effort to show that he was a statewide candidate and to be close to the offices of his major backers, Associated Industries and Ed Ball. The Smathers workers, known as the Goon Squad, fanned out across the state to organize each county. The strength of the Smathers organization was clear when car caravans were organized to accompany the candidate. On April 25, four hundred cars led Smathers into Tampa, and later in North Florida the motorcade reached seven hundred.[30] The motorcades served two purposes: they rallied the faithful, and they were excellent at drumming up publicity and attention for the candidate's appearances.

Pepper's campaign harked back to an earlier era, while Smathers was rewriting the rules for Florida campaigns. Smathers introduced direct mail, with letters tailored to the individual interests of thousands of Florida voters. Within days of his announcement, the letters began filling mailboxes throughout the state. To doctors went letters stating, "We are engaged in a struggle of two basic philosophies—our Democratic way of life and communism. Your individual initiative and freedoms are being threatened today and various attempts are being made to socialize the professions of our nation."[31] To a member of the Junior Chamber of Commerce, Smathers wrote, "As a fellow Jaycee and past president of the Dade County Junior Chamber of Commerce I have always enjoyed a close relationship and pleasant association with Jaycees throughout the state."[32] To a businesswoman he wrote, "The Federation of Business and Professional Women Clubs has upheld the motto, 'Better Businesswomen for a Better Business World.' I more than appreciate the part that women are playing in shaping the destiny and future of our state."[33] Other voters received a Smathers-Gram, which looked like a telegram and read "George Smathers is a liberal. Not a Radical."[34] And to one of the state's most significant groups of voters, the alumni of the University of Florida, the Smathers appeal highlighted his university ties: "Today as a candidate for the Senate of the United States, I am confident that the same spirit displayed on the campus will be revitalized by fellow alumni in the forthcoming campaign."[35] Smathers noted that the university alumni "are legion and there's one of them in virtually every cross roads community from Pensacola to Key West. Usually they're pretty influential locally."[36]

Smathers also used sophisticated advertisements placed in newspapers. One, supposedly from a North Florida farmer, was addressed to the People of Florida:

I know plenty of families right here and I know how they get their money to live on. They get it from the Government—I call it PEPPER PROSPERITY. I know one family that gets $50 a month assistance. I know another who gets blind assistance but who can see well enough to get around and get drunk, for I paid $15 one time to get him out of the jail house. . . . I offered them land and a mule to plow to make a garden, but they could not turn their fishing down! . . . This is the kind of folks our government is sponsoring—just laziness and no work! It is ruining our country![37]

The Smathers campaign even had its own newspaper, the *St. Augustine Observer*, an eight-page publication with headlines such as "Pepper and Commie Front Organizations" and "Pepper Hot Over Negro Photo Spread." Inside were pictures of Pepper with far-left icons Henry Wallace and Paul Robeson.[38]

But Smathers's best tool was a forty-eight-page booklet entitled *The Red Record of Senator Claude Pepper*. It was a collection of newspaper clippings documenting Pepper appearances before left-wing groups and his comments about friendly relations with Russia. On the cover was an unflattering photograph of Pepper, with his eyes bulging. Taken together, it was a devastating document. Many of the stories were from the *Daily Worker*. The booklet was put together by Lloyd C. Leemis, a former FBI agent who once worked with campaign chief Richard Danner, and was published in Jacksonville. Although it carried a price of one dollar, tens of thousands of copies were given away throughout the state. Smathers claimed that he did not print or distribute the booklet. It appears likely, in fact, that friends of Ed Ball paid for it. "Ed Ball was running his own campaign against Pepper," Smathers said.[39]

FBI agents in Florida kept director J. Edgar Hoover informed about the campaign, and an April memo to Hoover speculated that Leemis had help from Associated Industries, which was largely financed by Ball companies and Ball associates. Both Leemis and Associated Industries were working out of the Graham Building. "It is believed that former Special

Agent Leemis was probably assisted in the compilation of the material in this book by an organization known as Associated Industries of Florida. . . . This organization is reported to have some remote connection with the Ball-DuPont interests in Florida, and to serve as a confidential information service for the Ball-DuPont's many business interests."[40]

The booklet was nothing new for Ball. Backing Herbert Hoover during the 1928 presidential election, he organized Florida Democrats for Hoover and arranged to print 150,000 leaflets carrying a photograph of a Negro man dictating a letter to a white girl. The caption said, "If you want this to happen in Florida, vote for Alfred E. Smith."[41]

Smathers referred to the "Red Pepper" booklet in his speeches: "These are grave and serious charges to bring against a public official, but they are supported by the record which is open for all to see. It is these charges and the indisputable proof of them that is giving my opponent so much concern and discomfort now that the truth is out."[42] Pepper responded that it was "The most scurrilous and vicious document ever to besmirch a Florida political campaign."[43]

The first poll of the campaign, conducted by the *Jacksonville Journal* in late February and early March, surveyed eleven key counties and found Smathers ahead by an astounding two-to-one margin. According to the poll, Smathers held commanding leads in Duval (Jacksonville), Volusia (Daytona Beach), and Pinellas (St. Petersburg) counties and ran even in Dade (Miami), Escambia (Pensacola), and Hillsborough (Tampa).[44]

Pepper had hoped that he might use the issue of relations with Russia to become president. But instead of putting him into the White House, his calls for better relations with Russia threatened to end his political career. Not only did Pepper have to fight Smathers, he had to battle world events. It was difficult to find a major event between mid-1948 and mid-1950 that did not work against Pepper. In June 1948 the Russians began a blockade of Berlin, which threatened to lead to war and resulted in the Berlin Airlift. In December 1948, former State Department officer Alger Hiss was accused of handing over government secrets to the Soviets and indicted for perjury; in January 1950 Hiss was convicted and sentenced to five years in prison. In March 1949 Judith Coplon, a Justice Department employee, was arrested while carrying secret documents she was thought to be delivering to a Russian agent.

In September 1949 the Russians detonated a nuclear bomb. The importance of the explosion did not immediately register with the American people; Truman, although he had thought the Soviets were three years away from a successful A-test, was calm and gave no indication that anyone should be concerned. But by early 1950 the calm turned to alarm. The White House responded by announcing development of an even more powerful hydrogen bomb. Adding to the perception of threat, in October 1949, China with its five hundred million people—a quarter of the world's population—fell under communist rule.

The Republicans recognized that communism was the best issue they had to fight the Democrats. In the 1948 presidential campaign, Republican nominee Dewey accused Truman of allowing "Communists and fellow travelers" to land jobs in his administration.[45] The Republicans lost the 1948 presidential election, but they had found an issue that worked. For the next two years they continued to label the Democrats as either unwitting pawns or outright supporters of communism. By 1950, Republicans all over the country were counting on the issue to help them take control of Congress. On February 9, Wisconsin senator Joseph McCarthy told the Republican Women's Club of Wheeling, West Virginia, that he had a list of State Department employees who were members of the Communist Party—so many that he did not have time to name all of them. Smathers had already made communism his lead issue, and McCarthy's remarks turned the issue into a national obsession. Historian Arnold Toynbee saw the cold war lasting until the end of the century.[46]

Even good news for the nation seemed to work against Pepper. In May 1949 the eleven-month Berlin Blockade finally came to an end, convincing many that Truman's tough strategy of dealing with the Russians worked. In February 1950, Secretary of State Dean Acheson called for the United States to negotiate from a position of strength. His plan included furnishing allies with more military aid.[47]

In America in 1950, communists were seen everywhere. This was rather odd because, amid the growing obsession with a Red Menace, the Communist Party USA was dwindling fast. The 1939 Hitler-Stalin pact had already cost the party much of its prewar peak membership of 55,000.[48]

Politicians had been using communism to gain votes since 1919, when Democratic attorney general Mitchell Palmer tried to use it to capture the Democratic presidential nomination. He failed, but the Red Scare he fanned ruined thousands of lives. In 1936 Alf Landon's running mate, Frank Knox, charged that Roosevelt was leading the United States toward Moscow. Eight years later the Republican vice presidential candidate, John W. Bricker, charged that American Communist Party leader Earl Browder had been released from prison to organize party members to vote for Roosevelt's fourth term. In 1948 Earl Warren, the Republican nominee for vice president, said Truman was soft on the communists. The presidential nominee, New York governor Thomas Dewey, promised, "There will not be any Communists in the Government after January 20."[49]

Pepper tried to rebut the allegations of procommunism against him by linking Smathers to McCarthy. But Smathers responded by ridiculing Pepper's own words. He asked his audience if they "prayed today for a long life for Joe Stalin." He could always count on a chorus of "no's." Then Smathers would tell the crowd, "For every one of you who wants to preserve our great American heritage, the time has come to take off your coat . . . and join our holy crusade to preserve America for honest-to-God Americans."[50] Pepper had in fact never said he prayed for Stalin, but in those turbulent times, what he did say back in 1945 in a Moscow radio address—"People everywhere are looking prayerfully toward us and counting upon us to fulfill our great missions to mankind"[51]—was seen as supportive of the man most blamed for the cold war.

Anticommunism was sweeping the country. In the 81st Congress, a total of thirty-eight anticommunist bills were introduced. The one that passed was the McCarran Act of 1950, which created the five-member Subversive Activities Control Board to identify communist, communist-front, and communist-infiltrated organizations.[52]

Many suggest that Truman and the Democrats were not the victims of what became known as McCarthyism, but its architects. It was the Truman administration that legitimized red-baiting with its loyalty-oath programs and the creation of communist-front lists by the attorney general.[53] In 1946 Truman set up a committee to review loyalty programs and recommend changes. On March 25, 1947, he issued an executive order instituting a new loyalty program, resulting in thousands of Americans either losing government jobs or being denied employment.

Pepper's attempts to deny that he supported communism suffered a decisive setback in April when the *Daily Worker* endorsed his candidacy. The endorsement, written by state party leader George Nelson, said, "The Communist party of Florida has called upon all voters to work for the defeat of Smathers. . . . His victory would strengthen the Dixiecrat-KKK forces in Florida as well as throughout the South." The endorsement said the party, with the aid of the CIO's Political Action Committee and the AFL's Political Education Committee, would work to register 250,000 black voters for the primary.[54]

The *Daily Worker* endorsement was a disaster for Pepper's already struggling campaign. Throughout the state, pro-Smathers newspapers displayed the endorsement on their front pages. Pepper tried to portray it as a political dirty trick: "They know that I, fighting always for a stronger America, am a more formidable foe of Communists than those who would weaken America. I strongly denounce the Communists and communism and very much suspect that the Communists and our opposition in this matter are fellow travelers."[55] Nelson, the author of the endorsement, said that representatives of the Pepper and Smathers camps had both approached him about endorsing the other. He said the endorsement was sincere, although he added that the endorsement was more anti-Smathers than pro-Pepper.[56] Smathers rejected Pepper's charge that it was a trick, saying, "Year after year my opponent has received the endorsement, the praise and the favorable comment of Communist writers. But this is the first time he has hollered 'trickery.'"[57]

Pepper asked Ross C. Beiler, a professor of government at the University of Miami, for help in dealing with the communist issue. Beiler urged Pepper to try humor and make light of Smathers's accusations. "When dealing with the Communist and FEPC charges, couple some unimpeachable associations that reveal the insincerity of these charges with gentle, droll ridicule that makes Smathers appear ridiculous, and not merely mistaken or overzealous in his charges."[58] Pepper took the advice. At political rallies he would turn his coat collar up, put his head down mysteriously, and say, "The other crowd would have you believe that I slipped out of the house while my wife was asleep . . . crept along the wall of the Kremlin until I came to a door marked 'Stalin,' knocked on the door, and when the man came, I said: 'Joe, here's Claude.'"[59] The technique was unconvincing. *Life* magazine dismissed his strategy by saying Pepper "tried to clown his way out of the accusations he was a Communist sympathizer."[60]

On March 28, Smathers announced that every day until the May primary he would name a different communist-front organization that Pepper had addressed. Smathers claimed there were twenty-three such groups. He kicked off his list with the American Slav Congress, listed as subversive by the attorney general. One of the organizations Smathers named, the Southern Conference for Human Welfare, was not on the attorney general's list, and, as with many of those Smathers named, Pepper had spoken to the groups before they were put on the attorney general's list.[61] The so-called "attorney general's list" was created by Attorney General Francis Biddle, who was trying to come up with some type of standard to guide the Department of Justice, as government officials who were interviewing job applicants could not judge whether an applicant's list of organizations was suspect or not. Names such as Friends of the Soviet Union clearly set off alarm bells, but could the interviewer know that the Detroit Youth Assembly was also suspected of being linked to communists? The list was intended only as a guide. Then Martin Dies, the chairman of the House Un-American Activities Committee, obtained a copy of the list and inserted it in the *Congressional Record*. Quickly it went from a guide to a blacklist. Despite Truman's protest that the list was only a "factor to be taken into consideration," membership in the groups on the list cost many their jobs.[62] A Smathers newspaper advertisement said, "Pepper spent most of his time in the period 1945 to 1948 visiting Joe Stalin, Russia, and the satellite states and thereafter making speeches to radical organizations from coast to coast praising Dictator Joe Stalin, instead of working for Florida's interest in Washington."[63] The communist issue kept Pepper on the defensive throughout the campaign. Although Pepper was certainly not a communist or a fellow traveler, his actions between 1944 and 1950 created the impression that he had at the very least been duped by the communists. No matter how much he denied the charges hurled by Smathers, Pepper could not overcome his meeting with Stalin, his opposition to the Truman Doctrine, his endorsement by the *Daily Worker*, and his association with groups identified as communist fronts.

9

The Campaign and Civil Rights

Although communism was the main issue that Smathers used against Pepper, he also hammered away at a short but effective list of domestic issues led by civil rights. Opponents in previous elections had used the race issue against Pepper, but it was effective only when used by Park Trammell in 1934. In 1938 and 1944 Pepper carefully maintained his support for segregation.

Pepper's position on civil rights was a hodgepodge of shifting sentiments and a desire both to be attractive to northern liberals and to retain office in Florida. During his 1944 reelection campaign, he declared that the "South will allow nothing to impair white supremacy."[1] In the Senate he never voted for a civil rights measure, although he stopped joining his fellow southerners in filibusters against bills to outlaw lynching and the poll tax.

Pepper enjoyed a measure of protection under Roosevelt, whose domestic program never included any civil rights measures. Roosevelt believed that if he pushed civil rights legislation, key southern politicians would scuttle his New Deal agenda. But northern congressmen tried time and again to push through antilynching bills. In one speech opposing the legislation, Pepper said, "Whatever may be written into the Constitution, whatever may be placed upon the statute books of this nation, however many soldiers may be stationed about the ballot boxes of the Southland, the colored race will not vote, because in doing so under present circumstances they endanger the supremacy of a race to which God has committed the destiny of a continent, perhaps a world."[2]

Like many, Pepper was undone largely by his own words. For years he tried to appeal to both a national audience and a southern audience. Ultimately, by the 1950 campaign, Smathers was able to make Pepper appear to be both a racist and a civil rights champion while he himself avoided being a target entirely. As with many issues, Smathers was able to exploit inconsistencies and put Pepper on the defensive.

By 1950 civil rights had moved to center stage. In 1946 Truman created the President's Committee on Civil Rights, which produced a report urging federal action to overcome racial discrimination in the United States, and on February 2, 1948, the president called on Congress to pass antilynching laws, abolish the poll tax, outlaw segregation in interstate transportation, and establish the Fair Employment Practices Commission as a permanent body. Truman's proposals forced moderate southern politicians to take a stand, and nearly all came out in opposition to any civil rights program.

Blacks returning from World War II were not willing to settle for the second-class citizenship awaiting them in the South. Some three million African Americans registered for the military, and half a million men were stationed overseas. In the United States, nearly a million blacks moved into factory jobs.[3] At the same time, the Supreme Court was handing down decisions favorable to blacks. The Court ruled in *Smith v. Allwright* (1944) that blacks could not be barred from voting in Democratic primaries, in *Morgan v. Virginia* (1946) that it was unconstitutional to require segregation on carriers moving across state lines, and in *Shelley v. Kraemer* (1948) that state judicial enforcement of racially restrictive covenants violated the Fourteenth Amendment.

The combination of the court rulings, Truman's civil rights legislation, and the growing militancy of blacks alarmed southerners, who responded with violence. In 1946 in Batesburg, South Carolina, returning veteran Isaac Woodward was removed from a bus, beaten, and blinded by the chief of police.[4] In Columbia, Tennessee, two blacks were shot and killed as Ku Klux Klansmen terrorized the town.[5] In Monroe, Georgia, four blacks being transported by a white farmer were shot to death.

But one of the most violent places was Florida, where a resurgent Klan operated not only with impunity but often with the support of law enforcement officials. The sheriff of Orange County, home of Orlando, was a Klansmen whose Apopka chapter carried out beatings and murders. In early 1950, as the campaign began, there were cross burnings across the state. Five took place in Jacksonville, ten in Orlando and Winter Park, seventeen in and around Tallahassee.[6] A report by the Workers Defense League stated, "Terror is spreading in Florida." A synagogue and a public housing project were bombed in Miami. Just months after the 1950s primary, Florida NAACP executive director Harry T. Moore and his wife were killed when their home in Mims, Florida, was bombed by Klansmen. The WDL found that "more forms of forced labor are more widely practiced in Florida than in any other state. Its legislature, by successive enactments, has most consistently attempted to evade or ignore U.S. Supreme Court decisions."[7]

One of the most sensational cases occurred in Florida in 1949. Early in the morning of July 16, 1949, in the tiny Central Florida community of Groveland, a white woman named Norma Padgett told officials she was raped by four black men. Sammy Shepherd, Walter Irwin, Ernest Thomas, and Charles Greenlee were identified as suspects in the rape case. Three were quickly arrested, but Thomas eluded police for a week before being shot and killed two hundred miles north of Lake County.[8]

The NAACP, entering the case to help the three defendants, questioned whether Padgett was in fact raped or was seeking to cover up a beating by her husband. Even before the trial began, the *Orlando Morning Sentinel* ran a front-page editorial cartoon showing electric chairs and demanding justice.[9] There was little doubt about the outcome of the case. The three were convicted after the jury deliberated just ninety minutes. Irwin and Shepherd were sentenced to death, but sixteen-year-old Greenlee was spared the death penalty.

Pepper had nothing to do with the case and had not made any public comment about it, but in April 1950 the Groveland case became a campaign issue and added to Pepper's woes. The *St. Petersburg Times* published a series of articles questioning how Greenlee could have been involved in the rape of Padgett inasmuch as, at the time the alleged assault took place, he was being arrested nineteen miles away. The *Times* also substantiated alibis for Shepherd and Irwin, who were near Orlando the night the alleged attack took place.[10] The stories were critical of the methods used by the courts and police.

Lake County state attorney J. W. Hunter, who prosecuted the case, was a major Pepper supporter in Central Florida, where Pepper needed all the help he could get. One year earlier Hunter wrote to Pepper, "If you are defeated, there will be no one in Florida to stand against two aggregations of capital—the Dupont monopoly in business and the Perry monopoly in the newspaper field."[11] Hunter demanded that Pepper repudiate the *Times* stories. Pepper replied that he had not seen the articles and saw no reason to get involved. Hunter angrily denounced Pepper and threw his support to Smathers.

As a result of the 1944 Supreme Court decision in *Smith v. Allwright*, blacks could no longer be kept from registering to vote in the Democratic Party. In 1944 there were no blacks registered as Democrats in Florida, and about 20,000 registered as Republicans. By 1950 there were 106,420 blacks registered as Democrats. The number of registered black Republicans fell to 9,725 during that period.[12]

The elections of 1946 were the first in which Florida blacks could vote as Democrats. Despite the ruling by the Supreme Court and a statement by Florida attorney general Tom Watson stating that "for the first time in modern history, Negro citizens of Florida will cast their votes in the Democratic primary in the coming month of May," thousands of blacks were still denied the right to register by local election officials, who came up with dozens of excuses for denying blacks their rights.[13]

Moore, the leader of the Florida NAACP, began sending regular letters to blacks urging them to fight for their rights.[14] Moore formed the Progressive Voters League to encourage black registration and to endorse candidates. The PVL endorsed Truman's reelection in 1948 and was active in turning out black voters. Moore's PVL was beginning to be heard by the state's politicians. In the fall of 1949, Moore held meetings with Florida governor Fuller Warren, attorney general Richard Ervin, and state education superintendent Thomas D. Bailey. The *Miami Times*, a black-owned newspaper, commented that "not since the Reconstruction Period have Negroes representing a state-wide political organization been able to sit down and talk with high state officials as full-fledged voting citizens."[15]

In 1948 Pepper made a series of startling declarations indicating that he backed Truman's civil rights program. In February he gave a vague statement linking it to the rising prodemocracy movement around the world: "We must practice it as well as preach it."[16] But he realized that any support of civil rights might cost him votes in Florida. He wrote in his diary, "Troubled by the civil rights issue and foreign policy especially."[17] A few days later, in a national broadcast, he announced, "I can say that I am generally in favor of the president's civil rights program."[18] At the end of the year, at a gathering of Young Democrats at the University of Florida, Pepper stunned everyone by announcing that it was his "intention to support President Truman's whole program of civil rights even if it beats me in the next election." Pepper said he did not think his stand would have much effect on his support because of the fairness of the American people.[19] But when the 1950 campaign began, he told crowds that he was "absolutely opposed to any attempt by the government to abolish or interfere in any way with the customs and traditions of the Southland."[20] Smathers pointed to Pepper's promise to support civil rights and said, "Where is this courageous fellow now?"[21]

Pepper had never voted for a civil rights bill, leaving Smathers to search for a concrete issue connected to civil rights. He found it in the Fair Employment Practices Commission. The FEPC went from an obscure agency to a litmus test for every southern politician. In 1941 Roosevelt issued an executive order forbidding discrimination in defense industries and made nondiscrimination clauses in defense contracts mandatory. To enforce this, he created a five-member commission to evaluate complaints. Even though the FEPC's guidelines were voluntary, it seemed a dastardly civil rights measure to white southern politicians. Roosevelt knew that he could count on southern members of Congress blocking attempts to finance the commission, so he paid for it with a discretionary fund and some small legislative appropriations.

There were numerous attempts by southerners in Congress to kill the commission, primarily by eliminating funding. On June 20, 1944, Pepper voted against a motion by Senator Richard Russell of Georgia to kill a $500,000 appropriation for the FEPC. At the same time, he voted against another motion to strip the commission of what little power it did have. When Truman became president, he asked Congress to make the commission permanent and its rulings binding. In 1945 Pepper voted against creating a permanent commission, and in 1946 he voted against even holding hearings to discuss keeping the FEPC alive. With the southerners conducting a filibuster, the legislation died and the FEPC died with it.[22] Even though its demise was due in part to Pepper's opposition, Smathers successfully used the FEPC against him four years later in 1950.

The FEPC allowed Smathers to raise the race issue without appearing to join the southern politicians who had turned race baiting into a campaign staple. Smathers pointed out that after running as a white supremacist in the 1944 election, Pepper turned around and voted in the Senate Labor Committee to continue FEPC.[23] In Belle Glade, Smathers hammered on the FEPC issue: "I would have had a lot more respect for my opponent if he had just one stand on this issue. But he has two stands. It appears to depend entirely on whether he is making a speech before a northern audience or whether he is making it down here in the South. You have green peppers and red peppers. Keep the green ones too long and they turn red."[24] Smathers's campaign ran an advertisement stating, "The wily Senator Pepper, with his oily tongued oratory, is endeavoring to lead the unwary Florida voter into an FEPC–Civil Rights trap." Smathers also linked the FEPC to communism: "This vicious legislation, conceived in Communistic Russia in 1917, is sponsored by Senator Pepper in an attempt to regiment and control our way of life, and with whom we work, worship and associate."[25] In other speeches he said it came from the 1936 platform of the Communist Party, instead of the 1917 original, to "revolutionize the political, economic, and social relations between the whites and the Negroes in the South."[26] Smathers had white racial sensibilities on his side, and his advertisements hammered at Pepper's votes: "You will not find me guilty of voting for FEPC in non-election years and saying I am against it during election years."[27]

Pepper maintained that he voted for the FEPC only as a wartime measure and thereafter opposed the legislation: "For two hundred years I haven't had an ancestor who lived north of Virginia. I was born in Alabama and spent the last twenty-five years in Tallahassee. Is that young du Pont lawyer from Miami who was born in New Jersey . . . going to tell me how to handle problems like this?"[28] He waved a copy of Smathers's New Jersey birth certificate over his head in the rural areas and called him "that Miami lawyer from Sunset Island."[29] Pepper insisted that he was "in favor of retaining social segregation."[30]

Pepper produced a letter from Leslie Biffle, the secretary of the Senate, stating that Pepper did not introduce any FEPC legislation. Joseph McMurray, a staff member of the Senate Education and Labor Committee, sent a signed statement that Pepper voted against the measure in the committee.[31] Pepper told a Leesburg audience that the FEPC charges were part of a larger scheme to link him with blacks, which was Smathers's goal. Smathers warned crowds that "if they can pass the FEPC, which tells you whom you must hire without regard to race, creed, or color, it is a logical step for them to be telling you whom your daughter can marry without regard to race, creed, or color."[32]

In the midst of the campaign, Pepper issued a flier saying he was "ABSOLUTELY OPPOSED TO ANY ATTEMPT BY THE GOVERNMENT to abolish or interfere in any way with the customs and traditions of the Southland."[33]

Smathers's charge that Pepper was out of touch with other southern leaders on the race issue got an unexpected boost early in 1950 when Pepper was not included in a meeting of southern senators. Eighteen southern members of the Senate gathered in Raleigh, North Carolina, to come up with a plan to defeat Truman's civil rights proposals. Pepper's fellow southerners had not even bothered to invite him.[34] The other two southerners who were excluded were Frank Graham of North Carolina and Estes Kefauver of Tennessee, whose views on civil rights were suspect to white southerners. The snub provided another opportunity for Smathers to attack: "When you send me to the United States Senate you will find me with Dick Russell of Georgia, Spessard Holland of Florida, and other southern politicians."[35]

Smathers was a racial moderate by the standards of the 1940s. He had avoided the Dixiecrat platform of 1948 by endorsing Truman wholeheartedly, and he took the political middle ground by rejecting any call for civil rights legislation with the argument that it was simply not a federal matter and should be left to the states. Although Pepper was certainly the more moderate of the two, he was constantly forced to issue racist statements to defend himself. Meanwhile Smathers was able to escape criticism by both African Americans and racist whites. And so while Pepper was on the defensive, Smathers could oppose every single piece of civil rights legislation during his twenty-two years on Capitol Hill but still say, "I will never be motivated by racial or religious prejudices." He said that "all minorities will find me an outspoken and vigilant defender, and I will never be guilty of fanning the flames of class hatred and bigotry in order to secure votes."[36]

Smathers never did join his fellow southern senators in the race baiting that marked the era. Like many moderates, he relied on terms such as "states' right," and cautioned against the federal government's becoming involved in local matters. And yet, unlike Pepper, he remained on good terms with his fellow senators and earned their respect and friendship.

Both Smathers and Pepper wanted the black vote, but without white voters finding out. As Hugh Douglas observed in his study of black voting in Florida, "The Negro vote is too large for conservative candidates to risk indulging in undiluted Negro-baiting, but neither do liberal candidates dare expose a too pro-Negro program or make too open a bid for Negro support."[37] Or, as the *New York Times* noted, both Pepper and Smathers "are courting the Negro vote as much as they can without offending white voters."[38] The *St. Petersburg Times* reported an almost comical series of events involving Smathers's effort to get black votes. Two Smathers workers attended a meeting with black voters, but then denied they were there. The newspaper responded with an article asking, "Do Johnny Burroughs and Aubry Moorefield have doubles in St. Petersburg?" The paper reported that Burroughs's car was outside the meeting, and that people in the meeting identified Burroughs and Moorefield as the speakers. "Moorefield said last night he wasn't there. He said there were two or three fellows around town who looked like him. . . . Burroughs claims he and Moorefield and Smathers were in the Pheil Hotel at the time. . . . Furthermore he said no Smathers meeting with the Negroes was scheduled."[39] Smathers issued leaflets listing his contributions to blacks in his district, but devoted most of his efforts to warning blacks that whites were "watching to see whether you will prove that you are independent, free thinking citizens or whether your votes will be controlled by the red-tinged group who seeks to cause strife and bloodshed among the whites and Negro people."[40]

During the campaign, *Miami Life*, a newspaper aimed at black readers, published an article entitled "George Puts It in Black and White, A Few Things George Smathers Had Done for the Negro Race." It was based on a memo Smathers wrote, but when it appeared in print, Smathers assumed it was a Pepper trick. Smathers's Dade County coordinator, Sloan McCrea, sent a telegram to Pepper's campaign manager, Jim Clements, calling the article misleading. "It is unfortunate that this type of strategy which appears to be a desperate last-minute effort . . . should be injected into the campaign."[41] Clements responded that "as far as dissemination and circulation of malicious literature and advertising is concerned, your state committee is a past master at this game."[42]

The dangerous political game that Pepper played with the race issue was coming back in 1950 to haunt him. He could not moderate his racial views enough to become a national political candidate and still retain his seat as a southern senator. As the rising tide of civil rights spurred both blacks and whites to action, Pepper could no longer merely say he was against equal rights for blacks; white voters expected him to come up with plans to battle civil rights. His personal beliefs, and his desire for national office, kept him from joining the race baiters who were winning southern elections. But without such an approach in 1950, he could not win.

Old Friends, New Enemies

Pepper's decline from one of the state's most popular politicians to one of its least popular (in 1950, the most unpopular was certainly Governor Fuller Warren) took nearly a decade. It began with the opposition of Ed Ball during World War II, then escalated in the postwar period. In the elections of 1938 and 1944, Pepper could count on the support of nearly all of the state's newspapers and union members. By 1950 he lost nearly all of his newspaper support and the backing of one significant union. The state's physicians, who began to desert Pepper in 1944, organized a massive campaign to defeat Pepper over his support of a national health insurance plan.

Five days after Smathers announced his candidacy, Pepper supporter Jerry W. Carter, the Florida Democratic national committeeman, sent the first of several letters to leaders of the Congress of Industrial Organizations pleading for help, saying that Smathers and his backers "seem to have unlimited funds and have done some very effective work in coordinating and drilling the anti-Pepper forces and I will have to admit they have made considerable gains."[1]

Pepper believed he could count on strong labor support because he was one of labor's most loyal friends. To labor groups Pepper said, "You can help elect a friend of labor or you can permit the selfish anti-Roosevelt forces to put a man who has shown himself to be the enemy of both organized and unorganized labor" into the Senate.[2] Pepper opposed the Labor-Management Relations Act of 1947, known generally as the Taft-Hartley Act, while Smathers voted for it. Unions despised Taft-Hartley because it required unions to give sixty days' notice of a strike, restricted union political contributions, and outlawed the closed shop, in which all workers had to join the union if a majority voted for it.

Compared to Smathers's aggressive, modern campaign, Carter admitted that Pepper "knows nothing of the art of modern politics and is far from a shrewd political manipulator." One reporter noted, "If any real organization work has been done for Pepper, it was a closely guarded secret."[3] Carter asked the CIO "to come into this state of Florida and bring as many others as necessary to arouse labor and other groups to this danger and put them earnestly to work."[4] The CIO presence became a major campaign issue, working to Smathers's advantage in a state where union membership was small and the labor movement was unpopular.

Ten days later Carter wrote to Jack Kroll, the political director of the CIO: "I feel it is my duty as Democratic National Committeeman to send out the alarm and acquaint you with the definite fact that the enemies of the New Deal and the Fair Deal are making their most decisive efforts to capture Florida."[5] Kroll already knew that Pepper was in trouble. In mid-January the CIO's political research department listed seven Democrats, including Pepper, who it felt were in grave danger.[6]

CIO support was a double-edged sword for political candidates in the South. Endorsement by the labor federation brought money, organizing support, and votes. But the CIO supported a permanent Fair Employment Practices Commission, repeal of Taft-Hartley, and Truman's civil rights program, all measures opposed by most white southerners.

During World War II there was a dramatic increase in southern CIO membership, but most workers remained unorganized. In 1946 the CIO launched the Southern Organizing Committee to extend the membership gains in what became known as Operation Dixie. For the CIO there was the prospect of millions of potential members in textiles, steel mills, transportation, lumber, and other industries. The CIO Executive Board committed one million dollars to the effort and hired two hundred labor organizers.[7] The American Federation of Labor set up its own, less publicized, organizing campaign. There were some small victories, but the CIO drive sputtered and ended largely in failure. The union organizers anticipated opposition from the owners, but they were surprised to find that the employees too were often antagonistic. What the South offered was cheap labor. Workers knew that employers were abandoning plants in the North to move to the South. A generation later, those jobs would begin migrating overseas as owners found workers willing to work for even less money. Southern workers, frightened that any association with the union meant the end of what they considered very attractive jobs, sometimes turned on the union organizers, telling them to leave or in some cases physically assaulting them.[8]

The drive not only failed, it left a negative legacy in the South. Businessmen reacted with alarm at the mention of the CIO, and their anti-CIO effort convinced many voters that the CIO was in league with Joe Stalin. From its founding in 1935, the CIO counted communists and other radicals among its most ardent members. The communists provided organizing strength when the CIO was launched. In the 1940s, communists and their allies controlled nearly a dozen unions, led by the United Electrical, Radio and Machine Workers. The presence of communists gave a wide range of opponents the excuse they sought to work against the union. Employers could claim that they were not negotiating with the union because they refused to negotiate with communists, and could tell employees that by joining a CIO union they were helping communism. In 1949–50, CIO leaders drove eleven affiliated unions out of the federation as part of an anticommunist purge. This eliminated some problems for the CIO, but it also weakened the union and served to remind voters that Pepper's strongest ally had been a home for communists. As historian Robert Zieger noted, the loss of members "underscored the continuing weakness of the CIO as a central labor federation."[9]

The southern membership drive was not the only new activity by the CIO in the South. In 1946 Daniel Powell became the southern director for the CIO Political Action Committee. Like the union organizing drive, the CIO political operation arrived with flags flying. Each union member was supposed to contribute a dollar for political action, with half going to the national CIO-PAC and the remaining fifty cents divided between the local union and the member's local political action group.[10] It was difficult to get the members to contribute, however. Often an individual member's political views were in conflict with the national union's.[11]

Just as it did when the CIO launched Operation Dixie, the CIO Political Action Committee made its entry into Florida very public—and thereby made it difficult to determine whether the organization was trying to help Pepper or demonstrate its political influence. Even after it became clear that the CIO's involvement in the campaign provided Smathers with an important issue, the labor federation continued its efforts to promote its influence in the election. Just days before the election, Jack Kroll, the CIO political director, told an Alabama union meeting that "Pepper appeared to be a defeated man, but the CIO-PAC got busy, and now it begins to look as if he holds the edge."[12] Florida newspapers widely reported the speech.

The CIO-PAC sent Philip Weightman, a black official, to Florida to direct the registration of blacks. The gains in black voters since the 1944 Supreme Court ruling were dramatic, mainly due to the work of the Progressive Voters League and the CIO. Weightman was able to put together an organization in Miami, but he had trouble in Jacksonville, where he found "Negroes who are favorable but reluctant to take an active part on a committee on the Senator's behalf." Weightman found a black dentist to head the Pepper campaign in Miami but admitted that "among the Negro, there is a group who are opposed to the Senator's re-election because of his stand in support of National Health Insurance." He also found that there was no white organization supporting Pepper in Jacksonville.[13]

The CIO became a target for Smathers after he received a copy of a CIO report entitled "Survey of Negro Vote in Florida" showing that labor organizers were working to register black voters in Florida for Pepper. The report, from George Weaver, the assistant to the union's secretary treasurer, detailed efforts to register blacks primarily in Jacksonville, Miami, and Tampa.[14] Smathers held the speech above his head and told crowds, "We now have the full documentary proof to show that he conspired with the paid and imported organizers of the CIO . . . to register and deliver the Negro vote for him, as a bloc."[15] Smathers charged that northern labor bosses were using large slush funds to defeat him and that 150 paid labor organizers were in Florida to help register Pepper supporters, including blacks. Smathers alleged that "some Negroes had received $1.50 and $2.00 for registering, and in Miami we are told some were handed free movie passes."[16] Smathers ran a newspaper advertisement featuring a photograph of blacks waiting to register to vote and the caption "Doesn't this make your blood boil?"[17]

The registration effort no doubt hurt Pepper more than it helped. It did produce greater numbers of black voters in Jacksonville, Miami, and Tampa. But in some smaller counties there was no gain, and the attention may have actually discouraged blacks from registering and voting in rural counties. Newspapers around the state carried front-page stories about the registration efforts, which Smathers used to alarm whites. In late March the *Miami Herald* reported on one such effort under the headline "Voting List Is Swelled by Negroes." The newspaper reported, "In some areas, registration clerks were quoted to the effect that most Negroes were coming in to register in the company of the same four or five Negro men, and one courthouse report said the recruiters received twenty-five cents a head."[18]

The registration rolls closed on April 1 and showed 1,006,560 registered Democrats, including 106,420 African Americans.[19] But registration did not necessarily translate into votes. One Hillsborough County election official said after the election, "They had three months to get the Negroes registered but only one day to get them voted."[20]

Pepper pointed out that in the 1946 election Smathers asked for the union's endorsement in his race against Pat Cannon. Now, said Pepper, Smathers was "running against labor, trying to make the CIO the whipping boy." Smathers denied that he ever received union aid, but Pepper produced an affidavit from the assistant director of the CIO Political Action Committee that said, "Mr. Smathers said that if he were elected to Congress he would be known as a liberal Democrat by his voting record, and that he would approximate in the House of Representatives the record and work of Claude Pepper in the Senate."[21]

Pepper had the wholehearted support of the American Federation of Labor and its affiliate union the Brotherhood of Railway Clerks, but many Florida railroad workers campaigned to defeat him. At issue was Pepper's opposition to Ed Ball's acquisition of the Florida East Coast Railway. George M. Harrison, the national president of the Railway Clerks, wrote letters to Florida union members asking them to "join in the effort to return one of the greatest of Liberals to the Senate of the United States."[22] But W. F. Howard, chairman of the Florida Brotherhood of Railway Clerks, rejected the appeal. He sent his own letter to labor leaders urging members to vote against Pepper. "I do not, of course, know whether or not the du Pont interests are leading the fight to defeat Pepper, but I certainly hope and pray they are. Why should we be concerned over a strong financial interest leading a fight to defeat the man who is out to destroy our jobs and our homes? I think we should lend assistance to that strong financial interest." Howard said he did not care about Pepper's national union support, adding, "I would vote for anyone opposing Pepper. No one in my opinion could be any worse nor less desirable than Claude Pepper."[23] Local union members were at war with the national leadership. Frank Upchurch, a Ball ally from St. Augustine, where the FEC was based, sent out a letter saying that the Pepper-backed merger would "rob St. Augustine of its principal payroll, one-third of its population and reduce property values 50%."[24] Both the union members of the Florida East Coast Railway and the line's owner, Ed Ball, were working toward the same goal—defeating Pepper.

After the election, a friend wrote to Pepper, "It is my considered judgment that it is your activities in this ACL-FEC [Atlantic Coast Line–Florida East Coast] case which cost you reelection to the United States Senate."[25] The loyalty of the workers turned out to be misplaced. In 1964 the railroad unions struck the Florida East Coast Railway. Within days the owners announced a resumption of service without the workers. It then started hiring replacements and imposing new work rules.[26]

Just how much support Pepper had lost in Florida could be seen in the state's newspapers. In 1944 all but a few of the daily newspapers endorsed his reelection, but in 1950 the situation was reversed: only the *St. Petersburg Times* and the *Daytona Beach News Journal* supported Pepper. The opposition should not have come as a surprise to Pepper, because the editorial pages of most Florida newspapers had criticized him for five years.

The Perry newspapers, which had close financial links to Ed Ball, made defeating Pepper their primary goal. Although they were called the Perry newspapers, they were in fact the du Pont newspapers. By 1946 John Perry had acquired fourteen weekly newspapers, seven small daily papers, and four radio stations, all financed by Ed Ball through his Florida National Banks holding company.[27] As the 1950 election approached, Pepper decided to publicize the link between Perry and Ball, although he knew it would "intensify Perry's bitter fight against me but he has been carrying it on anyway so I don't think I have much to lose by letting the tie up between him and the du Ponts become public." Pepper said Perry came to Florida from New York to spread "Republican propaganda in over twenty newspapers throughout the state."[28]

Newspapers with no connection to Ball also opposed Pepper. The *Tampa Morning Tribune* sought Pepper's defeat as part of its crusade against big government. To the *Tribune*, Pepper's continued support for creating New Deal programs meant a bigger and more menacing national government. The *Miami Daily News* said that "Senator Pepper has gotten away from the people of Florida."[29] Pepper replied that the *News* "in its feeble way is spreading vicious venom."[30]

The *Miami Herald*, once a strong supporter of Pepper, praised Smathers as representing "basic Americanism, liberally interpreted and administered with a minimum of government control." The paper dismissed Pepper as supporting "the big welfare state, big government, deficit spending, and global largesse." The *Herald* said the election was "a trial of radicalism and extremism, with all of the United States as an observer."[31] The *Herald* publisher referred to Pepper as "Pink" and "Red Pepper."[32] The *Leesburg Commercial*, a Perry newspaper, also joined the parade to endorse Smathers, saying Pepper "has proclaimed Stalin one of the greatest men of history. He has shouted that he instinctively trusted Stalin. . . . We will vote for George Smathers and the welfare of this Republic."[33]

The *Orlando Morning Sentinel* was particularly hard on Pepper. First the newspaper ran a large front-page picture of Pepper shaking hands with a black voter, implying that he was seeking black support. Pepper reacted angrily, saying, "They planted several colored people in the audience and tried to rush them up to me. . . . They pushed a colored woman up to me, and as I reached out my hand they took a picture." The *Sentinel*, after running the picture, then became a champion of blacks. "Now, Claude, let's get right down to cases. What's wrong with shaking hands with a colored woman, especially one who has registered and, therefore, a full-fledged citizen with the right to vote? . . . There is nothing wrong with shaking hands with colored people, Claude."[34] Pepper said blacks were being planted at his rallies and at least one was paid twenty-five dollars to shake hands with him while a photographer took a picture.[35]

Meanwhile, the *Sentinel* lavished attention on Smathers. In December 1949, even before Smathers announced his candidacy, the paper found him to be "a good speaker, a fine able handshaker. Young people—especially those who went to the University of Florida with him—adore him and admire his intellect. Women think him handsome. His colleagues in Washington think him studious, brilliant."[36] Following Smathers's announcement of his candidacy, the *Sentinel* praised him again. "Those who saw and heard George Smathers launch his U.S. Senate campaign here Jan. 12 knew immediately that this was going to be a different kind of Florida political campaign."[37] Pepper said Martin Andersen, the publisher of the *Sentinel*, "turned against me because he became too rich to remain a Democrat."[38]

Anti-Pepper newspapers went to extraordinary lengths to deny his supporters access to voters. In late April, Washington columnist Drew Pearson criticized Smathers as a candidate of wealthy Republicans and business. But a number of newspapers friendly to Smathers refused to carry the column, and the Perry papers would not even run the column as a paid advertisement.[39]

Headlines in the pro-Smathers newspapers assailed Pepper. "Pepper's Campaign Sinks to Final Low," said the *Miami News*; "Pepper Has Many Wealthy Friends Ready to Help Meet His Vote Getting Costs," said the *Miami Herald*. Some of the headlines were designed to scare white voters, warning that "304 Negroes Register in Day."[40]

The two dailies and the handful of weeklies supporting Pepper did their best to help the incumbent. The *St. Petersburg Times* said Smathers was "a politician who tried to trim his sails to each new gust of public opinion. . . . Smathers launched his campaign with an appeal to ignorance, and prejudice and sly bigotry."[41] Days before the election, the newspaper said Smathers did "greater violence to our institutions of self-government than any single man in the past thirty years."[42]

As if the opposition of the newspapers and railway workers were not enough, Pepper faced another new group of powerful opponents in 1950: the state's doctors. The doctors were not so much concerned with electing Smathers as with defeating Pepper, whom they labeled the champion of "socialized medicine."[43]

Twice Pepper sponsored health insurance legislation, which he called an "an extension of social security, like unemployment compensation and other insurance."[44] Pepper said he wanted to create a way "by which every man or woman gainfully employed could pay for and get the health care they need."[45] Pepper first presented his views in a report prepared for the Senate Subcommittee on Wartime Health and Education and Labor. That study called for "a system of prepaid medical care," to be "financed by required contributions to the Social Security fund and by payments from general tax revenues." The report was ignored by nearly all senators (only three members of the subcommittee even bothered to sign it) but set off alarms among the nation's doctors, who almost uniformly opposed government-financed health care.[46]

The Truman administration proposed a plan to assist mothers and children with medical needs, and to provide more money for medical research, hospitals, and physicians. Pepper supported the administration proposal, but he wanted to go further. He said he wanted a comprehensive program of "complete medical, and hospital, dental and home nursing care."[47] As early as 1946, a medical journal carried an article about Pepper and "socialized medicine."[48]

Smathers charged that government-sponsored health insurance was "paving the way for a Soviet Union of the United States" and was lifted "from the Communist Party platform."[49] Pepper badly underestimated the power of the doctors. He met with Florida medical leaders but said he could not agree with their position. Pepper told them, "I'm sticking to the administration's health plan. I just don't care about your two thousand votes in this state." In response, the medical community worked hard to defeat Pepper. One of the leaders of the effort was Jacksonville physician Frank Slaughter, who was best known as the author of popular novels. His first best-selling novel, *That None Should Die*, published in 1941, dealt with a young doctor resisting a government takeover of the medical establishment. Slaughter said, "The immediate task of Florida doctors . . . is to unseat Claude Pepper, one of their high priests of the administration sect which seeks to control the people of this country through the socialist state."[50]

The doctors organized anti-Pepper efforts in every county and asked each physician to contribute $100 toward the effort. Money, however, was secondary to the involvement of the doctors themselves in every part of the state. After the election, an article in *Medical Economics* said, "Professional reserve melted away. Doctors got out their patient lists, dashed off hundreds of personal letters. . . . No politician running for office in this state will ever again discount the power of the physicians. . . . On election day, medical workers phoned every professional man in the state before noon. . . . In some small towns every phone number in the book was called."[51] Midway through the campaign, Pepper realized what his stand meant. "It might have been better for me politically to line up with the other side. . . . The medical lobby is trying to defeat me, but a man in politics has to make up his mind whether he is on the side of special interests."[52] One week before the election, the Florida Medical Association held its regular meeting in Hollywood, Florida, where Dr. Walter C. Payne, the FMA president, urged members to "elect members of Congress who will stand out against socialism."[53]

Less than a month before the election, Pepper said he was optimistic, even though the polls showed him trailing. The *New York Times* reported that "Senator Pepper and his associates remain confident. They believe their man is 'a slow starter and fast finisher,' that Representative Smathers 'reached his peak too soon' and is beginning to lose ground."[54] There was no reason for Pepper's optimism. All of the polls showed him trailing.

Pepper tried to portray Smathers as an ingrate who courted his support when convenient and then turned against him. Smathers said he had not betrayed the friendship, but rather that his faith in Pepper was destroyed by the appearances Pepper made with Henry Wallace and Paul Robeson. Smathers said he was putting "patriotism above friendship."[55] Smathers told audiences that he was walking through the streets of New York in the fall of 1946 when he suddenly looked up and saw a red banner announcing an appearance by "Claude Pepper, Henry Wallace, and Paul Robeson, the noted Communist Negro leader."[56] According to Smathers, "that was the beginning of the end of our friendship."[57] However, Smathers left unmentioned that his outrage did not prevent him from asking Pepper for assistance after that, or from continuing to call Henry Wallace "a good friend."[58]

As Smathers continued his attack, Pepper was repeatedly put on the defensive. Pepper claimed that he had "never been on the same platform with Henry Wallace after he was vice president or since he quit the Democratic Party."[59] Pictures of Pepper at rallies in New York and Washington were produced to show that the two indeed appeared together. At one point Pepper declared: "I never spoke anywhere with Henry Wallace after he got out of the vice presidency [in 1945]," even though the two appeared together in Madison Square Garden in 1946 and at a Southern Conference on Human Welfare meeting in Washington in 1947.[60]

Pepper took aim at those he said were behind Smathers, including Republicans, big business, and the du Pont interests. Speaking in Jacksonville on March 10, Pepper criticized what he called the "big monopoly crowd,"[61] and said, "No wonder the Republicans of Florida are teamed up solidly behind this kind of opposition. Having nothing to offer themselves, this desperate opposition has no weapon against me but money and smears."[62] Smathers replied that Pepper had received du Pont money in his 1938 election, and that the Pepper campaign manager in Dade County, William G. Wood, was the du Pont representative in South Florida.[63] Smathers did not mention that his own law firm was located in a Ball-owned building in Miami, and that the firm did work for Ball. Newspapers around the state carried the stories linking Pepper and du Pont.

Smathers charged Pepper with being both a friend to the communists and to du Pont. Pepper asked audiences how he could be working for Wall Street and for the Kremlin, and called the charges an "insult to the intelligence of the people of Florida."[64] Pepper accused Smathers of "conducting the most bigoted, prejudiced campaign against me in the history of Florida."[65]

Pepper searched for issues that resonated with the voters—anything that might put Smathers on the defensive. One tactic that Pepper thought was working was to link Smathers to the Republicans. But Smathers responded angrily that his support of Democratic legislation in the House was higher than anyone in the Florida delegation in the 80th Congress and second in the 81st Congress. When columnist Drew

Pearson tried to help Pepper by writing a column about the charge, Smathers labeled Pearson an unmitigated liar.

Still, Pepper continued to use the issue, especially in North Florida. "You won't find me getting elected as a Democrat, then voting with the Republicans," he told a Miami crowd.[66] Pepper tried to tie Smathers to a nationwide effort to roll back the work of the Roosevelt administration: "They are not interested in personalities; they are interested in whether the weather vane of national politics in Florida points towards the election of a Republican Congress in the fall. My opponent is the spokesman of the anti-Roosevelt forces in this state and this nation that are out to beat me. They think if they can knock me out, it will be the beginning of the end for the New Deal."[67]

There was ample evidence that the Republicans were supporting Smathers. The president of the Florida Young Republican Club told members to forget the party and concentrate on beating Pepper. A Young Republicans for Smathers Committee was formed.[68] Pepper produced a letter from Joseph S. Bair, the president of the Young Republican Club of Volusia County, allocating $2,455 to help Smathers win.[69]

In nearly every speech, Pepper mentioned his loyalty and commitment to Roosevelt and the New Deal. He talked of Roosevelt prosperity, and claimed that Smathers "has arrayed himself with the selfish groups who always fought Roosevelt."[70] Pepper ran full-page newspaper advertisements showing pictures of himself with Roosevelt.[71] He also invoked Truman's name, telling audiences that those who opposed him "fought Truman's election. . . . they fought me in every election."[72] He did not mention that he was one of those who fought Truman's election, even though he had tried repeatedly to deny renomination to the president in a variety of ways, including offering himself as an opposing candidate.

Smathers reacted with humor to Pepper invocations of Roosevelt, saying he would not have entered the race if he knew he was running against Roosevelt. He said that if the voters found Roosevelt's name on the ballot, "by all means vote for him."[73] He added that Pepper was running on Roosevelt's record "because he can't defend his own record."[74]

For years, political observers noted that Pepper had a knack of salvaging a bad situation at the last minute. At a meeting of campaign workers from each of the state's sixty-seven counties, Smathers warned of a letdown allowing Pepper to steal a victory. "We got him down. He's mortally wounded. Now all we've got to do is keep our foot on his neck until May third."[75]

Pepper's faith in Governor Warren's ability to deliver votes ended on February 20, when onetime Warren supporter C. V. Griffin broke with the governor and released secret financial documents that seriously discredited Warren's leadership. Griffin said that he contributed $154,000 to Warren's campaign and that two other men, financier Louis Wolfson and a dog-track operator named William Johnston, each contributed the same amount, even though candidates for governor were limited to spending a total of $15,000.[76] In exchange for the contributions, the three men virtually ran the state government, controlling most of the appointments to state office. One reporter noted that the problem with the Warren administration was the lack of Warren appointees in it.[77] A *Miami Herald* columnist said bluntly, "Actually there is not and never has been a Warren administration, since it has been divided from the start, like all Gaul, into three parts—the factions led by C. V. Griffin, Louis Wolfson and William H. Johnston."[78]

For Warren, the duties of being governor seemed to be more than he could handle. During the Pepper campaign, Warren said being governor was "the roughest, toughest, most terrifying task I ever confronted."[79] Warren did campaign with Pepper, but there was little indication that he was willing or able to put the state bureaucracy behind the Pepper effort. One reporter wrote, "Wags around the capitol are saying the Warren administration, despite the gnawing desire of the Governor to be helpful, is giving Senator Claude Pepper all aid short of actual assistance in his campaign for re-election."[80]

Pepper's campaign became increasingly isolated. One newspaper noted: "Some of his long-time friends appear to be afraid to cheer openly for him, probably fearing business or political reprisals. Many of them come around to his hotel with their well wishes when the public meeting is over. They assure him they're working for him—but quietly. No state political aspirants show up."[81]

In mid-March columnist Drew Pearson, one of the few Pepper loyalists in the national media, launched an attack on Smathers that backfired. Pearson questioned Smathers's patriotism by publishing excerpts from the letters Smathers sent to Pepper in 1945 requesting help in getting an early discharge. Smathers had written to a number of people, including Pepper, seeking a discharge after he returned to the United States from the Pacific theater. On June 11, 1945, Smathers wrote, "Can't possibly tell you how anxious I am to get out and start doing." Two days later there was another letter saying his "services could be better utilized in the Justice Department." He wrote that his military assignment was "equivalent to being 2nd deputy sheriff of Collier County. And I can't wear a star nor high top boots. . . . Let me assure you of my gratitude in rescuing me from this mental Sahara." Two weeks later he wrote, "Another lawyer . . . got out of the service last week. Senator Morris [Wayne Morse] of Oregon was his benefactor so it is being done." There was even a letter from Smathers's mother, Laura, saying "we are deeply appreciative for what you have done and are doing for our son George. We know you are a very busy man and a very big man. . . . We will continue to hope and pray that all goes well—and for your success too."[82]

Ordinarily such a charge by one of the nation's leading columnists would have seriously hurt Smathers, but it was clear that Smathers had served with distinction for thirty-nine months and that, when the request came, the war was all but over. Smathers was like millions of other soldiers who wanted to get back to their civilian lives as fast as possible.

Moreover, the column inadvertently brought into focus Pepper's war record, or more accurately his lack of a war record. His two months of service on the University of Alabama campus during the First World War stood in stark contrast to Smathers's lengthy service in the Pacific. Smathers even turned the Pearson column into another opportunity to attack Pepper in newspaper advertisements around the state. "Which will you believe?" a Smathers advertisement challenged. "The political propaganda of a desperate Senator with but 66 days service in two World Wars and on a University campus—or the open unbiased record of the greatest fighting Marines this country has ever known?"[83] To keep the issue alive, Smathers produced letters from Marine officers attesting to his service. The Veterans of Foreign Wars gave Smathers a boost when the state commander accused Pepper of using a VFW appreciation scroll, which was given as a thank-you to many people, as an endorsement.[84]

Only one of the letters Pepper released caused Smathers any embarrassment. During the 1946 campaign against Pat Cannon, Smathers had
asked for Pepper's help to delay a government project. Cannon told voters in Key West to expect an announcement that the naval station was
about to be expanded. Smathers told Pepper, "If that happens it will
ruin me there. Will you check into this and if possible find out why it
cannot be delayed at last until after May 7th"[85]—that is, after the election. Pepper also released copies of Smathers's letters requesting Pepper's help in the 1946 congressional race against Pat Cannon. But the
letters were released too late in the campaign to arouse much interest.
Smathers called it "a last desperation effort," and then stopped com-
menting on the letters.[86]

One of the lasting contributions of the Pepper-Smathers campaign
to the lore of American politics is a speech Smathers supposedly gave.
Two weeks before the election, *Time* magazine carried a report on the
Florida election and stated that Smathers prepared this speech just for
the state's Cracker voters. "Are you aware that Claude Pepper is known
all over Washington as a shameless extrovert? Not only that, but this
man is reliably reported to practice nepotism with his sister-in-law, and
he has a sister who was once a thespian in wicked New York. Worst of all,
it is an established fact that Mr. Pepper before his marriage habitually
practiced celibacy."[87]

There was no indication where the speech was given, but over the years
it has grown and become a legend. By 1987 the speech was nearly ten
times longer as people added to it: "His great-aunt expired from a degen-
erative disease. His nephew subscribed to a phonographic magazine. His
wife was a thespian before their marriage and even performed in front of
paying customers. And his own mother had to resign from an organization in her later years because she was an admitted sexagenarian."[88]

Word of the speech spread throughout the country, growing with
every retelling. In October *Time*'s sister publication *Life* reprinted the
Time quote.[89] In 1971 the speech acquired dramatic detail in the *Miami
Herald*'s version: "scenario of the spring of 1950: George Smathers, eyes
glinting like Clint Eastwood in an Italian-made Western, entertains—
and confuses—a gathering of North Floridians with the most famous
phraseology of the campaign."[90]

No other reporter claimed to have heard the speech. Pepper himself, in his autobiography, claims that Smathers did give the speech, but he offers no proof, merely writing, "Well, it strikes me as a little odd that *Time* would make that up."[91] But *Time* apparently reported the story with tongue in cheek. *Time* called the story a yarn and said it showed that "Smathers was capable of going to any length in campaigning." *Time* claimed that the quotes appeared in southern newspapers, but no one ever found those newspapers.[92]

The alleged speech may have been a joke that was started by a Pepper aide. Nine days after the *Time* magazine article appeared, George Dixon, in a column for King Features Syndicate, wrote that he knew the origin of the "speech." Dixon wrote that a Pepper spokesman, William Daffron, was in the bar at the National Press Club in late March or early April and began talking about an idea he had for a whispering campaign. Daffron said, "These Florida Crackers don't know any big words. Senator Pepper could use a batch of harmless words and those dumbbells would think he was accusing Smathers of unspeakable depravity." According to Dixon, those at the bar "fell into the spirit of the thing and began to offer suggestions. They finally agreed that 'extrovert' and 'thespian' and 'nepotism' were the most suggestive of the lot." The "speech" began to make the rounds, but as it spread, it was Smathers who was supposed to have given the speech, not Pepper.[93]

Another theory involved William H. Lawrence of the *New York Times* and Stephen Trumbull of the *Miami Herald*. They covered the Florida campaign and often heard the same speech six times a day. Trumbull noted that reporters could fill in for the candidates in case of illness because they knew the speeches so well.[94] The two may have played with variations of the speech and begun substituting different words. After the election, Smathers offered a $10,000 reward to anyone who could prove that he actually delivered such a speech. No one ever claimed the money.

As the campaign neared its end, Pepper desperately needed help, and his supporters argued that he should seek an endorsement from Truman. Although Pepper maintained in his memoirs that Truman offered to campaign for him in 1950, there is absolutely no indication that Truman wanted Pepper to win reelection.[95] After all, Pepper tried to deny Truman the vice presidency in 1944 and the presidency in 1948. Every private statement Truman made about Pepper was disparaging, but the Pepper supporters saw Pepper as the champion of Truman's Fair Deal and assumed the president preferred Pepper to Smathers. In mid-April Truman vacationed in Key West but said nothing about the primary contest. He came back to the state to make an appearance in the Panhandle, but again there was no endorsement.

Pepper tried unsuccessfully to appeal to the Florida tradition of one senator representing South Florida and the other North Florida. It was a tradition dating back to the days when senators were chosen by the state legislature rather than the voters. Pepper said that to elect Smathers meant there would be no senator from North Florida. But the concept did not have any resonance with the voters.

Both candidates were required to file financial disclosure statements, although these bore little resemblance to reality. In 1949 the Florida Legislature removed spending limits for candidates, requiring only that candidates file two financial disclosure forms, one on April 22, the second on June 2. In the first statement, the two candidates said they spent a total of $74,481.62. Pepper listed $43,723.59 in contributions and Smathers $30,758.03. Each side claimed that the other really spent hundreds of thousands of dollars (Pepper eventually said Smathers spent two million dollars), but determining the actual amount spent is impossible. Both sides had too many free agents working on their behalf: Pepper had the CIO and the AFL, and Smathers had Ed Ball.[96]

One month before the election, most of the predictions indicated a Smathers victory. John Kilgore, the state's leading political writer, saw a Smathers win by 26,000 votes.[97] The *New York Times* reported the race was "rated a toss-up." Pepper had no polls to show that he was ahead, but continued to maintain that he would win the election.

By the time the campaign neared its end, tempers were frayed, and there were reports of violence. The *Miami Herald* counted four violent acts, with the worst one coming in Fort Meade, a heavily unionized town.[98] Smathers said that when he reached the city limits there were trucks across the road to stop his car. When he attempted to speak, he was told, "Get out of here," but he refused to leave. As he spoke, the crowd began heckling and throwing things. As he left the podium, a woman approached and spat tobacco juice in his eyes. Smathers said that he fell to his knees and the crowd began clapping and saying, "Give it to him again, give it to him."[99]

On the eve of the election, both candidates believed their strategy had triumphed. Smathers calculated that he needed to win a 30,000-vote margin in Dade County, his home, to carry him to victory. Pepper thought he could carry Dade, or even lose by a small margin, then carry Duval, Hillsborough, Monroe, and Pinellas Counties and do well in North and West Florida.[100]

An hour after the polls closed, it became clear that Pepper's reelection was in trouble. Florida secretary of state R. W. Gray predicted that 60 percent of the state's one million registered Democrats would turn out.[101] Instead, 70 percent of the voters cast ballots. Smathers received 387,215 votes and Pepper 319,784. The Smathers margin of 67,431 votes was far more than anyone envisioned. Pepper, receiving barely 45 percent of the vote, became the first Florida senator to lose a reelection bid.

Pepper conceded at 1:15 a.m. on May 3 with only about 20 percent of the precincts reporting but with Smathers ahead by 50,000 votes. In county after county Pepper saw his percentage of the vote decline from the 1944 election. In Hillsborough County (Tampa) his percentage was down 6.6 percent, in Dade 7.7 percent, and in Orange County, where the *Orlando Morning Sentinel* led the crusade against him, he lost 25 percent of his 1944 vote.

Even in the counties where Pepper had tremendous support from local politicians and newspapers, his results were dismal. In Volusia County, where he had the active support of the daily newspaper and the sheriff, he lost by 4.1 percent. He also lost in Pinellas County, where the *St. Petersburg Times* was Pepper's most eloquent champion. St. Lucie County went to Smathers despite the backing of Vero Beach mayor Alex MacWilliam. Only in a handful of small counties did Pepper do better than in 1944. The one thing Pepper could point to with pride was that he carried Smathers's home county, Dade—by 914 votes.

As the votes were being counted, reporters began to assess Pepper's defeat. The *St. Petersburg Times* reported, "The tide that swept Pepper into defeat really started when he aligned himself with Henry Wallace."[102] The *Nation* also saw Pepper's relationship with Wallace as the major reason for his defeat. "Pepper was vulnerable to charges of leftist affiliation which are applicable to no other candidate except Glen Taylor of Idaho. . . . He was left without the full backing of either the right or the left wing of his party."[103]

Life magazine blamed Pepper. "In 14 years in the Senate, in saying Communism was no real danger and the U.S. could make friends Pepper had become a cocky, perplexing figure. . . . After the war he persisted with Stalin, whom he had visited and liked."[104] To the *New Republic*, a Pepper supporter, "The defeat of Claude Pepper in Florida demonstrates the power of the smear. Senator Pepper was driven from the office he has held with honor and distinction for 14 years by an emotional appeal to the basest prejudices of the Florida voters."[105]

Washington columnist David Lawrence blamed the CIO for Pepper's defeat. "The CIO is unintentionally responsible. . . . The defeat of Senator Claude Pepper by Representative Smathers was a clear case of labor union interference in the affairs of the State of Florida and an unwise stirring up of friction between whites and Negroes." But Lawrence also saw the FEPC as a major factor, making the election a contest "between whites and Negroes."[106] For the *New York Times*, "The primary campaign did no credit to either of the contestants, nor was it a compliment to the intelligence of the voters. Senator Pepper seems to have based his appeal largely on his ability to wangle extensive financial benefits out of Washington . . . while Representative Smathers apparently spent much of his considerable energies in attacking Senator Pepper for being too friendly to Negroes and to Communists."[107]

Commonweal said both men ran tawdry campaigns but noted that "Pepper was vulnerable. He had a deadly record of friendliness towards the Soviet Union."[108] The *Christian Century* also saw both men as having fought in the gutter: "Each tried to outdo the other in proclaiming his devotion to white rule and his abhorrence of President Truman's civil rights program. We believe both Mr. Smathers and Mr. Pepper to be better men than their campaigning indicated."[109]

The *Tampa Daily Times* said that "Senator Pepper brought it on himself. His crushing defeat by Representative Smathers in yesterday's Democratic primary for the nomination for United States Senator is plainly traceable to his headlong and reckless course toward radicalism since his last election six years ago. . . . Florida is now in the vanguard of the march back to sanity and sobriety in national affairs. It was a day to make the judicious celebrate."[110]

Pepper himself thought the issue that beat him was race. He wrote to Herbert M. Davidson, publisher of the *Daytona Beach News Journal* (one of the two daily newspapers to support him), "That's what made the children in the schools display the antagonism which they manifested and it was the thing which stole away from us thousands of working men and women to whom I devoted myself and my political career." But Pepper added that Truman bore part of the blame: "The President told me some time ago that he wanted me to win and did what he could to help me without sticking his neck out. They didn't do much, if anything—a rather sad commentary upon the faithfulness which with I have supported the Administration."[111] Pepper wrote to Hugh DeLacy, the director of the Ohio Progressive Party, "No man in the South's history has ever gone as far and stayed in office as long as I. But they finally got me." Pepper said his loss was the result of "the combination of all the reactionary forces working in concert."[112]

Two days after Pepper's defeat, Truman was asked if the loss was a setback for the Fair Deal. He bluntly replied, "No." However, when asked about the defeat of Senator Frank Graham in North Carolina the following month, Truman said it was one of the "most serious losses for the administration."[113] Truman's assistant press secretary, Evan A. Ayers, noted in his diary on the day after the Florida primary that Truman mentioned that he doubted that Pepper would be renominated. Ayers quoted Truman as saying that Smathers "could have won if he [had] gone ahead on his record and never mentioned Pepper. . . . The president said he had told Smathers what he told us."

Nowhere was there praise of Smathers and the campaign he waged. Smathers ran a brilliant, flawless campaign, and yet the consensus was that Pepper was victimized by a brutal, unfair opponent. In his 1968 book *Gothic Politics in the Deep South: Stars of the New Confederacy*, author Robert Sherrill called his chapter on the 1950 primary "George Smathers, the South's Golden Hatchetman." Smathers spent the rest of his life explaining and defending what happened—and what people thought happened—during the 1950 campaign. Meanwhile Pepper, who strayed far from the Florida voters and who ran a miserable campaign, was viewed as the victim.

11

Aftermath

What is amazing is that Pepper did as well as he did. He managed to capture 45 percent of the vote in the primary despite more than six years of constant negative publicity. Moreover, Pepper did not receive a single break in the campaign; he had alienated the sitting president; he received national negative publicity for his stand on the Soviet Union; and he was opposed by a bright and attractive candidate who had all but two of the state's newspapers behind him and the support of business leaders and doctors.

Pepper needed a shift of just 34,000 votes to defeat Smathers. His victories in 1938 and 1944 gave him a false sense of security. He made dozens of mistakes, and avoiding any one of them could have changed the outcome.

What could Pepper have done to win the election of 1950?

If he had not antagonized Harry Truman by challenging him in 1944 and 1948, Truman might not have urged Smathers to run.

If he had not angered Ed Ball, Pepper might have retained Ball's support. His victory in 1944 convinced him that he could overcome the opposition of Ed Ball, even though Ball saw 1944 as just a trial run and spent six years preparing for 1950. Pepper's efforts to deny Ball control of the Florida East Coast Railway failed miserably. By challenging Ball's control of the railroad, he also angered the line's workers, who almost certainly would have voted for him, but who ended up not only voting against him but urging others to do the same. With the exception of

Dade County, Pepper lost every single county the Florida East Coast Railway passed through.

If he had not challenged the state's doctors, he would have avoided their grassroots campaign against him.

But Pepper's biggest mistake was in losing touch with his state. For six years he ignored the warning signs of discontent in Florida. The state's newspapers criticized him continually for his position on Russia, his friendship with Henry Wallace, and his liberal views. Between 1944 and 1950 he slowly lost support. In 1944 he received 51 percent of the vote in the Democratic primary. The next time around, he received 45 percent, a drop of just 6 points in six years. He did as well as he did in his final Senate primary because he was able to provide favors for thousands of constituents, there was still a strong appreciation of the New Deal in Florida, and Pepper was a great speaker who could still electrify a crowd.

In his classic study of politics, Samuel Lubell blamed the defeat of Pepper on three trends in the South in the late 1940s: the failure of labor's drive to organize southern workers (he said that Operation Dixie turned into Operation Fizzle), the rise of a more politically conservative middle class, and the reaction by whites to the increasing number of black voters.[1] Lubell found that although Pepper and Smathers were both Democrats, the contest was a trial run for an approaching Republican-southern alliance, with Smathers cast as the Republican and Pepper as the Democrat. He showed that in the North Carolina primary—where incumbent Frank Graham likewise lost—and in Florida, the precinct results were close to those in the 1948 presidential election. Smathers did well where Dewey and Strom Thurmond did well. He won the ten counties Dewey carried and the three counties Thurmond carried. Pepper did well in areas where Truman did well. Pepper ended with about the same percentage of the Florida vote as Truman.[2] But Truman ran in a four-candidate race, while Pepper had just one opponent.

Lubell's theory about the importance of race in the election was rejected by Hugh Douglas, who found that "Pepper's greatest loss of strength, in comparison to his successful 1944 campaign, was not in the racially sensitive Suwannee-Apalachicola region, but in the towns and small cities of Central Florida and the East Coast."[3] Herbert J. Doherty wrote that Smathers was able to take away the lower-class support that returned Pepper to office twice before. Doherty, in examining voting patterns in Florida, found that Pepper was particularly hurt in North Florida, "the section most receptive to Pepper's stand on economic questions but also the most susceptible to racist fears." Doherty also found, as others did, that Smathers did well among upper-income voters.[4]

The Republicans saw the victory as a defeat for the Truman administration. Republican National Chairman Guy Gabrielson said he was jubilant over the Smathers victory and claimed it marked a Republican trend away from Truman's Fair Deal.[5] Smathers fired back, "I campaigned as a Democrat who had a high record of the support of the Democratic Administration in the 80th and 81st Congresses."[6] He sent a telegram to Truman stating, "In my opinion our victory does not mean a trend toward Republicanism nor in any sense does it mean a repudiation of the Democratic Party or the Democratic principles, but rather a repudiation of extremism and radicalism. My record reveals that I am a liberal Democrat."[7] Truman wrote back, "I appreciate your telegram of the fourth and I was also highly pleased to receive the copy of the message which you sent to Mr. Gabrielson. . . . When I get back from the Western trip, I'll be glad to see and talk with you."[8]

The Pepper-Smathers campaign was over, but its legacy was to endure. In the years since 1950, the defeat of Claude Pepper has been attributed to McCarthyism and the fear of communism. It is important to note that Wisconsin senator Joseph McCarthy did not make his first speech on the subject until February 9, 1950, more than a month after the Florida campaign started and just three months before the Florida primary. By that time Smathers had already begun to hammer Pepper for his relationship with left-wing groups, closeness to Russia, support of the FEPC, and failure to denounce civil rights measures with enough vigor. It was Smathers, not McCarthy, who first showed how these issues could be used in a political campaign.

Smathers created a blueprint for other candidates to use. It was a blueprint that could be readily adapted to other campaigns in which a liberal Democrat was the opponent. For example, the FEPC issue and civil rights might be dropped in the North and West, but the communism issue worked well everywhere. Candidates used it for more than a decade, railing at the Democrats in Washington, and usually pointing to the State Department as a home for fellow travelers, communists, and left-wingers. McCarthy followed the traditional pattern, criticizing the Democratic administration for what he saw as foot-dragging in removing communists from government and for its liberal policies toward the Soviets, and demanding the removal of the bureaucrats he claimed were communists. What was different about Smathers's criticisms was his target: Smathers aimed his charges not at the Truman administration or at faceless bureaucrats but at his opponent. He linked Pepper to left-wing groups, communist fronts, and Russia. While never saying that Pepper was a communist, he left the clear impression that Pepper was either a dupe of the Russians, a deluded admirer of Joe Stalin, or perhaps a fellow traveler.

The theory that McCarthy was influential in securing the defeat of incumbent Democratic senators in 1950 has been questioned by a number of historians, including Robert Griffith, who asserted that, "though Pepper's loss resulted from plural causes, and McCarthyism was not the chief of them, some observers erroneously exaggerated the impact of Smathers's Red-baiting." Griffith argued that in all of the 1950 elections, "Thanks to the unique conditions that prevailed in 1950 and to miscalculations on the part of the press and the politicians, an overstated assessment of McCarthy's electoral influence was born. This exaggeration, by producing an expanded perception of McCarthy's power, ultimately enlarged his power itself."[9]

Griffith is correct is discounting the importance of McCarthyism in the Florida election, but he fails to understand that what Smathers did was different from McCarthy's tactics. And the results indicate that the Smathers approach was more effective than the McCarthy technique in defeating incumbent Democrats. The Florida primary was the earliest in the nation and, since Pepper's campaign in 1938, was seen as a weathervane, first for Roosevelt's New Deal, then for Truman's Fair Deal. A look at the 1950 Senate elections shows that those candidates who followed Smathers's plan of attacking opponents on a laundry list of issues, including links with the CIO, being soft on communism, and in some cases on racial issues, did well. Those who failed to link their Democratic opponent with communism, but simply attacked the

Truman administration and talked about communists in high government jobs, did not do as well.

The first place the Smathers method was tried following Pepper's defeat was in North Carolina, where challenger Willis Smith was struggling to unseat incumbent U.S. senator Frank Graham. The Florida results came three weeks before the North Carolina Democratic primary. According to historians Julian Pleasants and Gus Burns, Smith's supporters seized on the Pepper defeat as proof that Frank Graham could be beaten.[10] Jonathan Daniels, editor of the *Raleigh News and Observer* and a Graham supporter, tried to downplay the Florida results. He wrote that it would be similar to the Florida campaign only if one of the North Carolina candidates used Smathers's techniques. But Willis Smith was immediately heartened by the results and said the vote was a "great victory for levelheaded citizens."[11] Graham did have many of the same political weaknesses as Pepper. Like Pepper, he was involved with what many viewed as left-wing groups, and the CIO Political Action Committee operatives who worked hard—if not successfully—for Pepper had packed their bags and moved to North Carolina to "help" Graham. As in Florida, the CIO endorsement was a very mixed blessing, generating more opposition than support. Lubell, in his analysis of the election, found that the CIO support was the "kiss of defeat" for Graham in North Carolina.[12]

It had obviously not registered on the CIO leadership that its endorsement could be deadly for political candidates in the South. Smith seized the issue just as Smathers did in Florida, asserting that labor support meant that Graham supported their agenda, including the FEPC and socialized medicine.[13]

The CIO workers were not the only ones going north. Dan Crisp, the Ball operative who was so successful in helping to defeat Pepper, immediately moved to North Carolina to help Smith. Crisp claimed that he took with him money from supporters in Florida and literature used in the Smathers-Pepper race.[14]

In the first primary in North Carolina in late May, Graham came within a hair of winning, getting 49.1 percent of the vote, while Smith received 40 percent. Graham was just 5,673 votes short of avoiding a runoff.[15] A friend wrote to Graham, "What happened happily in the recent senatorial election in Florida would happen here but for the wide popular knowledge of your personal excellence."[16] Smith agonized over whether to call for a runoff, but in the end he decided to request one.

The second campaign lasted just seventeen days. Using a Pepper technique, Graham tried to label Smith as a Republican in disguise. Smith, like Smathers, railed against the FEPC and the CIO. Truman was clearly a Graham supporter, writing, "Graham must win—we can't possibly have a loss there."[17] But Smith's campaign gained strength, and he upset Graham in the runoff by 20,000 votes.

The Graham defeat illustrates how Truman felt toward Pepper. After the election, Truman became a one-person employment agency for Graham, offering him a number of jobs including the presidency of the American Red Cross. For Pepper, there was not a single job offer from Truman.[18]

The Smathers campaign method was also used in California by one of Smathers's closest friends, Richard Nixon. The relationship between Smathers and Nixon was unusual. Smathers, Nixon, and John Kennedy all came to Washington in the same Congress, members of the class of 1946. They were all veterans of the war, all served in the Pacific, and all were ambitious. Smathers became one of Kennedy's closest friends, and he also became friends with Nixon. It was Smathers who first invited Nixon to Miami and introduced him to Bebe Rebozo, who became Nixon's best friend. Smathers was an usher in Kennedy's wedding. When Nixon became president, he purchased the Smatherses' Key Biscayne home. Smathers had the ability to make anyone a friend. The outgoing Kennedy was attracted to Smathers just as the shy Nixon was.

In 1950, Nixon ran for the Senate against Democrat Helen Gahagan Douglas. The race was a carbon copy of the Florida election. When Smathers won in May, the headline in the *Los Angeles Herald Express* was "Nixon Jubilant." Nixon said, "I am confident that the people of California, like those in Florida, also will register their disapproval at the polls this year."[19] Like Pepper, Douglas was involved in left-wing causes and was susceptible to charges that she was overly friendly toward Russia. While visiting Florida in 1950, Nixon asked Smathers for his strategy in the Florida campaign. Nixon used the plan well. While Pepper was

"Red Pepper," Douglas became the "Pink Lady."[20] Nixon won a convincing victory.

Other 1950 elections were also affected by Smathers-style tactics. In Ohio, Senator Robert Taft successfully used the CIO-PAC as a whipping boy to help defeat Joseph T. Ferguson. A study found that Taft's overwhelming margin was the result of support from Catholics, Jews, and even labor union members, who resented labor's aggressive support of Ferguson.[21] In Idaho, Glen Taylor, who along with Pepper had been identified as the most left-wing member of the Senate, was particularly vulnerable. His primary challenger used the communism issue and made sure newspapers received copies of *The Red Record of Senator Claude Pepper*, which featured Taylor prominently. The *Daily Statesman* in Boise ran excerpts from the booklet. Taylor lost in a close battle.[22]

Even the Republican National Committee picked up on the Smathers campaign, producing a booklet called *Red Herring and Whitewash*, a pale imitation of *Red Record*, featuring pictures of communists and newspaper clippings about what the Republicans saw as the rising tide of communism.[23]

One of the most misleading postelection developments was the filing of financial forms by the candidates. Smathers reported collecting $63,767.75 and spending $63,711.88. Pepper claimed that he spent $78,644.81 but collected just $59,849.50.[24] Of course, neither side listed the in-kind contributions from rich businessmen, doctors, unions, and others with a stake in the outcome. The election was the first held in Florida without spending limits and was such a disaster that the legislature reformed the campaign spending rules. Both Pepper and Smathers claimed that the other spent much more money, and as the years passed, the amounts grew. Even before the election year began, there were predictions about the amount of money to be spent. The *Jewish Floridian* claimed that the du Pont interests were prepared to spend "millions" to defeat Pepper.[25] Each side could point to a big spender who was willing to come up with millions for one side or the other. Pepper had Jacksonville businessman Lou Wolfson on his side, and, of course, Smathers had Ball. But neither candidate seemed to have large amounts of money to spend. Pepper ran a traditional campaign of stumping and radio talks. Smathers also stumped, but, as he did in 1946, he relied on his Goon

Squad to carry much of the burden. Ball was never known for giving away money; rather, he was much better at encouraging others to contribute to causes he was interested in. The real amount of money spent was never known—even to the candidates themselves.

After losing in the May primary, Pepper spent eight months in the Senate as a lame duck. During that time he ran into Ed Ball at a Washington dinner sponsored by the Florida Industrial Council. The annual event brought together elected representatives, lobbyists, and Florida business leaders. Pepper was no longer seated at the head table, although Ball was. Pepper congratulated Ball on what Pepper called Ball's victory. Ball replied that he was happy to have won the last round. Pepper replied that perhaps it was not the last round. As the crowd fell silent, Ball yelled at Pepper, "Claude, if you ever run for public office in Florida again we'll lick you so bad you'll think this time was a victory."[26]

Late on the night of December 22, 1950, Pepper made his final speech to the Senate. It was a somber address. "This is the darkest period of American history, if not human history. It is the first time that through the dark, impenetrable veil of the future there is no glimmer of that light of hope, save the confidence that is our faith."[27]

Pepper found it difficult to adjust to life out of politics. His standing with the business community was such that they did not want him as an attorney or lobbyist, and his labor friends offered nothing. He joked, "I have returned to Tallahassee to represent the Florida Medical Association. Since they worked so hard to get me out of Washington and back to Tallahassee, they must want me to represent them."[28] He again entertained the idea of moving to New York and entering politics there, but Cardinal Francis J. Spellman discouraged him.[29] Pepper was not, however, through in politics. In 1952 he briefly considered running against Florida's other senator, Spessard Holland. In 1956 he gave serious thought to taking on Smathers in a rematch. He talked with his friends in labor and wrote in his diary, "I shall have to start early for '58, or abandon the idea of the senate again," but he knew that things had changed and reflected, "I guess it would not be the same as in the old days."[30] Pepper claimed that he asked a friend to meet with Smathers about promising support in a future race if Pepper stayed out of the 1956 primary. Pepper said Smathers was pleased by the approach and saw it as an opportunity to help his standing with labor. "If he double-crosses me, labor will be embittered against him in the future," Pepper wrote in his diary. "Smathers can be taken care of later if he does not show himself worthy of confidence."[31] He decided against challenging Smathers, but he ran in the Democratic primary in 1958 against Holland. As in 1950, he received about 45 percent of the vote.

In 1962 Pepper reentered national politics, winning election to the U.S. House of Representatives from a Miami district created as a result of the state's population growth in the 1960 census. There were four candidates for the Democratic nomination, with state senator W. C. Herrell considered the favorite. Herrell was part of the state's political machine and had the endorsement of the *Miami Herald*. As he had done with Roosevelt three decades earlier, Pepper campaigned as a complete supporter of President John Kennedy. He produced a polite letter from Kennedy expressing the hope that someday Pepper would return to office. Even though it was written before the district was created, Pepper claimed a Kennedy endorsement. He won the election without a runoff by 59 votes.

If Ball thought he had heard the last of Pepper in 1950, he was mistaken. Pepper joined forces with Wisconsin senator William Proxmire to strike at the heart of the Ball empire. Congress passed legislation to force charitable organizations, such as the one Ball ruled, to divest the controlling interest in businesses. For Ball, this meant parting with the majority control of his beloved Florida National Banks. Other legislation further limited the ability of Ball to use the Nemours Foundation of his late brother-in-law, Alfred du Pont, to create a largely tax-exempt business empire for himself.

Pepper also had some vindication in his feud with Ball over the Florida East Coast Railway. The railroad's union employees abandoned him in 1950—even campaigned against him—when he warned that they should not trust Ball. Once back in Washington, Pepper's view was substantiated. In September 1961, eleven unions served notice on the National Railroad Conference demanding wage increases and work rule changes. A special board established by Kennedy recommended a pay increase, and the unions and 192 railroads agreed to the proposal. But one railroad did not. Ball refused to go along with the national settlement, and 1,200 FEC personnel went on strike. The FEC workers, who had roundly rejected Pepper in favor of Ball, now found that Pepper had been right. Pepper declined to play an active role, and the strike became the longest-running work stoppage in the nation's history.

With an influx of Cuban refugees, the makeup of Pepper's district began to change. Pepper became strongly anticommunist, supporting the embargo against Cuba. No opponent would ever again be able to claim that he was helping communism. He also changed his position on civil rights, voting for both the Civil Rights Act of 1964 and the Voting Rights Act of 1965, and he held his House seat until his death in 1989.

George Smathers served three terms in the Senate, becoming one of its most popular members. Smathers was able to become close personal friends with three fellow senators who were known for their differences—Richard Nixon, John F. Kennedy, and Lyndon Johnson. He introduced Nixon to Miami, was in Kennedy's wedding, and was asked by Johnson to become Senate majority leader. But after Kennedy's 1963 assassination, the fun went out of politics for Smathers, and he did not seek reelection in 1968.[32] Much to his displeasure, the story about the speech he supposedly made using words such as "thespian" kept growing, becoming longer and funnier with each retelling. In 1954, William F. Buckley coauthored a book entitled *McCarthy and His Enemies* and quoted from what he said was Smathers's speech.[33] Smathers wrote that he never made the remarks. Buckley wrote back, "You will have a difficult time persuading the general public that you did not in fact make these remarks."[34]

Pepper had gambled with his Senate seat and lost. He bet that he could tailor his views to attract a national audience without losing his Florida constituency. It was not until the 1980s, when he became a champion of the elderly, that he was finally able to enjoy both a national reputation and a safe seat. Pepper's commitment to the New Deal led him to believe that it was the answer to both national and international problems. He did not see that the nation was moving away from the New Deal by the late 1940s, and that for many voters the New Deal became synonymous with bloated bureaucracy, government control, and excessive spending. On the international level, Pepper pushed for a loan to the Soviet Union as he would a New Deal spending program. He believed the loan would have allowed the Soviets to rebuild from World War II and be a peaceful member of the world community. Two decades later another New Deal stalwart, Lyndon Johnson, used the same strategy to try to bring the North Vietnamese to the negotiating table.

Pepper was in his sixties when he returned to Congress, a body where the seniority system is the most important element in advancing. When he was defeated in 1950, his emphasis was on foreign affairs. When he returned as a representative in 1963, he all but ignored international matters—except to rail at Fidel Castro's Cuba. As he did with Roosevelt's New Deal, he embraced Lyndon Johnson's Great Society, supporting dozens of programs and participating in the creation of many others. Just as it had been in the 1940s, his name again became a household term. In the 1970s, during the administration of Richard Nixon, the nation swung to the right, and this time Pepper went with the tide, becoming a crime fighter. In 1971, when there was rioting at the Attica Correctional Facility in upstate New York, Pepper showed up at the prison—with reporters in tow—to say he was launching an investigation. No matter what the mood of the nation, Pepper could find a way to gain maximum publicity.

He had first made the cover of *Time* magazine back in 1938 during his primary campaign for reelection to the Senate. Half a century later, he returned to the cover for his work in expanding social programs.

Smathers retired from the Senate in 1969, still mourning the death of his friend John Kennedy. He told his Senate colleagues, "I was too near the one we mourn to sum up his career and contributions. I regret I do not have the words for the poignancy of the loss I feel."[35]

While he devoted a great deal of time to improving relations with Latin America, Smathers rejected calls to take a leadership role in the Senate. In the remainder of his term after Kennedy's 1963 assassination, Smathers failed to take courageous stands during the debate on civil rights legislation. Although he never engaged in the virulent race baiting that marked so many Southern politicians, he was a reliable "no" vote on civil rights and other progressive legislation. As the civil rights movement gained strength, Smathers turned to the old tried-and-true southern chant of states' rights. In a letter to the *Miami Daily News*, Smathers said he was in favor of ending racial discrimination, but without the aid of the federal government—or, as he put it, "the intrusion of federal authorities."[36] The proposed legislation might "destroy this right of a man to control his own property," Smathers claimed, and "invade the right of privacy of every race, color and creed to a degree that would endanger basic principles of individual rights long established in our Constitution."[37]

When Pepper died in 1989 after twenty-seven years in the House, his passing was a national story and he was mourned on the front pages of newspapers. He had become a champion for the nation's elderly and supported the dramatic expansion of a host of social programs including Social Security, Medicare, and Medicaid. Millions of Americans receive a check every month because of legislation Pepper worked for.

Smathers died in 2007, largely forgotten. He had made a fortune in real estate and other business ventures, but despite being one of the best-liked men in the Senate, he left little political legacy. He remains best remembered for the 1950 campaign, and perhaps for the speech he never gave. When his obituary appeared in the nation's newspapers, it was pointed out correctly that he was an early and enthusiastic champion of the Alliance for Progress, which pumped billions of dollars into Latin America, and that he was one of the first in Washington to warn about the threat posed by Fidel Castro. But the obituaries also noted his opposition to civil rights reforms, his offer to post bail for Dr. Martin Luther King Jr. in St. Augustine if King promised to leave Florida, and The Speech. Although the obituaries used terms such as "according to legend" and "supposedly," and even included outright denials, they still offered excerpts from the speech that never was, using the sentences that were never said: "Are you aware that Claude Pepper is known all over Washington as a shameless extrovert? Not only that, but this man is reliably reported to practice nepotism with his sister-in-law, and he has a sister who was once a thespian in wicked New York. Worst of all, it is an established fact that Mr. Pepper before his marriage habitually practiced celibacy." It was a most unusual way to be remembered.

Notes

Chapter 1. The Making of a Liberal

1. "Biographical Sketch of Senator Pepper," in Claude D. Pepper Papers, Mildred and Claude Pepper Library, Florida State University, Tallahassee (hereafter Pepper Papers).

2. Stewart, "Serious Senator Pepper," 7.

3. Pepper, *Pepper*, 5.

4. *Radiator* (Camp Hill High School yearbook), 1917, Pepper Papers.

5. Pepper to Dorothy Sara, 16 August 1948, Pepper Papers.

6. *Miami Herald*, 18 October 1936.

7. Stewart, "Serious Senator Pepper," 7.

8. Pepper to former congressman William Joseph Sears Jr., 11 May 1940, Pepper Papers. *Miami Herald*, 18 October 1936.

9. Claude Pepper Harvard diary, 23 December 1922, Pepper Papers.

10. Stewart, "Serious Senator Pepper," 7.

11. Harvard diary (see note 9), 1 November 1921.

12. Harvard diary, 21 June 1922.

13. Pepper to parents, 16 February 1922, Pepper Papers.

14. Pepper to parents, 6 December 1922, Pepper Papers.

15. Pepper to Mrs. Frances Collinson, 4 December 1941, Pepper Papers.

16. Harvard diary, 19 November 1921.

17. Harvard diary, 7 May 1922.

18. Harvard diary, 25 December 1922.

19. Harvard diary, 6 May 1922.

20. Pepper to Julian Pennington, 11 April 1929, Pepper Papers.

21. Ibid.

22. Gannon, *Florida: A Short History*, 77.

23. Ibid.

24. Pepper to parents, n.d., Pepper Papers.
25. Gannon, *Florida: A Short History*, 82–83.
26. Pepper to Franklin D. Roosevelt, 22 December 1928, Pepper Papers.
27. Pepper, *Pepper*, 41–42.
28. *Perry Herald*, 5 June 1930.
29. Stewart, "Serious Senator Pepper," 8.
30. *Washington Herald*, 2 August 1934.
31. Pepper, 1934 announcement of candidacy, n.d., Pepper Papers.
32. John H. Perry to Oscar Johnson, 31 March 1934, Pepper Papers.
33. Pepper, campaign speech, n.d., Pepper Papers.
34. Florida, *Tabulation of . . . Democratic Primary Election, . . . 1934*, 3.
35. "Trammell for Senator Club," handbill, n.d., Pepper Papers.
36. *Ocala Morning Banner*, 20 June 1934.
37. Florida, *Tabulation* (see note 34), 8.
38. Pepper to Park Trammell, 28 June 1934, Pepper Papers.
39. Edwin D. Lambright to Pepper, 9 July 1934, Pepper Papers.
40. *Orlando Morning Sentinel*, 7 August 1934.
41. *Leesburg Commercial*, 16 October 1936.

Chapter 2. The Junior Senator

1. Davidson et al., *Nation of Nations*, 731.
2. Leuchtenburg, *Roosevelt and the New Deal*, 235.
3. Ibid., 236.
4. *Congressional Record*, 75th Cong., 2nd sess., 1937, 82: 167.
5. *Congressional Record*, 75th Cong., 3rd sess., 1938, 83: 975.
6. Kabat, "From New Deal to Red Scare," 70.
7. Weiss, *Farewell to the Party of Lincoln*, 35–40.
8. Pepper radio address, manuscript, 12 November 1937, Pepper Papers.
9. Ibid.
10. *Lake Wales News*, 13 January 1938.
11. *Miami Herald*, 7 February 1938.
12. Mark Wilcox, 1938 campaign flier, Pepper Papers.
13. Burns, *Roosevelt: The Lion and the Fox*, 343.
14. Pepper to George A. Smathers, 4 January 1938, Pepper Papers.
15. Smathers to Pepper, n.d., Pepper Papers.
16. *Time*, 2 May 1938, cover.
17. Florida, *Tabulation of . . . Democratic Primary Election, . . . 1938*, 1.
18. Pepper to Franklin D. Roosevelt, 4 May 1968, Pepper Papers.
19. *Congressional Record*, 76th Cong., 1st sess., 1939, 84: 11165–11168.
20. "The Effigy," *Time*, 2 September 1940, 14.
21. Entry for 28 August 1940 in Personal Diaries, 1937–49, Mildred and Claude D. Pepper Foundation, McLean, Virginia (hereafter Pepper Diaries).
22. Pepper to George Atkins, 2 April 1943, Pepper Papers.
23. Burns, *The Crosswinds of Freedom*, 153.

24. Turner Catledge, "We Take Action 'Short of War' to Aid Allies," *New York Times*, 9 June 1940.

25. *Congressional Record*, 76th Cong., 3rd sess., 1940, 86: 7577.

26. Wesley Price, "Pink Pepper," *Saturday Evening Post*, 13 August 1946, 117.

27. *Tampa Morning Tribune*, 7 October 1940.

28. "The Effigy," *Time*, 2 September 1940, 14.

29. Pepper speech, 17 July 1939, Pepper Papers.

30. *Congressional Record*, 79th Cong., 1st sess., 1945, 91: 8069.

31. Nixon, "Changing Political Philosophy of the South," 247.

32. Grantham, *Solid South*, 102.

33. Biles, *South and the New Deal*, 151.

34. Freedman, *Roosevelt and Frankfurter*, 282–283.

35. Grantham, *Solid South*, 119.

36. Cooper and Terrill, *The American South*, 684.

37. Grantham, *Solid South*, 115.

38. Tindall, *Emergence of the New South*, 103–104.

Chapter 3. Making Enemies

1. Mason and Harrison, *Confusion to the Enemy*, 8.

2. Ibid., 20.

3. *Wilmington Morning News*, 19 March 1974.

4. Lincoln, "The Terrible Tempered Mr. Ball," 158.

5. Ed Ball to Pepper, 5 January 1944, Pepper Papers.

6. Danese, "Claude Pepper and Ed Ball," 199–201.

7. "Syndicate to Sell East Coast Bonds," *New York Times*, 5 August 1942.

8. "Tax Bill Veto Message," *New York Times*, 23 February 1944.

9. Danese, "Claude Pepper and Ed Ball," 201.

10. Ibid., 206.

11. Ibid.

12. Pepper Diaries, 23 February 1944.

13. Pepper Diaries, 24 February 1944.

14. Danese, "Claude Pepper and Ed Ball," 208.

15. "President Asked to Spare Army Hospital and Stop Order to Give Up Palm Beach Hotel," *New York Times*, 8 April 1944.

16. Ibid.

17. "Roosevelt Landslide Foreseen by Pepper," *New York Times*, 7 October 1944.

18. Danese, *Claude Pepper and Ed Ball*, 148.

19. Ibid., 210–211.

20. Spessard L. Holland to Ed Ball, 3 July 1958, box 812, file 77, Spessard Holland Papers, Florida State University, Tallahassee.

21. "Statement Regarding Reorganization Proceedings of the Florida East Coast Railway by the Trustees of the Alfred I. duPont Estate," July 1947, Pepper Papers.

22. Interstate Commerce Commission, Finance Docket 13170, 252 ICC 423, 1942, Pepper Papers.

23. Interstate Commerce Commission, Finance Docket 13170, in re Florida East Coast Railway Reorganization, "Memorandum by Senator Claude Pepper of Florida in support of a rehearing in this case, filed in his capacity as a citizen of Florida and on behalf of the public," 13 April 1945, Pepper Papers.

24. Danese, "Claude Pepper and Ed Ball," 216.

25. St. Augustine Chamber of Commerce, "Why the Florida East Coast RWY. Should Be an Independent Railroad," Pepper Papers.

26. Champion Davis to Pepper, 1 November 1945, Pepper Papers.

27. Pepper to James C. Clements, 3 November 1945, Pepper Papers.

28. *Jacksonville Journal*, 6 November 1945.

29. Transcript of Interstate Commerce Commission hearing, October 9, 1946, 4599–4601, Pepper Papers.

30. Pepper to Moorman M. Parrish, 29 December 1945, Pepper Papers.

31. Ollie Edmunds to Fred M. Ivey, 20 January 1934, Pepper Papers.

32. Mrs. Ronald Slye, interview by Evans Johnson, 13 June 1985.

33. Crosby S. Haddock Sr., interview by author, 15 December 1985.

34. Key, *Southern Politics in State and Nation*, 98.

35. *Miami Herald*, 25 April 1944.

36. Slye, interview.

37. Sherrill, "Golden Hatchetman," 143–144.

38. *Orlando Morning Sentinel*, 2 May 1944.

39. Wallace, *The Price of Vision*, 328.

40. *Pensacola Journal*, 25 March 1944.

41. *Jacksonville Journal*, 21 March 1944.

42. *DeLand Sun News*, 29 April 1944.

43. *Miami Daily News*, 5 April 1944.

44. *Orlando Morning Sentinel*, 29 March 1944.

45. *DeLand Sun News*, 12 April 1944.

46. *Florida Chief* (Winter Haven), 13 April 1944.

47. *Lakeland Ledger*, 7 April 1944.

48. *Miami Herald*, 1 April 1944.

49. *St. Petersburg Times*, 10 May 1944.

50. Haddock, interview.

51. *Orlando Morning Sentinel*, 26 April 1944.

52. Grismer, *Story of St. Petersburg*, 142–143.

53. Ibid.

54. Florida, *Tabulation of . . . Democratic Primary Election, . . . 1944*, 6.

55. Lincoln, "The Terrible Tempered Mr. Ball," 158.

Chapter 4. The Search for Peace

1. Pepper to Raymond Robins, 28 January 1942, Pepper Papers.

2. Senate Resolution 135, *Congressional Record*, 78th Cong., 1st sess., 1943.

3. Pepper to Sherman Minton, 10 March 1945, Pepper Papers.

4. Pepper to Robins, 21 May 1945, Pepper Papers.

5. *Chicago Sun Times*, 22 July 1944.

6. Pepper Diaries, 28 January 1945.

7. Pepper to Minton, 10 March 1945, Pepper Papers.

8. Franklin Roosevelt to Pepper, 9 April 1945, Pepper Papers.

9. McCullough, *Truman*, 220.

10. Pepper Diaries, 24 and 29 April 1945.

11. Goulden, *The Best Years*, 61.

12. Chafe, *The Unfinished Journey*, 82.

13. Hamilton, *Lister Hill*, 133.

14. P. Griffith, "Truman and the Historians," 34.

15. Hartmann, *Truman and the 80th Congress*, 113–214.

16. Donovan, *Conflict and Crisis*, 113.

17. Chafe, *The Unfinished Journey*, 81.

18. Wallace, *The Price of Vision*, 575.

19. Goulden, *The Best Years*, 61.

20. Diggins, *The Proud Decades*, 101.

21. *Congressional Record*, 79th Cong., 2nd sess., 1946, 92: 5819–5822.

22. Wallace, *The Price of Vision*, 575.

23. Ibid., 464–465.

24. Unsigned memorandum to Pepper, 30 July 1945, Pepper Papers.

25. Walker, *The Cold War*, 29–30.

26. Ibid.

27. Pepper Diaries, 25 July 1941.

28. *American Forum of the Air*, radio transcript, 5 June 1945, Pepper Papers.

29. *American Forum of the Air*, radio transcript, 18 January 1945, Pepper Papers.

30. "Pepper Off to Europe," *New York Times*, 15 August 1945.

31. Pepper, "Stalin Voices Aim for Amity and Aid of U.S. in the Peace," *New York Times*, 1 October 1945.

32. Pepper, "Russia in Transition," newspaper column, 27 September 1945, Pepper Papers.

33. Kennan, *Memoirs, 1925–1950*, 278.

34. Embassy of the USSR, information bulletin, 2 October 1945, Pepper Papers.

35. See note 31.

36. Ibid.

37. See note 32.

38. Pepper, notes, 14 September 1945, Pepper Papers.

39. Ibid.

40. *Daily Worker*, 7 February 1945.

41. *Fort Lauderdale News*, 21 September 1945.

42. Moorman M. Parrish to James C. Clements, 20 November 1945, Pepper Papers.

43. R. K. Lewis to Robert W. Fokes, 22 October 1945, Pepper Papers.

44. Pepper to Parish, 17 December 1945, Pepper Papers.

45. Walker, *The Cold War*, 31.

46. Ibid., 36–37.

47. Gaddis, *Origins of the Cold War*, 284.

48. Ibid., 289.

49. Ibid., 299.

50. Hamby, *Beyond the New Deal*, 154.

51. Diggins, *The Proud Decades*, 105.

52. *Daily Worker*, 27 February 1946.

53. Gaddis, *Origins of the Cold War*, 309.

54. *Congressional Record*, 79th Cong., 2nd sess., 1946, 92: 2463.

55. *Daily Worker*, 21 March 1946.

56. *Congressional Record*, 79th Cong., 2nd sess., 1946, 92: 3087.

57. Gaddis, *Origins of the Cold War*, 315.

58. Leffler, *A Preponderance of Power*, 106.

59. "Pepper's Apology Demanded," *New York Times*, 6 April 1946.

60. *Daily Worker*, 6 April 1946.

61. "Soviet Press Hails Iranian Oil Treaty," *New York Times*, 10 April 1946.

62. *Washington Post*, 10 April 1946.

63. Pepper, "A Program for Peace," 471.

64. Department of State (Moscow embassy), telegram to Secretary of State, 28 June 1945, in Federal Bureau of Investigation, Claude D. Pepper file (hereafter FBI Pepper file), 94-4-684-47.

65. D. M. Ladd to J. Edgar Hoover, 1 May 1946, FBI Pepper file, 94-4-684-54.

66. Hoover to Brigadier General Harry Vaughan, 9 May 1946, FBI Pepper file.

67. Ladd to Hoover, 28 March 1947, FBI Pepper file.

68. Ibid.

69. Ibid.

70. Latham, *Communist Controversy in Washington*, 110, 121.

71. Sayers and Kahn, *Great Conspiracy Against Russia*, 1.

72. Pepper to Robins, 5 June 1946, Pepper Papers.

Chapter 5. The Controversial Politician

1. "More Third Party Talk," *Daily Worker*, 6 June 1946.

2. "Senator Pepper's Emergence as Champion of Left-Wing Groups," *United States News*, 7 June 1946, 56.

3. *Washington Times-Herald*, 12 September 1946.

4. "Pink Pepper," *Saturday Evening Post*, 31 August 1946, 19, 118.

5. Editorial, "The Democratic Keynote," *Hartford Courant*, 17 September 1946.

6. Pepper Diaries, 23 August 1946.

7. *United States News*, 27 September 1946, 64–65.

8. *Newsweek*, 30 September 1946, 29.

9. *American Mercury*, October 1946, 389, 396.

10. *Medical Economics*, October 1946, 73–81.

11. Pepper, speech to the American-Soviet Institute, 7 May 1946, Pepper Papers.

12. *Daily People's World*, 2 September 1946.

13. *Newsweek*, 20 September 1946, 29.

14. Paterson, *Cold War Critics*, 120–122.

15. Francis E. Townsend to Pepper, 15 August 1946, Pepper Papers. Dexter, "Wanted: A Leader," 108.

16. United Press, 13 August 1946, Box 56, President's Secretary's Files, in Papers of Harry S. Truman, Harry S. Truman Library, Independence, Missouri (hereafter Truman Papers).

17. *Boston Herald*, 10 October 1946.

18. *Detroit Free Press*, 26 October 1946.

19. Hamby, *Beyond the New Deal*, 154.

20. Donovan, *Conflict and Crisis*, 223.

21. James A. Hagerty, "Wallace Warns on 'Tough' Policy Toward Russia," *New York Times*, 13 September 1946.

22. Ibid.

23. "Russian Radio Thanks Wallace and Pepper," *New York Times*, 17 September 1946.

24. Gaddis, *The Long Peace*, 341.

25. Donovan, *Conflict and Crisis*, 229.

26. Ibid., 230.

27. *Lakeland Ledger*, 16 September 1946.

28. William S. White, "Party Campaign Ban Shaped for Both Wallace, Pepper," *New York Times*, 21 September 1946.

29. "Pepper Hits Back at Party's 'Purge,'" *New York Times*, 23 September 1946.

30. Jay Walz, "GOP Sees Wallace a Blow to the Peace," *New York Times*, 23 September 1946.

31. Pepper Diaries, 24 September 1944.

32. "Pepper Demands Help for Labor," *New York Times*, 18 September 1946.

33. *Miami Herald*, 18 September 1946.

34. Pepper to Raymond Robins, 14 October 1946, Pepper Papers.

35. *New York News*, 5 November 1946.

36. *New York Mirror*, 5 November 1946.

37. Shalett, "The Paradoxical Mr. Pepper," 71.

38. Pepper to Mike Monroney, 23 October 1946, Pepper Papers.

39. Pepper Diaries, 20 September 1946.

40. Pepper Diaries, 2 June 1946.

41. Pepper Diaries, 4 November 1946.

42. Special Agent in Charge to J. Edgar Hoover, FBI Pepper file, 64-4480-467.

43. Charles E. Marsh to Pepper, n.d., Pepper Papers.

44. Robins to Carleton, 10 August 1945, William G. Carleton Papers, P. K. Yonge Library of Florida History, University of Florida.

45. Salzman, *Reform and Revolution*, 365.

46. *Tampa Morning Tribune*, 18 July 1949.

47. Salzman, *Reform and Revolution*, 374–376.

48. Carleton to Raymond Robins, 27 February 1946, Pepper Papers.

49. *PM*, 7 January 1947.

50. Pepper to Robins, 9 January 1947, Pepper Papers.

51. *Tampa Morning Tribune*, 9 January 1947.

52. *Chicago Star*, 1 March 1947.

53. National Catholic Welfare Conference, *Newsletter*, 21 March 1947.

54. *New York World Telegram*, 22 April 1947.

55. "Red Pepper," *Newsweek*, 7 April 1947, 25.

56. Cohen, *America in the Age of Soviet Power*, 38–39.

57. Leffler, "American Conception of National Security," 368.

58. *Congressional Record*, 80th Cong., 1st sess., 1947, 93: 3281–3289.

59. Ibid., 3592.

60. Pepper, column for Florida newspapers, 27 March 1947, Pepper Papers.

61. *Miami Herald*, 9 March 1947.

62. Pepper to Robins, 5 May 1947, Pepper Papers.

63. "Red Pepper," *Newsweek*, 7 April 1947, 25.

64. Ibid.

65. C. P. Trussell, "Pepper Embroils Senate on Russia," *New York Times*, 18 April 1947.

66. Pepper to Robins, 5 May 1947, Pepper Papers.

67. Ibid.

68. *Newsweek*, 12 May 1947, 29.

Chapter 6. Pepper and the 1948 Election

1. "Democrats: Through the Looking Glass," *Time*, 25 August 1947, 16.

2. Ibid.

3. Pepper to Sherman Minton, 14 September 1947, Pepper Papers.

4. Pepper to William Carleton, 30 June 1947, Pepper Papers.

5. Carleton to Pepper, 22 March 1946, Pepper Papers.

6. Pepper to Raymond Robins, 6 March 1948, Pepper Papers.

7. *Miami Herald*, 3 August 1947.

8. *Miami Herald*, 12 September 1948.

9. *Orlando Morning Sentinel*, 10 January 1948.

10. Florida Democratic Club, "Statement of Policy," n.d., Pepper Papers.

11. Chester Dishong to Pepper, 2 April 1948, Pepper Papers.

12. Pepper to John G. Ward, 16 February 1948, Pepper Papers.

13. *Washington Evening Star*, 29 March 1948.

14. Pepper to Robins, 6 March 1948, Pepper Papers.

15. Pepper, press release, 24 January 1948, Pepper Papers.

16. Pepper to James C. Sheppard, 10 June 1948, Pepper Papers.

17. Kabat, "From New Deal to Red Scare," 247.

18. "Students Group Asks Douglas Head Ticket," *New York Times*, 19 April 1948.

19. *Los Angeles Post*, 14 April 1948.

20. Clayton Knowles, "Truman Expected to Ease Zion Blow," *New York Times*, 24 March 1948.

21. Pepper to Robins, 6 March 1948, Pepper Papers.

22. *Miami Herald*, 1 April 1948.

23. Florida Democratic Club, "Sample Ballot," n.d., Pepper Papers.

24. *Tampa Daily Times*, 9 June 1948.

25. Pepper to Robins, 28 May 1948, Pepper Papers.

26. Ibid.

27. *Miami Herald*, 2 May 1948.

28. A. H. Raskin, "Clothing Workers Condemn 3d Party," *New York Times*, 14 May 1948.

29. Pepper to Robins, 28 May 1948, Pepper Papers.

30. Ibid.

31. Leonard Finder to Pepper, 26 June 1948, Pepper Papers.

32. Pepper to Raymond A. deGroat, 7 June 1948, Pepper Papers.

33. Ross, *The Loneliest Campaign*, 112.

34. Tilford E. Dudley, memorandum, n.d., in Jack Kroll Papers, Library of Congress, Washington, D.C. (hereafter Kroll Papers).

35. McCullough, *Truman*, 635.

36. Warren Moscow, "Eisenhower Says He Couldn't Accept Nomination," 6 July 1948.

37. James Roosevelt to Pepper, 5 July 1948, Pepper Papers.

38. Warren Moscow, "O'Dwyer Abandons Stop-Truman Move," *New York Times*, 9 July 1948.

39. Pepper to Dwight D. Eisenhower, 6 July 1948, Pepper Papers.

40. "Pepper Proposes New Party Policy," *New York Times*, 7 July 1948.

41. Truman diary, 6 July 1948, Truman Papers.

42. Eisenhower to Pepper, 9 July 1948, Pepper Papers.

43. Pepper, *Pepper*, 164.

44. Ross, *The Loneliest Campaign*, 83.

45. Donovan, *Conflict and Crisis*, 401.

46. James A. Hagerty, "Pepper Gets Wire," *New York Times*, 10 July 1948.

47. Dudley memo (see note 35), Kroll Papers.

48. Ibid.

49. Ibid.

50. Ibid.

51. Ibid.

52. "Truman Foes Hint Ballots for Pepper," *New York Times*, 11 July 1948.

53. Pepper, *Pepper*, 166.

54. Ibid.

55. W. H. Lawrence, "Pepper Comes Out as a Truman Rival," *New York Times*, 12 July 1948.

56. *New York World Telegram*, 12 July 1948.

57. Dudley memo (see note 35), Kroll Papers.

58. Ibid.

59. *New York World Telegram*, 12 July 1948.

60. W. H. Lawrence, "Oratory Is Torrid," *New York Times*, 13 July 1948.

61. *St. Petersburg Times*, 12 July 1948.

62. See note 56; William S. White, "Texas Unit Fights Bolt from Truman," *New York Times*, 13 July 1948.

63. Pepper Diaries, 6 December 1940.

64. *Fort Lauderdale News*, 13 July 1948.

65. *Miami Daily News*, 12 July 1948.

66. *Tampa Morning Tribune*, 12 July 1948.

67. *Miami Herald*, 13 July 1948.

68. *Lake Worth Leader*, 13 July 1948.

69. *St. Petersburg Times*, 12 July 1948.

70. Truman to A. J. Angle, 12 July 1948, Truman Papers.

71. Pepper, handwritten note, n.d., Pepper Papers.

72. "Pepper Withdraws to Avoid Bolt Tie," *New York Times*, 14 July 1948.

73. *New York Herald Tribune*, 14 July 1948.

74. Pepper to William Carlton, 12 August 1948, Pepper Papers.

75. Ibid.

76. *Miami Daily News*, 16 July 1948.

77. A. J. Angle to Truman, 14 September 1948, Truman Papers.

78. Angle to Pepper, 1 November 1948, Pepper Papers.

79. Ibid.

80. *Fort Lauderdale News*, 23 July 1948.

81. Truman to Mrs. Frank Smathers, 29 November 1948, Truman Papers.

82. Paterson, *Cold War Critics*, 132–134.

Chapter 7. The Opponent

1. George Smathers, interview by Donald Ritchie, 1 August 1989, Senate Historical Office, Washington, D.C.

2. Ibid.

3. Smathers, interview by author, 27 February 1987.

4. *Miami Daily News*, 7 May 1941.

5. *Miami Herald*, 10 May 1941.

6. *Miami Herald*, 12 July 1941.

7. *Miami Herald*, 25 July 1941.

8. Ibid.

9. *Miami Herald*, 10 May 1941.

10. Smathers, interview by author, 27 February 1987.

11. Crispell, *Testing the Limits*, 10.

12. Memo, William Paisley to Tom C. Clark, 6 June 1945, in Attorney General files, box 73, papers of Tom C. Clark, Harry S. Truman Library, Independence, Missouri (hereafter Clark Papers).

13. Smathers to Clark, 2 July 1945, Clark Papers.

14. Crispell, "Smathers and the Politics of Cold War," 21.

15. *Miami Herald*, 29 April 1946, 1 May 1946.

16. *Miami Herald*, 1 May 1946.

17. *Palm Beach Post*, 30 September 1945.

18. Smathers to Grace Stuart, n.d., Clark Papers.

19. Crispell, *Testing the Limits*, 15.

20. *Miami Herald*, 6 January 1946.

21. *Miami Herald*, 27 January 1949.

22. Goulden, *The Best Years*, 229.

23. *Miami Herald*, 7 February 1946.

24. *Miami Herald*, 6 February 1946.

25. "George Smathers speech, n.d., George Smathers Papers, University of Florida Library, Gainesville (hereafter Smathers Papers).

26. Ibid.

27. *Miami Herald*, 27 April 1946.

28. *Miami Daily News*, 1 May 1946.

29. Crispell, *Testing the Limits*, 25.

30. *Miami Herald*, 2 April 1946. McGill, "Can He Purge Senator Pepper?" 33.

31. *Miami Herald*, 4 May 1946.

32. *Miami Herald*, 7 May 1946.

33. Crispell, *Testing the Limits*, 25.

34. *Miami Daily News*, 30 April 1946.

35. Memo, 8 October 1946, box 561, President's Personal File, Truman Papers.

36. Colburn, *From Yellow Dog Democrats to Red State Republicans*, 28–29.

37. *Miami Daily News*, 8 November 1948.

38. Pepper to James Flanagan, 28 February 1949, Pepper Papers.

39. Pepper to Raymond Robins, 13 May 1949, Pepper Papers.

40. Ibid.

41. Pepper to Robins, 22 August 1949, Pepper Papers.

42. Senate Committee on Labor and Public Welfare, *Labor Relations, Hearings on S.249*, 81st Cong., 1st sess., 1949, 2370.

43. *Washington Evening Star*, 20 February 1949.

44. *Tampa Morning Tribune*, 23 February 1949.

45. *Orlando Morning Sentinel*, 3 September 1949.

46. Smathers, interview by author, 27 February 1987.

47. Transcript of Truman-Smathers meeting, 10 August 1949, official file, box 977, Truman Papers.

48. Smathers, interview by author, 27 February 1987.

49. Smathers, interview by Tracy E. Danese, 4 June 1996.

50. Danese, "Claude Pepper and Ed Ball," 293.

51. Ibid., 293–294.

52. McGill, "Can He Purge Senator Pepper?" 33.

53. *Orlando Morning Sentinel*, 4 September 1949.

54. Smathers, interview by author, 27 February 1987.

55. *Miami Herald*, 13 November 1949.

56. Pepper, *Pepper*, 196.

57. Pepper to Robins, 22 August 1949, Pepper Papers.

58. Pepper to Robins, 17 October 1949, Pepper Papers.

59. *Los Angeles Daily News*, 6 April 1948.

Chapter 8. The Campaign Begins

1. Gannon, *New History of Florida*, 328.

2. Cooper, *Air-Conditioning America*, 143.

3. Arsenault and Mormino, "From Dixie to Dreamland," 162.

4. Scicchitano and Scher, "Florida: Political Change," 229.

5. *Miami Herald*, 13 January 1950, 14 January 1950.

6. *Miami Herald*, 13 January 1950.

7. *Miami Herald*, 18 January 1950.

8. Smathers to Matthew J. Connelly, 19 January 1950, Truman Papers.

9. *Congressional Quarterly*, 10 February 1950, 140–141.

10. *St. Petersburg Times*, 14 January 1950.

11. *Miami Herald*, 27 January 1950.

12. Ibid.

13. Key, *Southern Politics in State and Nation*, 98.

14. *Tampa Morning Tribune*, 3 March 1950.

15. Ibid.

16. Pepper, campaign speech, 2 March 1950, Pepper Papers.

17. *Miami Herald*, 11 March 1950.

18. *St. Petersburg Times*, 22 January 1950.

19. FBI memo, 14 October 1949, FBI Pepper file, 94-4-684-69.

20. *Miami Herald*, 19 April 1950.

21. *Miami Herald*, 6 April 1950.

22. James Horrell, campaign report, n.d., Smathers Papers.

23. "Information from the Files of the Committee on Un-American Activities," 18 November 1949, Smathers Papers.

24. *Miami Herald*, 12 March 1950.

25. *Miami Herald*, 26 April 1950.

26. *Miami Herald*, 23 February 1950.

27. *Miami Herald*, 2 April 1950.

28. *Miami Herald*, 31 March 1950.

29. *Tallahassee Democrat*, 26 April 1950.

30. *Tallahassee Democrat*, 1 May 1950.

31. Smathers to D. A. Dixon, 7 April 1950, Pepper Papers.

32. Smathers to Al Block, 18 January 1950, Pepper Papers.

33. Smathers to Blanche M. Maddox, 23 January 1950, Pepper Papers.

34. Smathers, "Smathers-Gram," n.d., Pepper Papers.

35. Smathers to Hugh McArthur, 26 January 1950, Pepper Papers.

36. *Miami Herald*, 10 April 1950.

37. *Pensacola Journal*, 13 April 1950.

38. *St. Augustine Observer*, 22 April 1950.

39. Smathers, interview by author, 27 February 1987.

40. Special Agent in Charge, Miami, to Hoover, 22 April 1950, FBI Pepper file, 94-4-684-71.

41. Lincoln, "The Terrible Tempered Mr. Ball," 159.

42. *Florida Times-Union*, 31 March 1950.

43. *Miami Herald*, 30 April 1950.

44. *Jacksonville Journal*, 4 March 1950; Rose, *The Cold War Comes to Main Street*, 22.

45. Morgan, *Reds*, 310–311.

46. Pleasants and Burns, *1950 Senate Race in North Carolina*, 97.

47. R. Griffith, "Truman and the Historians," 30.

48. Schrecker, *The Age of McCarthyism*, 7–8.

49. Fried, "Electoral Politics and McCarthyism," 194.

50. *Miami Herald*, 4 April 1950.

51. Pepper, radio address, 18 September 1945, Pepper Papers.

52. Weisberger, *Cold War, Cold Peace*, 119.

53. Theoharis, *Seeds of Repression*, 28–192.

54. *Daily Worker*, 9 April 1950.

55. *Miami Herald*, 9 April 1950.

56. *Miami Herald*, 11 April 1950.

57. Ibid.

58. Ross C. Beiler to Pepper, 23 March 1950, Pepper Papers.

59. W. H. Lawrence, "Pepper Campaigns on Roosevelt Ties," *New York Times*, 9 April 1950.

60. *Life*, 15 May 1950, 40–41.

61. *St. Petersburg Times*, 2 April 1950.

62. Goulden, *The Best Years*, 313.

63. *Florida Times-Union*, 1 May 1950.

Chapter 9. The Campaign and Civil Rights

1. *Miami Herald*, 5 April 1944.

2. *Congressional Record*, 75th Cong., 2nd sess., 1937, 8757.

3. Marable, *Race, Reform and Rebellion*, 14.

4. F. Murray, *The Negro Handbook, 1949*, 102–103.

5. Berman, *Politics of Civil Rights*, 45–46.

6. *Miami Herald*, 12 February 1950.

7. Workers Defense League report, April 1949, Workers Defense League Papers, Reuther Library, Wayne State University.

8. Lawson, Colburn, and Paulson, "Groveland," 4.

9. *Orlando Morning Sentinel*, 21 July 1949.

10. *St. Petersburg Times*, 2 April 1950.

11. Jesse Walton Hunter to Pepper, 26 March 1949, Pepper Papers.

12. Douglas, "The Negro and Florida Politics," 200.

13. NAACP papers, part 4, reel 6, Library of Congress, Washington, D.C.

14. Ibid.

15. *Miami Times*, 19 November 1949.

16. Clayton Knowles, "South in Congress Backs Rights Test," *New York Times*, 9 February 1948.

17. Pepper Diaries, 6 March 1948.

18. *Meet the Press* transcript, 9 March 1949, Pepper Papers.

19. *Florida Alligator*, 17 December 1948.

20. Campaign memorandum, n.d., Pepper Papers.

21. *Miami Herald*, 23 April 1950.

22. Billington, *Political South*, 83–84.

23. *Miami Herald*, 14 March 1950.

24. *Miami Herald*, 2 April 1950.

25. *Florida Times-Union*, 14 March 1950.

26. *Tampa Morning Tribune*, 7 March 1950.

27. *Florida Times-Union*, 17 February 1950.

28. *Miami Herald*, 1 April 1950.

29. *Miami Herald*, 31 March 1950.

30. *Tallahassee Democrat*, 20 January 1950.

31. Joseph McMurray, statement, 11 April 1950, Pepper Papers.

32. *Tampa Morning Tribune*, 7 March 1950.

33. "Claude Pepper and the Compulsory FEPC," campaign memorandum, n.d. [1950], Pepper Papers.

34. *Miami Herald*, 27 January 1950.

35. *Florida Times-Union*, 16 March 1950.

36. Draft of Smathers speech, 16 February 1950, Smathers Papers.

37. Douglas, "The Negro and Florida Politics," 217.

38. *New York Times*, 8 April 1950.

39. *St. Petersburg Times*, 8 April 1950.

40. "An Important Message to Our Negro Citizens," n.d., Pepper Papers.

41. Sloan McCrea to Jim Clements, n.d., Pepper Papers.

42. Clements to McCrea, n.d., Pepper Papers.

Chapter 10. Old Friends, New Enemies

1. Jerry W. Carter to Jack Kroll, 27 January 1950, Kroll Papers.

2. Pepper statement, 2 April 1950, Kroll Papers.

3. *Jacksonville Journal*, 21 January 1950.

4. CIO-PAC Research Department report, 19 January 1950, Kroll Papers.

5. See note 1.

6. See note 4.

7. Zieger, *The CIO, 1935–1955*, 231.

8. Ibid., 236.

9. Ibid., 277.

10. Zieger, "A Venture into Unplowed Fields," 158, 164–165.

11. Ibid., 164–165.

12. *Tampa Morning Tribune*, 25 April 1950.

13. Philip Weightman, report, 16 February 1950, Daniel Augustus Powell Papers, Southern Historical Collection, Wilson Library, University of North Carolina, Chapel Hill.

14. *Miami Herald*, 26 April 1950.

15. *Miami Herald*, 27 April 1950.

16. *Miami Herald*, 6 April 1950.

17. *Florida Times-Union*, 30 April 1950.

18. *Miami Herald*, 29 March 1950.

19. Florida, *Report of the Secretary of State . . . , 1949–1950*, 264.

20. Moore, "Good Reason, Bad Reason, No Reason At All!" 20.

21. *Miami Herald*, 29 April 1950.

22. George M. Harrison to W. F. Howard, 26 January 1950, Pepper Papers.

23. Howard to Harrison, 5 February 1950, Pepper Papers.

24. Frank D. Upchurch to "Friends," 26 April 1950, Pepper Papers.

25. Robert G. Smith to Pepper, 30 May 1950, Pepper Papers.

26. Elliott, "Road from Serfdom" (part 1), 3.

27. *Time*, 24 June 1946.

28. Pepper to James W. Flanagan, 12 January 1948, Pepper Papers.

29. *Miami Daily News*, 30 April 1950.

30. *Miami Sunday News*, 20 April 1945.

31. *Miami Herald*, 26 April 1950.

32. Ibid.

33. *Leesburg Commercial*, 27 April 1950.

34. *Orlando Morning Sentinel*, 6 April 1950.

35. Affidavit of Willie Singleton, 1 April 1950, Pepper Papers.

36. *Orlando Morning Sentinel*, 15 December 1949.

37. *Orlando Morning Sentinel*, 2 April 1950.

38. *Orlando Morning Sentinel*, 30 April 1950.

39. *Miami Herald*, 1 May 1950.

40. *Miami Daily News*, 27 April 1950. *Miami Herald*, 13 April 1950. *Miami Herald*, 19 March 1950.

41. *St. Petersburg Times*, 12 March 1950.

42. *St. Petersburg Times*, 30 April 1950.

43. *Nation*, 4 March 1950, 199.

44. *Tampa Morning Tribune*, 18 February 1950.

45. Pepper, campaign speech, 2 March 1950, Pepper Papers.

46. Senate Subcommittee on Wartime Health and Education, *Health Insurance Report*, 28–29.

47. Ibid.

48. Harlow, "Pepper—With a Grain of Salt," 73.

49. *Tallahassee Democrat*, 22 March 1950.

50. *St. Petersburg Times*, 15 November 1949.

51. Lewis, "New Power at the Polls," 78.

52. *Miami Herald*, 6 April 1950.

53. *Miami Herald*, 25 April 1950.

54. W. H. Lawrence, "Pepper-vs.-Smathers Race Close," *New York Times*, 7 April 1950.

55. *Miami Herald*, 5 March 1950.

56. *Florida Times-Union*, 1 May 1950.

57. Ibid.

58. Smathers to Helen Robeson, 16 January 1946, Smathers Papers.

59. *Tampa Morning Tribune*, 4 March 1950.

60. *Tallahassee Democrat*, 5 March 1950.

61. *Miami Herald*, 11 March 1950.

62. *Miami Herald*, 5 March 1950.

63. *Miami Herald*, 30 March 1950.

64. *Tallahassee Democrat*, 5 April 1950.

65. *Miami Herald*, 26 March 1950.

66. *Miami Herald*, 14 April 1950.

67. *St. Petersburg Times*, 27 April 1950.

68. *St. Petersburg Times*, 22 February 1950.

69. Joseph S. Bair, Letter to Young Republican members, 2 February 1950, Pepper Papers.

70. *St. Petersburg Times*, 2 April 1950.

71. *Florida Times-Union*, 30 April 1950.

72. *Miami Herald*, 4 March 1950.

73. *Florida Times-Union*, 25 April 1950.

74. *Atlanta Constitution*, 30 April 1950.

75. *Miami Herald*, 17 April 1950.

76. *Tampa Morning Tribune*, 26 February 1950.

77. *Jacksonville Journal*, 25 February 1950.

78. Colburn and Scher, *Florida's Gubernatorial Politics*, 138.

79. *Miami Herald*, 8 February 1950.

80. *St. Petersburg Times*, 9 April 1950.

81. *Miami Herald*, 3 April 1950.

82. Smathers to Pepper, 11–26 June 1945, Pepper Papers.

83. *Tallahassee Democrat*, 1 May 1950.

84. *Miami Herald*, 6 April 1950.

85. Smathers to Pepper, n.d., Pepper Papers.

86. *Miami Herald*, 17 April 1950.

87. "Anything Goes," *Time*, 17 April 1950.

88. *Tallahassee Democrat*, 1 November 1987.

89. *Life*, 23 October 1950, 28.

90. *Miami Herald*, 2 May 1971.

91. Pepper, *Pepper*, 204.

92. "Anything Goes," *Time*, 17 April 1950, 27–28.

93. *Baltimore Sun*, 26 April 1950.

94. *Miami Herald*, 18 March 1950.

95. Pepper, *Pepper*, 168.

96. *Miami Herald*, 23 April 1950.

97. *Miami Herald*, 30 April 1950.

98. *Miami Herald*, 3 April 1950.

99. Smathers, interview by author, 27 February 1987.

100. *Miami Herald*, 2 May 1950.

101. *Miami Herald*, 30 April 1950.

102. *St. Petersburg Times*, 6 May 1950.

103. "Exit Senator Pepper," *Nation*, 13 May 1950, 15.

104. *Life*, 15 May 1950, 40–41.

105. "Lessons of the Primaries," *New Republic*, 15 May 1950, 5.

106. *Washington Evening Star*, 4 June 1950.

107. Editorial, "The Florida Primary," *New York Times*, 4 May 1950.

108. *Commonweal*, 19 May 1950, 141–142.

109. *Christian Century*, 17 May 1950, 605.

110. *Tampa Daily Times*, 3 May 1950.

111. Pepper to Herbert M. Davidson, 28 August 1950, Pepper Papers.

112. Pepper to Hugh DeLacy, 5 September 1950, Pepper Papers.

113. Savage, *Truman and the Democratic Party*, 172.

Chapter 11. Aftermath

1. Lubell, *Future of American Politics*, 106–115.

2. Ibid., 113–114.

3. Douglas, "Negro and Florida Politics," 220.

4. Doherty, "Voting Patterns in Florida," 413–414.

5. *St. Petersburg Times*, 5 May 1950.

6. Smathers to Guy Gabrielson, 4 May 1950, Truman Papers.

7. Smathers to Truman, 4 May 1950, Truman Papers.

8. Truman to Smathers, 5 May 1950, Truman Papers.

9. Fried, "Electoral Politics and McCarthyism," 197–198.

10. Pleasants and Burns, *1950 Senate Race in North Carolina*, 148.

11. Lubell, *Future of American Politics*, 244.

12. Ibid., 267.

13. Ibid., 167.

14. Sherrill, "Golden Hatchetman," 151.

15. Pleasants and Burns, *1950 Senate Race in North Carolina*, 186.

16. Ibid., 189.

17. Ibid., 210.

18. Ibid., 279.

19. *Los Angeles Herald Express*, 3 May 1950.

20. Smathers, interview by author, 27 February 1987.

21. Savage, *Truman and the Democratic Party*, 184.

22. L. Griffith, *Ed Ball: Confusion to the Enemy*, 201.

23. Mitchell, *Tricky Dick and The Pink Lady*, 127–128.

24. *Miami Herald*, 3 June 1950.

25. *Jewish Floridian*, 4 November 1949.

26. Lincoln, "The Terrible Tempered Mr. Ball," 158.

27. *Congressional Record*, 81st Cong., 2nd sess., 1950, 96: 17002.

28. *Jacksonville Journal*, 30 December 1950.

29. Pepper Diaries, 11 October 1951.

30. Pepper Diaries, 29 February 1956.

31. Pepper Diaries, 1 March 1956.

32. Smathers, interview by author, 27 February 1987.

33. Buckley and Bozell, *McCarthy and His Enemies*.

34. Smathers to Buckley, 10 June 1954, Smathers Papers. Buckley to Smathers, 17 March 1955, Smathers Papers.

35. Crispell, *Testing the Limits*, 182.

36. Smathers to William Baggs, 1 July 1963, Smathers Papers.

37. Crispell, *Testing the Limits*, 176–177.

Bibliography

Primary Sources

MANUSCRIPT COLLECTIONS

Carleton, William G. Papers. P. K. Yonge Library of Florida History, University of Florida, Gainesville.

Carter, Jerry. Papers. Robert M. Strozier Library, Florida State University, Tallahassee.

Clark, Tom C. Papers. Harry S. Truman Library, Independence, Mo.

Holland, Spessard. Papers. Spessard Holland Collection, Special Collections, Florida State University Library, Tallahassee.

Kroll, Jack. Papers. Library of Congress, Washington, D.C.

National Association for the Advancement of Colored People. Papers. Library of Congress, Washington, D.C.

Pepper, Claude D. Papers. Mildred and Claude Pepper Library, Florida State University, Tallahassee.

———. Personal Diaries: 1937–1949. Mildred and Claude D. Pepper Foundation, McLean, Va.

Political Campaign 1950. Papers. P. K. Yonge Library of Florida History, University of Florida, Gainesville.

Powell, Daniel Augustus. Papers. Southern Historical Collection. Wilson Library, University of North Carolina, Chapel Hill.

Robins, Raymond. Papers. Wisconsin State Historical Society, Madison.

Smathers, George A. Papers. P. K. Yonge Library of Florida History, University of Florida, Gainesville.

Truman, Harry S. Papers. Harry S. Truman Library, Independence, Mo.

Workers Defense League. Papers. Wayne State University, Reuther Library, Detroit, Mich.

INTERVIEWS

Haddock, Crosby S., Sr. Interview by author. Jacksonville, 15 December 1985.

Slye, Mrs. Ronald. Interview by Evans Johnson. Jacksonville, 13 June 1985. DuPont-Ball Library, Stetson University, DeLand, Fla.

Smathers, George. Interview by author. Washington, D.C., 27 February 1987.

———. Interview by Tracy E. Danese. 4 June 1996. Transcript provided by Danese.

———. Interview by Donald Ritchie. 1 August 1989. Senate Historical Office, Washington, D.C.

PUBLIC DOCUMENTS

Congressional Record. Washington, D.C., 1936–1950.

Federal Bureau of Investigation (FBI). Claude D. Pepper File 94-4-684. Washington, D.C.

Florida. Office of the Secretary of State. *Report of the Secretary of State of the State of Florida: 1943–1944*. Tallahassee: State Printer, 1944.

———. *Report of the Secretary of State of the State of Florida: 1949–1950*. Tallahassee: State Printer, 1950.

———. *Tabulation of Official Vote, Florida Democratic Primary Election, June 5, 1934, and June 26, 1934*. Tallahassee: State Printer, 1934.

———. *Tabulation of Official Vote, Florida Democratic Primary Election, May 3, 1938, and May 24, 1938*. Tallahassee: State Printer, 1938.

———. *Tabulation of Official Vote, Florida Democratic Primary Election, May 2, 1944*. Tallahassee: State Printer, 1944.

———. *Tabulation of Official Vote, Florida Democratic Primary Election, May 2, 1950*. Tallahassee: State Printer, 1950.

———. *Tabulation of Official Vote, Florida General Election, November 7, 1944*. Tallahassee: State Printer, 1944.

———. *Tabulation of Official Vote, Florida General Election, November 1, 1948*. Tallahassee: State Printer, 1948.

President's Committee on Civil Rights. *To Secure These Rights: The Report of the President's Committee on Civil Rights*. Washington, D.C.: U.S. Government Printing Office, 1947.

U.S. Senate. Committee on Finance. *Revenue Act of 1943: Hearings on H.R. 3687*. 78th Cong., 1st sess., 29 December 1943.

———. Committee on Foreign Relations. *Hearings on Assistance to Greece and Turkey*. 80th Cong., 1st sess., 1947.

———. Committee on Labor and Public Welfare. *Labor Relations: Hearings on S. 249*. 81st Cong., 1st sess., 1949.

———. Subcommittee on Wartime Health and Education of the Committee on Education and Labor. *Health Insurance Report*. 79th Cong., 2nd sess., 1946.

———. Subcommittee on Wartime Health and Education of the Committee on Education and Labor. *Investigation of Manpower Resources*. 77th Cong., 2nd sess., 1942.

Secondary Sources

Acheson, Dean. *Present at the Creation: My Years in the State Department*. New York: W. W. Norton, 1969.

Alperovitz, Gar. *Atomic Diplomacy: Hiroshima and Potsdam*. New York: Vintage Press, 1965.

Altman, Burton. "'In the Public Interest?' Ed Ball and the FEC Railway War." *Florida Historical Quarterly* 64 (July 1985): 32–37.

Ambrose, Stephen E. *Eisenhower: Soldier, General of the Army, President-Elect, 1890–1952*. New York: Simon & Schuster, 1983.

———. *Nixon: The Education of a Politician, 1913–1962*. New York: Simon & Schuster, 1987.

Arsenault, Raymond, and Gary R. Mormino. "From Dixie to Dreamland: Demographic and Cultural Change in Florida, 1880–1980." In *Shades of the Sunbelt: Essays on Ethnicity, Race, and the Urban South*, edited by Randall Miller and George E. Pozzetta, 161–192. Westport, Conn.: Greenwood Press, 1988.

Bartley, Numan V. *The New South, 1945–1980*. Baton Rouge: Louisiana State University Press, 1995.

Bartley, Numan V., and Hugh D. Graham. *Southern Politics and the Second Reconstruction*. Baltimore: Johns Hopkins University Press, 1975.

Bendiner, Robert. "Maytime Politics." *Nation*, 29 April 1950, 380–391.

Berman, William C. *The Politics of Civil Rights in the Truman Administration*. Columbus: Ohio State University Press, 1970.

Biles, Robert. *The South and the New Deal*. Lexington: University Press of Kentucky, 1994.

Billington, Monroe Lee. *The Political South in the Twentieth Century*. New York: Charles Scribner's Sons, 1975.

Black, Earl, and Merle Black. *Politics and Society in the South*. Cambridge, Mass.: Harvard University Press, 1987.

Boylan, James R. *The New Deal Coalition and the Election of 1946*. New York: Garland, 1981.

Brinkley, Alan. *The End of Reform: New Deal Liberalism in Recession and War*. New York: Alfred A. Knopf, 1995.

———. *Liberalism and Its Discontents*. Cambridge, Mass.: Harvard University Press, 1998.

Brock, Clifton. *Americans for Democratic Action: Its Role in National Politics*. Washington, D.C.: Public Affairs Press, 1962.

Buckley, William F., Jr., and L. Brent Bozell. *McCarthy and His Enemies: The Record and Its Meaning*. Chicago: Regnery, 1954.

Burns, James MacGregor. *The Crosswinds of Freedom: From Roosevelt to Reagan*. Vol. 3 of *The American Experiment*. New York: Alfred A. Knopf, 1989.

———. *Roosevelt: The Lion and the Fox*. New York: Harcourt Brace, 1956.

Carleton, William G. "Can Pepper Hold Florida?" *Nation*, 4 March 1950, 198–200.

Caute, David. *The Great Fear: The Anti-Communist Purge Under Truman and Eisenhower*. New York: Simon & Schuster, 1978.

Chafe, William H. *The Unfinished Journey: America Since World War II*. 2nd ed. New York: Oxford University Press, 1991.

Clark, James C. "The 1944 Florida Democratic Senate Primary." *Florida Historical Quarterly* 66 (July 1988): 365–384.

———. "Claude Pepper and the Seeds of His 1950 Defeat, 1944–1948." *Florida Historical Quarterly* 74 (Summer 1994), 1–22.

Clayton, Bruce, and John A. Salmond, eds. *The South Is Another Land: Essays on the Twentieth-Century South*. Westport, Conn.: Greenwood Press, 1987.

Cochran, Bert. *Harry Truman and the Crisis Presidency*. New York: Funk & Wagnalls, 1973.

Cohen, Warren I., ed. *America in the Age of Soviet Power, 1945–1991*. Vol. 4 of *The Cambridge History of American Foreign Relations*. Cambridge: Cambridge University Press, 1993.

Colburn, David R. *From Yellow Dog Democrats to Red State Republicans: Florida and Its Politics Since 1940*. Gainesville: University Press of Florida, 2007.

Colburn, David R., and Richard K. Scher. *Florida's Gubernatorial Politics in the Twentieth Century*. Gainesville: University Presses of Florida, 1980.

Colby, Gerard. *Du Pont Dynasty*. Secaucus, N.J.: Lyle Stuart, 1984.

Collier, Bert. "Pepper versus Smathers," *New Republic*, 1 May 1950, 14–15.

Congressional Quarterly. *Guide to U.S. Elections*. Washington, D.C.: Congressional Quarterly, 1975.

Conquest, Robert. *The Great Terror: A Reassassment*. New York: Oxford University Press, 1990.

———. *The Harvest of Sorrow*. New York: Oxford University Press, 1986.

Cooper, Gail. *Air-Conditioning America: Engineers and the Controlled Environment, 1900–1960*. Baltimore: Johns Hopkins University Press, 1998.

Cooper, William J., Jr., and Thomas E. Terrill. *The American South: A History*. New York: Alfred A. Knopf, 1990.

Craig, Stephen C. "Politics and Elections." In *Government and Politics in Florida*, edited by Robert J. Huckshorn, 77–110. Gainesville: University of Florida Press, 1991.

Crispell, Brian Lewis. "George Smathers and the Politics of Cold War America, 1946–1969." Ph.D. diss., Florida State University, 1996.

———. *Testing the Limits: George Armistead Smathers and Cold War America*. Athens: University of Georgia Press, 1999.

Dallek, Robert. *Franklin D. Roosevelt and American Foreign Policy*. New York: Oxford University Press, 1979.

Danese, Tracy E. "Claude Pepper and Ed Ball: A Study in Contrasting Political Purposes." Ph.D. diss., Florida State University, 1997.

———. *Claude Pepper and Ed Ball: Politics, Purpose, and Power*. Gainesville: University Press of Florida, 2000.

Davidson, James West, et al. *Nation of Nations: A Narrative History of the American Republic*. 3rd ed. New York: McGraw-Hill, 1997.

Dexter, Charles. "Wanted: A Leader—Claude Pepper," *Reader's Scope*, September 1946, 108–110.

Diggins, John Patrick. *The Proud Decades: America in War and in Peace, 1941–1960*. New York: W. W. Norton, 1988.

Doherty, Herbert J., Jr. "Liberal and Conservative Voting Patterns in Florida." *Journal of Politics* 14 (August 1952): 403–417.

Donovan, Robert J. *Conflict and Crisis: The Presidency of Harry S. Truman, 1945–1948*. New York: W. W. Norton, 1977.

Douglas, Hugh. "The Negro and Florida Politics, 1944–1954." *Journal of Politics* 17 (May 1955): 198–220.

Drury, Allen. *A Senate Journal: 1943–1945*. New York: McGraw-Hill, 1963.

Dunn, James W. "The New Deal and Florida Politics." Ph.D. diss., Florida State University, 1971.

Eden, Robert, ed. *The New Deal and Its Legacy: Critique and Reappraisal*. Westport, Conn.: Greenwood Press, 1989.

Egerton, John. "Claude Pepper's Last Crusade." In *Shades of Gray: Dispatches from the Modern South*, 146–163. Baton Rouge: Louisiana State University Press, 1991.

Elliott, J. Richard. "Road From Serfdom: The Florida East Coast Is Signaling the Way." 2 parts. *Barron's*, 11 May 1964, 1, 3, 14–17; 18 May 1964, 3, 10, 12–15.

Farris, Charles D. "The Re-Enfranchisement of Negroes in Florida." *Journal of Negro History* 39 (October 1954): 259–283.

Ferrell, Robert H. *Choosing Truman: The Democratic Convention of 1944*. Columbia: University of Missouri Press, 1994.

Fleming, Denna Frank. *The Cold War and Its Origins, 1917–1950*. Garden City, N.Y.: Doubleday, 1961.

Foster, James Caldwell. *The Union Politic: The CIO Political Action Committee*. Columbia: University of Missouri Press, 1975.

France, Royal Wilbur. "Five Against Pepper." *Nation*, 29 April 1944, 507–508.

Fraser, Steve, and Gary Gerstle, eds. *The Rise and Fall of the New Deal Order, 1930–1980*. Princeton, N.J.: Princeton University Press, 1989.

Freedman, Max, ed. *Roosevelt and Frankfurter: Their Correspondence, 1928–1945*. Boston: Little, Brown, 1967.

Fried, Richard M. "Electoral Politics and McCarthyism: The 1950 Campaign." In Griffith and Theoharis, *The Specter*, 190–222.

Gaddis, John Lewis. *The Long Peace: Inquiries into the History of the Cold War*. New York: Columbia University Press, 1987.

———. *The United States and the Origins of the Cold War: 1941–1947*. New York: Oxford University Press, 1972.

Gannon, Michael. *Florida: A Short History*. Gainesville: University Press of Florida, 1993.

———, ed. *The New History of Florida*. Gainesville: University Press of Florida, 1996.

Gimbel, John. *The Origins of the Marshall Plan*. Stanford, Calif.: Stanford University Press, 1976.

Glazer, Nathan, and Seymour Martin Lipset. "The Polls on Communism and Conformity." In *The New American Right*, edited by Daniel Bell, 141–165. New York: Criterion, 1955.

Goldfield, David R. *Black, White, and Southern: Race Relations and Southern Culture, 1940 to the Present*. Baton Rouge: Louisiana State University Press, 1990.

Goulden, Joseph C. *The Best Years, 1945–1960*. New York: Atheneum, 1976.

Grantham, Dewey W. *The Life and Death of the Solid South: A Political History*. Lexington: University Press of Kentucky, 1988.

———. *The South in Modern America*. New York: HarperCollins, 1994.

Griffith, Barbara S. *The Crisis of American Labor: Operation Dixie and the Defeat of the CIO*. Philadelphia: Temple University Press, 1981.

Griffith, Leon Odell. *Ed Ball: Confusion to the Enemy*. Tampa: Trend House, 1975.

Griffith, Robert. "Truman and the Historians: The Reconstruction of Postwar American History." *Wisconsin Magazine of History* 59 (Autumn 1950), 20–50.

Griffith, Robert, and Athan G. Theoharis, eds. *The Specter: Original Essays on the Cold War and the Origins of McCarthyism*. New York: New Viewpoints, 1974.

Grismer, Karl H. *The Story of St. Petersburg: The History of Lower Pinellas Peninsula and the Sunshine City*. St Petersburg, Fla.: P. K. Smith, 1948.

Hamby, Alonzo L. *Beyond the New Deal: Harry S. Truman and American Liberalism*. New York: Columbia University Press, 1973.

Hamilton, Virginia Van der Veer. *Lister Hill: Statesman from the South*. Chapel Hill: University of North Carolina Press, 1987.

Harbutt, Fraser J. *The Iron Curtain: Churchill, America, and the Origins of the Cold War*. New York: Oxford University Press, 1986.

Harlow, Robert M. "Pepper—With a Grain of Salt." *Medical Economics*, October 1946, 73–81.

Harney, Diane. "A Content Analysis Technique for Analyzing Newspaper Content: The 1950 Democratic Senatorial Primary Between Claude Pepper and George Smathers." Master's thesis, Florida State University, 1987.

Hartmann, Susan M. *Truman and the 80th Congress*. Columbia: University of Missouri Press, 1971.

Heale, M. J. *McCarthy's Americans: Red Scare Politics in State and Nation, 1935–1965*. Athens: University of Georgia Press, 1998.

Herken, Gregg. *The Winning Weapon: The Atomic Bomb in the Cold War, 1945–1950*. New York: Alfred A. Knopf, 1980.

Hewlett, Richard Greening. *Jessie Ball duPont*. Gainesville: University Press of Florida, 1992.

Hutto, Richard. "Political Feud in the Palmettos: A Chronology and Analysis of the 1950 Florida Senatorial Campaign." Graduate term paper, Florida State University, 1968.

James, Marquis. *Alfred I. duPont: The Family Rebel*. Indianapolis: Bobbs-Merrill, 1941.

Kabat, Ric A. "From New Deal to Red Scare: The Political Odyssey of Senator Claude D. Pepper," Ph.D. diss., Florida State University, 1995.

Kazin, Michael. *The Populist Persuasion*. New York: Basic Books, 1995.

Kennan, George F. *Memoirs: 1925–1950*. Boston: Little, Brown, 1967.

Key, V. O. *Southern Politics in State and Nation*. New ed. Knoxville: University of Tennessee Press, 1984.

Kirkendall, Richard S., ed. *The Truman Period as a Research Field: A Reappraisal, 1972.* Columbia: University of Missouri Press, 1974.

Klehr, Harvey. *The Heyday of American Communism: The Depression Decade.* New York: Basic Books, 1984.

Klingman, Peter D. *Neither Dies Nor Surrenders: A History of the Republican Party in Florida, 1867–1970.* Gainesville: University of Florida Press, 1984.

Langer, William L., and S. Everett Gleason. *The Challenge to Isolation, 1937–1940.* New York: Council on Foreign Relations, 1952.

Latham, Earl. *The Communist Controversy in Washington: From the New Deal to McCarthy.* Cambridge, Mass.: Harvard University Press, 1966.

Lawson, Steven F. *Black Ballots: Voting Rights in the South, 1944–1969.* New York: Columbia University Press, 1976.

Lawson, Steven F., David R. Colburn, and Darryl Paulson. "Groveland: Florida's Little Scottsboro." *Florida Historical Quarterly* 65 (July 1968): 1–26.

Leemis, Lloyd C. *The Red Record of Senator Claude Pepper.* Jacksonville: Lloyd C. Leemis, 1950.

Leffler, Melvyn P. "The American Conception of National Security and the Beginnings of the Cold War, 1945–1948." *American Historical Review.* 89 (April 1984): 346–381.

———. *A Preponderance of Power: National Security, the Truman Administration, and the Cold War.* Stanford, Calif.: Stanford University Press, 1992.

Leuchtenburg, William E. *Franklin D. Roosevelt and the New Deal.* New York: Harper & Row, 1963.

Lewis, R. Cragin. "New Power at the Polls." *Medical Economics,* January 1951, 73–78.

Lincoln, Freeman. "The Terrible-Tempered Mr. Ball." *Fortune,* November 1952, 143–162.

Lipsitz, George. *Rainbow at Midnight: Labor and Culture in the 1940s.* Chicago: University of Illinois Press, 1994.

Loving, Rush, Jr. "Ed Ball's Marvelous, Old-Style Money Machine." *Fortune,* December 1974, 170–185.

Lubell, Samuel. *The Future of American Politics.* 2nd ed. Garden City, N.Y.: Doubleday, 1956.

Malafronte, Anthony. "Claude Pepper, Florida Maverick: The 1950 Florida Senatorial Primary." Master's thesis, University of Miami, 1963.

Marable, Manning. *Race, Reform, and Rebellion: The Second Reconstruction in Black America, 1945–1982.* New York: Macmillan, 1984.

Marshall, F. Ray. *Labor in the South.* Cambridge, Mass.: Harvard University Press, 1967.

Mason, Raymond K., and Virginia Harrison. *Confusion to the Enemy: A Biography of Edward Ball.* New York: Dodd, Mead, 1976.

Matthews, Donald R., and James W. Prothro. *Negroes and the New Southern Politics.* New York: Harcourt, Brace & World, 1966.

McCoy, Donald R. *The Presidency of Harry S. Truman.* Lawrence: University Press of Kansas, 1984.

McCullough, David. *Truman.* New York: Simon & Schuster, 1992.

McGill, Ralph. "Can He Purge Senator Pepper?" *Saturday Evening Post*, 22 April 1950, 32–38.

McWilliams, Tennant S. *The New South Faces the World: Foreign Affairs and the Southern Sense of Self, 1877–1950*. Baton Rouge: Louisiana State University Press, 1988.

Messer, Robert L. *The End of an Alliance: James F. Byrnes, Roosevelt, Truman, and the Origins of the Cold War*. Chapel Hill: University of North Carolina Press, 1982.

Mitchell, Greg. *Tricky Dick and the Pink Lady: Richard Nixon vs. Helen Gahagan Douglas—Sexual Politics and the Red Scare, 1950*. New York: Random House, 1998.

Moore, John. "Good Reason, Bad Reason, No Reason at All! The Florida Senatorial Primary of 1950." Honors thesis, Harvard University, 1951.

Moore, Winfred B., Jr., Joseph F. Tripp, and Lyon G. Tyler, Jr., eds. *Developing Dixie: Modernization in a Traditional Society*. Westport, Conn.: Greenwood Press, 1988.

Morgan, Ted. *Reds: McCarthyism in Twentieth-Century America*. New York: Random House, 2003.

Morris, Roger. *Richard Milhous Nixon: The Rise of an American Politician*. New York: Henry Holt, 1990.

Mosley, Leonard. *Blood Relations: The Rise and Fall of the du Ponts of Delaware*. New York: Atheneum, 1980.

Murray, Florence, ed. *The Negro Handbook, 1949*. New York: Macmillan, 1949.

Murray, Robert K. *Red Scare: A Study in National Hysteria, 1919–1920*. Minneapolis: University of Minnesota Press, 1955.

Nation. "Exit Senator Pepper." 13 May 1950, 15.

New Republic. "Lessons of the Primaries." 15 May 1950, 5.

Newsweek. "Fireworks in Florida." 10 April 1950, 23.

———. "Red Pepper." 7 April 1947, 25.

Nixon, H. C. "The Changing Political Philosophy of the South." *Annals of the Academy of Political and Social Sciences* 153 (January 1931): 246–250.

O'Neill, William L. *A Better World: The Great Schism: Stalinism and the American Intellectuals*. New York: Simon & Schuster, 1982.

Paterson, Thomas G., ed. *Cold War Critics: Alternatives to American Foreign Policy in the Truman Years*. Chicago: Quadrangle, 1971.

Pepper, Claude D. "Address to Progressive Citizens of America." *PM*, 27 October 1947, 12.

———. "America and the Peace Crisis." *Soviet Russia Today*, June 1946, 9, 29.

———. "A Foreign Policy to Win the War, Keep the Peace, and Promote the Welfare of Our Nation and the World." *Foreign Policy Reports*, October 1944, 167–176.

———. "Hands Across the Elbe." *Soviet Russia Today*, July 1945, 31.

———. "International Organization an Imperative Necessity." *Free World*, December 1943, 508–509.

———. "Isn't Health Important to the Nation?" *New York Times Magazine*, 20 May 1945, 12, 33–34.

———. "The Liberated Nations and the New Order." *Free World*, August 1943, 110–113.

———. "Militarism Breeds Militarism." *Parents*, November 1944, 16.

———. "A More Perfect United Nations—How and When?" *Annals of the American Academy of Political and Social Science*, July 1943, 40–46.

———. "The New Deal—Dead or Alive?" *Everybody's Digest*, October 1946, 21–24.

———. *Pepper: Eyewitness to a Century*. With Hays Gorey. San Diego: Harcourt Brace Jovanovich, 1987.

———. "A Program for Peace." *New Republic*, 8 April 1946, 470–473.

———. "Things We Forgot About Russia." *Churchman*, May 1946, 13–14.

———. "Two Senators State the Campaign Issues." *New York Times Magazine*, 3 September 1944, 12, 38–40.

Peterson, F. Ross. *Prophet Without Honor: Glen H. Taylor & the Fight for American Liberalism*. Lexington: University of Kentucky Press, 1974.

Pleasants, Julian M., and Augustus M. Burns III. *Frank Porter Graham and the 1950 Senate Race in North Carolina*. Chapel Hill: University of North Carolina Press, 1990.

Price, Hugh Douglas. *The Negro and Southern Politics: A Chapter of Florida History*. New York: New York University Press, 1957.

Price, Wesley. "Pink Pepper." *Saturday Evening Post*, 31 August 1946, 19, 102, 117–118.

Reed, Linda. *Simple Decency & Common Sense: The Southern Conference Movement, 1938–1963*. Bloomington: Indiana University Press, 1991.

Reed, Merl E. *Seedtime for the Modern Civil Rights Movement: The President's Committee on Fair Employment Practice, 1941–1946*. Baton Rouge: Louisiana State University Press, 1991.

Reeves, Thomas C. *The Life and Times of Joe McCarthy: A Biography*. New York: Stein & Day, 1982.

Roady, Elston. "The Expansion of Negro Suffrage in Florida." *The Journal of Negro Education* 26 (Winter 1957): 297–306.

Rodell, Fred. "Senator Claude Pepper." *American Mercury*, October 1946, 389–396.

Rose, Lisle A. *The Cold War Comes to Main Street: America in 1950*. Lawrence: University Press of Kansas, 1999.

Ross, Irwin. *The Loneliest Campaign: The Truman Victory of 1948*. New York: New American Library, 1968.

Salzman, Neil V. *Reform and Revolution: The Life and Times of Raymond Robins*. Kent, Ohio: Kent State University Press, 1991.

Savage, Sean J. *Truman and the Democratic Party*. Lexington: University Press of Kentucky, 1997.

Sayers, Michael, and Albert E. Kahn. *The Great Conspiracy Against Russia*. New York: International Workers Order, 1946.

Schapsmeier, Edward L., and Frederick H. Schapsmeier. *Prophet in Politics: Henry A. Wallace and the War Years, 1940–1965*. Ames: Iowa State University Press, 1970.

Schrecker, Ellen. *The Age of McCarthyism: A Brief History with Documents*. Boston: Bedford Books of St. Martin's Press, 1994.

Schulzinger, Robert D. *American Diplomacy in the Twentieth Century*. 3rd ed. New York: Oxford University Press, 1994.

Schwarz, Jordan A. *The New Dealers: Power Politics in the Age of Roosevelt*. New York: Alfred A. Knopf, 1993.

Scicchitano, Michael J., and Richard K. Scher. "Florida: Political Change, 1950–1996." In *The New Politics of the Old South: An Introduction to Southern Politics*, edited by

Charles S. Bullock III and Mark J. Rozell, 263–284. Lanham, Md.: Rowman & Littlefield, 1998.

Shalett, Sidney. "The Paradoxical Mr. Pepper." *New York Times Magazine*, 3 November 1946, 16, 69, 71.

Sherrill, Robert. "George Smathers, the South's Golden Hatchetman." In *Gothic Politics in the Deep South: Stars of the New Confederacy*, 136–193. New York: Grossman, 1968.

Sirevåg, Torbjörn. *The Eclipse of the New Deal and the Fall of Vice-President Wallace: 1944.* New York: Garland, 1985.

Sitkoff, Harvard. "Harry Truman and the Election of 1948: The Coming of Age of Civil Rights in American Politics." *Journal of Southern History* 37 (November 1971): 597–616.

Sosna, Morton. *In Search of the Silent South: Southern Liberals and the Race Issue.* New York: Columbia University Press, 1977.

Stewart, Kenneth. "Serious Senator Pepper." *PM Magazine*, 1 June 1947, 7–9.

Stoesen, Alexander R. "Road from Receivership: Claude Pepper, the duPont Trust, and the Florida East Coast Railway." *Florida Historical Quarterly* 52 (October 1973), 132–156.

———. "The Senatorial Career of Claude D. Pepper." Ph.D. diss., University of North Carolina at Chapel Hill, 1964.

Sullivan, Patricia. *Days of Hope: Race and Democracy in the New Deal Era.* Chapel Hill: University of North Carolina Press, 1996.

Theoharis, Athan G. *Seeds of Repression: Harry S. Truman and the Origins of McCarthyism.* Chicago: Quadrangle, 1971.

Time. "Anything Goes." 17 April 1950, 27–28.

———. "The Effigy." 2 September 1940, 14–15.

———. "First Lame Duck." 15 May 1950, 25.

———. National Politics. 21 February 1938, 19–23.

———. National Politics. 15 March 1948, 23–30.

Tindall, George Brown. *The Emergence of the New South, 1913–1945.* Baton Rouge: Louisiana State University Press, 1967.

Tygiel, Jules. *Baseball's Great Experiment: Jackie Robinson and His Legacy.* Expanded ed. New York: Oxford University Press, 1997.

Vickers, Raymond B. *Panic in Paradise: Florida's Banking Crash of 1926.* Tuscaloosa: University of Alabama Press, 1994.

Walker, Martin. *The Cold War: A History.* New York: Henry Holt, 1993.

Wall, Joseph Frazier. *Alfred I. du Pont: The Man & His Family.* New York: Oxford University Press, 1990.

Wallace, Henry A. *The Price of Vision: The Diary of Henry A. Wallace, 1942–1946.* Edited by John Morton Blum. Boston: Houghton Mifflin, 1973.

Walton, Richard J. *Henry Wallace, Harry Truman, and the Cold War.* New York: Viking Press, 1976.

Warren, Fuller. *How to Win in Politics.* Tallahassee: Peninsular Publishing, 1949.

Weisberger, Bernard A. *Cold War, Cold Peace: The United States and Russia since 1945.* New York: American Heritage, 1985.

Weiss, Nancy J. *Farewell to the Party of Lincoln: Black Politics in the Age of FDR.* Princeton, N.J.: Princeton University Press, 1983.

Woods, Randall B., and Howard Jones. *Dawning of the Cold War: The United States' Quest for Order.* Athens: University of Georgia Press, 1991.

Woodward, C. Vann. *Origins of the New South: 1877–1913.* Baton Rouge: Louisiana State University Press, 1951.

Yergin, Daniel. *Shattered Peace: The Origins of the Cold War and the National Security State.* Boston: Houghton Mifflin, 1977.

Zieger, Robert H. *The CIO, 1935–1955.* Chapel Hill: University of North Carolina Press, 1995.

———, ed. *Southern Labor in Transition, 1940–1995.* Knoxville: University of Tennessee Press, 1997.

———. "A Venture into Unplowed Fields: Daniel Powell and CIO Political Action in the Postwar South." In *Labor in the Modern South,* edited by Glenn T. Eskew, 158–181. Athens: University of Georgia Press.

Index

Page numbers in italics refer to illustrations.

James C. Clark is a member of the History Department faculty at the University of Central Florida. He is the author of four books, including *Faded Glory: Presidents Out of Power*. He lives in Orlando.

Florida Government and Politics

SERIES EDITORS, DAVID R. COLBURN AND SUSAN A. MACMANUS

Florida has emerged today as a microcosm of the nation and has become a political bellwether in national elections. The impact of Florida on the presidential elections of 2000, 2004, and 2008 suggests the magnitude of the state's influence. Of the four largest states in the nation, Florida is the only one that has moved from one political column to the other in the last three national elections. These developments suggest the vital need to explore the politics of the Sunshine State in greater detail. Books in this series will explore the myriad aspects of politics, political science, public policy, history, and government in Florida.

The 57 Club: My Four Decades in Florida Politics, by Frederick B. Karl (2010)

The Political Education of Buddy MacKay, by Buddy MacKay, with Rick Edmonds (2010)

Immigrant Prince: Mel Martinez and The American Dream, by Richard E. Foglesong (2011)

Reubin O'D. Askew and the Golden Age of Florida Politics, by Martin A. Dyckman (2011)

Red Pepper and Gorgeous George: Claude Pepper's Epic Defeat in the 1950 Democratic Primary, by James C. Clark (2011)